D1094313

DISCARD

Sir Thomas WYATT and Henry HOWARD, Earl of Surrey

a reference guide

A
Reference
Guide
to
Literature

Everett Emerson
Editor

Sir Thomas WYATT and Henry HOWARD, Earl of Surrey

a reference guide

CLYDE W. JENTOFT

G.K.HALL&CO.

70 LINCOLN STREET, BOSTON, MASS.

Copyright © 1980 by Clyde W. Jentoft

Library of Congress Cataloging in Publication Data

Jentoft, Clyde W
  Sir Thomas Wyatt and Henry Howard, Earl of
Surrey, a reference guide.

  (Reference guides to literature)
  Includes index.
  1. English poetry—Early modern, 1500-1700—
Bibliography. 2. Wyatt, Thomas, Sir, 1503?-1547—
Bibliography. 3. Surrey, Henry Howard, Earl of,
1517?-1547—Bibliography. I. Title. II. Series.
Z2014.P7J46 [PR521] 016.821'2 80-16434
ISBN 0-8161-8176-4

iv

Contents

Preface

This Reference Guide is an annotated list of writings about Sir Thomas
Wyatt and Henry Howard, Earl of Surrey, from 1542, the year of Wyatt's
death, through 1977 and into 1978. It provides annotated entries for
books, monographs, articles, notes, unpublished American doctoral dissertations, and significant English-language reviews of books about
the two poets, as well as introductions, prefaces, memoirs, and commentaries in important editions of their works and significant chapters
or sections about them in more inclusive studies; it also lists reprints and revisions of books devoted exclusively to them. It does
not include foreign-language dissertations or reviews, passing references to them in larger modern surveys or anthologies, reprints and
revisions of books not focused exclusively on them, or English-language
reviews that simply summarize content or offer general praise; it is
somewhat selective in recording allusions to them in uncritical comments by their contemporaries and immediate successors, and it includes
only the more important treatments of them in histories of English
prosody. Its primary sources of information are the PMLA, SP, and MHRA
bibliographies, CBEL and YWES, Michael C. O'Neel's bibliography of
Wyatt [W 1970.4] and Burton Fishman's compilation of recent studies of
both poets [WS 1971]. It also takes into account the bibliography in
the May, 1979 issue of RES (n.s. 30, no. 118) and Joseph Wittreich's
bibliographical essay on "Recent Studies in the Renaissance" in SEL,
19, no. 1 (Winter, 1979), 143-73.

The Guide is divided into three sections: one on Wyatt [W], one
on Surrey [S], and one on studies that compare them or discuss them
together in relation to more inclusive subjects [WS]. The latter part,
while admittedly awkward, is necessitated by the durable convention
that has coupled their names since the sixteenth century; to ignore it
would produce a flood of multiple entries and cross references. (The
only double entry is Berdan's Early Tudor Poetry [W 1930, S 1920],
which devotes a whole chapter to Surrey but includes Wyatt as part of
other sections.)

The annotations for most items reflect the points of view of their
authors. Others describe subject, purpose, and/or scope. All reproduce their authors' spelling and punctuation of first lines/titles of

Preface

Wyatt and Surrey works. Some provide additional information or cross references to related entries in brackets. Pagination for studies devoted wholly to Wyatt or Surrey includes material in Roman as well as Arabic numerals.

On those occasions when I was unable to examine an item personally, I followed one of two procedures: if the necessary information was available only in a reprint, a later edition, or a collection, I entered the item in the year of its original publication, annotated the later version, and cited the later version in brackets; items that I was unable to examine personally in any form bear asterisks and the sources in the Guide where they are mentioned. All other annotations, including those for dissertations, are based on personal examination of the original items. To the best of my knowledge, the Guide contains entries for all the significant statements written about Wyatt and Surrey with the exception of those in the categories I mention above.

The preliminary material includes an introductory survey of Wyatt and Surrey criticism, a list of printed and unprinted sources containing their works, and a list of abbreviations used in the Guide. The list of sources does not pretend to include every collection or anthology containing the verse of the two poets; however, it does include, in addition to the major sources, those minor ones that may have some significance. The abbreviations, with the exception of the collections edited by G. Gregory Smith and Joel E. Spingarn, correspond to those in the PMLA bibliography.

This project would have been significantly longer and more difficult were it not for the invaluable help with research, proofreading, indexing, and, most particularly, translating provided by my wife Eve and for the wise counsel and efficient help of my colleague and friend Professor Thomas M. Davis. I also acknowledge the assistance of the Kent State University Library's Office of Interlibrary Loan, particularly that of Mr. Dan Fleming; the financial aid provided by Kent State's Office of Research and Sponsored Programs, directed by Dean Eugene Wenninger; and the graduate assistance furnished by the Kent State English Department. The Widener Library, Harvard, the Sterling Library, Yale, and the Ohio State University Libraries furnished me with many items I could find nowhere else. Professor Yoshinobu Hakutani of the Kent State English Department translated Japanese publications, and Wilma Crawford of the Kent State Honors College has been an uncommonly patient and efficient typist.

Manuscripts, Editions and Collections

I. Major Manuscripts

    The Arundel Harington Manuscript

    The Blage Manuscript

    BM Add. MS. 36529

    BM Devonshire MS. 17492

    BM Egerton MS. 2711

    BM Hargrave MS. 205

    BM Harleian MS. 78

    BM Royal MS. 17A, xxii

    Parker MS. 168

II. Minor Manuscripts

    The Bannatyne Manuscript

    BM Add. MS. 28635

    BM Add. MS. 28636

    BM Add. MS. 31392

    BM Add. MS. 31922

    BM Add. MS. 31992

    BM Add. MS. 33271

    BM Add. MS. 33933

    BM Harleian MS. 282

    BM Loan MS. 15

    BM Royal App. 58

    BM Royal MS. 20B

    BM Stowe MS. 389

    BM Vespasian MS. C. vii

BM Vespasian MS. P. xiii

California MS. AC 523

Folger MS. 448.16

Petyt MS. no. 47

III. Major Editions and Printed Sources

The Aeneid of Henry Howard Earl of Surrey, ed. Florence H. Ridley. Berkeley and Los Angeles: University of California Press, 1963.

The Arundel Harington Manuscript of Tudor Poetry, ed. Ruth Hughey. 2 vols. Columbus, Ohio: The Ohio State University Press, 1960.

Baldwyn, William. A treatise of Morall Phylosophie, contayning the sayinges of the wyse. London: Edwarde Whitchurche, 1547 [STC 1253].

Camden, William. Remaines of a Greater Worke, concerning Briaine.... London: printed by G. E. for Simon Waterson, 1605 [STC 4521].

Certain Bokes of Virgiles Aenis turned into English meter, by Henry Earle of Surrey. London: Richard Tottel, 1557 [STC 24798].

Certayn Chapters of the prouerbes of Salomon drawen into metre by Thomas sterneholde [STC 2760].

Certayne Psalmes chosen out of the Psalter of David commonly called the vii penytentiall Psalmes, drawen into Englyshe meter by sir Thomas Wyat knyght, whereunto is added a prologe of the auctore before every Psalme very pleasant and profettable to the Godly reader. London: T. Raynauld for J. Harrington, 1549.

Collected Poems of Sir Thomas Wyatt, ed. Kenneth Muir. London: Routledge and Kegan Paul, 1949; Cambridge, Massachusetts: Harvard University Press, 1950.

Collected Poems of Sir Thomas Wyatt, eds. Kenneth Muir and Patricia Thomson. Liverpool English Texts and Studies, ed. Kenneth Muir. Liverpool: Liverpool University Press, 1969.

The Court of Venus, ed. Russell A. Fraser. Durham, North Carolina: Duke University Press, 1955.

An excellent Epitaffe of syr Thomas Wyat, With two other compendious dytties, wherin are touchyd, and set furth the state of
mannes lyfe. London: Iohn Herforde for Robert Toye, 1542
[STC 26054].

Flügel, Ewald. "Die handscriftliche Überlieferung der Gedichte
von Sir Thomas Wyatt." Anglia, 18 (1896), 263-290, 455-516;
19 (1897), 175-210, 413-450.

The Fourth Boke of Virgill...drawne into a strange metre by
Henrye, late Earle of Surrey. London: John Day for William
Owen, 1554.

Griffith, Reginald H. and Robert A. Law. "'A Boke of Ballets'
and 'The Courte of Venus.'" University of Texas Studies in
English, no. 10 (1930), pp. 1-12.

Harrier, Richard C. The Canon of Sir Thomas Wyatt's Poetry.
Cambridge, Massachusetts: Harvard University Press, 1975.

Henry Howard, Earl of Surrey: Poems, ed. Emrys Jones. Clarendon Medieval and Tudor Series, ed. J. A. W. Bennett. Oxford:
Clarendon Press, 1964.

Muir, Kenneth. Life and Letters of Sir Thomas Wyatt. Liverpool:
Liverpool University Press, 1963.

Nugae Antiquae: Being a Miscellaneous Collection of Original
Papers in Prose and Verse...By Sir John Harington. 3 vols.
London: J. Dodsley and T. Shrimpton, 1769-1775, 1779, 1792;
rev. ed. Thomas Park. 2 vols. London: J. Wright for Vernor
and Hood, Poultry, and Cuthell and Martin, 1804.

Padelford, Frederick Morgan. "The Manuscript Poems of Henry
Howard, Earl of Surrey." Anglia, 29 (1906), 273-338.

Plutarch's Quyete of Mynde Translated by Thomas Wyat, ed.
Charles Read Baskervill. Huntington Library Publications.
Cambridge, Massachusetts: Harvard University Press, 1931.

The Poems of Henry Howard Earl of Surrey, ed. Frederick Morgan
Padelford. University of Washington Publications in Language
and Literature. Vol. 5. Seattle, Washington: University of
Washington Press, 1920; rev. ed., 1928; rpt. 1966.

The Poems of Sir Thomas Wiatt, ed. A. K. Foxwell. 2 vols.
London: University of London Press, 1913; rpt. 1964.

Sir Thomas Wyatt and His Circle: Unpublished Poems, ed. Kenneth
    Muir. English Reprints Series, No. 18, ed. Kenneth Muir.
    Liverpool: Liverpool University Press, 1963.

Sir Thomas Wyatt: Collected Poems, ed. Joost Daalder. London:
    Oxford University Press, 1975.

SONGES AND SONETTES, written by the ryght honorable Lorde Henry
    Haward late Earle of Surrey, and other. London: Richard
    Tottel, 1557 [STC 13860].

Surrey's Fourth Boke of Virgill, ed. Herbert Hartman. London:
    John Johnson (Oxford University Press) for Carl H. Pforz-
    heimer, 1933.

Tottel's Miscellany (1557-1587), ed. Hyder Edward Rollins.
    2 vols. Cambridge, Massachusetts: Harvard University Press,
    1929-1930.

The Works of Henry Howard Earl of Surrey and of Sir Thomas Wyatt
    the Elder, ed. George Frederick Nott. 2 vols. London:
    T. Bensley for Longman, Hurst, Rees, Orme, and Brown, 1815-
    1816.

IV. Unpublished Editions

"The Poetry of Henry Howard, Earl of Surrey," ed. Charles Willi-
    son Eckert. Ph.D. dissertation, Washington University,
    St. Louis, 1960.

"The Poetry of Sir Thomas Wyatt," ed. Richard Charles Harrier.
    Ph.D. dissertation, Harvard, 1952.

V. Minor Editions, Selections, Collections

Early Sixteenth Century Lyrics, ed. Frederick Morgan Padelford.
    Boston and London: D. C. Heath & Co., 1907.

Five Courtier Poets of the English Renaissance, ed. Robert M.
    Bender. New York: Washington Square Press, 1969.

The Original Poems of Henry Howard, Earl of Surrey. London:
    Aquila Press, 1929.

Poems: Henry Howard, Earl of Surrey, and Sir Thomas Wyatt, eds.
    G. D. H. and M. I. Cole. London, 1928.

Poems of Henry Howard, Earl of Surrey. With the Poems of Sir
    Thomas Wiat. London, 1717.

The Poems of Henry Howard Earl of Surrey. The Aldine Edition of
the British Poets. London: Bell and Daldy, 1831; rpts.
1866, 1871.

Poetical Works of Henry Howard, Earl of Surrey, Minor Contemporaneous Poets and Thomas Sackville, Lord Buckhurst, ed.
Robert Bell. The Annotated Edition of the English Poets,
ed. Robert Bell. London: John W. Parker and Son, 1854.

The Poetical Works of Sir Thomas Wyatt. The Aldine Edition of
the British Poets. London: Bell and Daldy, 1831; rpt. 1854,
1870.

The Poetical Works of Sir Thomas Wyatt. London: William Pick-
ering, 1831.

Poetical Works of Sir Thomas Wyatt, ed. Robert Bell. The Annotated Edition of the English Poets, ed. Robert Bell. London:
John W. Parker and Son, 1854.

The Poetical Works of Sir Thomas Wyatt, ed. Charles C. Clarke.
Edinburgh, 1868.

The Poetical Works of Sir Thomas Wyatt. With a Memoir and Critical Dissertation, ed. George Gilfillan. Edinburgh: James
Nichol; London: James Nisbet & Co.; Dublin: W. Robertson,
1858.

The Poetical Works of Sir Thomas Wyatt, ed. James Yeowell.
London: George Bell and Sons, 1904.

The Poetical Works of Sir Thomas Wyatt and Henry Howard Earl of
Surrey. With a Memoir of Each. 2 vols. Boston: Houghton
Mifflin; Cambridge: Riverside Press, n.d.

Silver Poets of the Sixteenth Century, ed. Gerald Bullett.
London and New York: Everyman's Library, 1947.

Some Poems of Sir Thomas Wyatt, ed. Alan Swallow. Books of The
Renaissance. New York: Swallow Press and William Morrow &
Co., 1949.

The Surrey and Wyatt Anthology, 1509-1547 A.D., ed. Edward Arber.
London, 1900.

Three Early Tudor Poets: A Selection from Skelton, Wyatt and
Surrey, ed. Nicholas Bielby. Wheaton Studies in Literature.
Oxford and Elmsford, New York: Pergamon Press, A. Wheaton &
Co., 1976.

Tillyard, E. M. W. <u>The Poetry of Sir Thomas Wyatt: A Selection and a Study</u>. London: Scholartis Press, 1929; rpts. 1949, 1978.

<u>To a Lady: The Songs and Sonnets of the Earl of Surrey</u>, ed. Douglas Geary. London: Forbes Robertson, 1957.

<u>The Works of the English Poets from Chaucer to Cowper</u>, ed. Alexander Chalmers. Vol. 2. London: J. Johnson, 1810.

Abbreviations

AN&Q	American Notes and Queries
AS	American Speech
AnM	Annuale Mediaevale
AUMLA	Journal of the Australasian Universities Language and Literature Association
BB	Bulletin of Bibliography and Magazine Notes
BC	Book Collector
BuR	Bucknell Review
CESC	Critical Essays of the Seventeenth Century, ed. J. E. Spingarn. 3 vols. Oxford: Clarendon Press, 1908.
CEJ	California English Journal
CL	Comparative Literature
CLJ	Cornell Library Journal
CQ	The Cambridge Quarterly
E&S	Essays and Studies by Members of the English Association
ECE	Elizabethan Critical Essays, ed. G. Gregory Smith. 2 vols. London: Oxford University Press, 1904.
EIC	Essays in Criticism
Eigo S	Eigo Seinen [The Rising Generation] (Tokyo)

Abbreviations

ELH	Journal of English Literary History
ELN	English Language Notes
ELR	English Literary Renaissance
EM	English Miscellany
ES	English Studies
ESt	Erlanger Studien
FMLS	Forum for Modern Language Studies (University of St. Andrews, Scotland)
HLQ	Huntington Library Quarterly
JEGP	Journal of English and Germanic Philology
JRUL	Journal of the Rutgers University Library
KR	Kenyon Review
Lang&S	Language and Style
LCUT	Library Chronicle of the University of Texas
LWU	Literatur in Wissenschaft und Unterricht (Kiel)
M&L	Music and Letters
MLN	Modern Language Notes
MLQ	Modern Language Quarterly
MLR	Modern Language Review
MP	Modern Philology
NA	Nuova Antologia
N&Q	Notes and Queries
NLH	New Literary History
PBSA	Papers of the Bibliographical Society of America
PLL	Papers on Language and Literature
PMLA	Publications of the Modern Language Association of America

Abbreviations

PQ	Philological Quarterly
REL	Review of English Literature
Ren&R	Renaissance and Reformation/Renaissance et Reförme
RES	Review of English Studies
RN	Renaissance News
RQ	Renaissance Quarterly
SB	Studies in Bibliography
SCN	Seventeenth-Century News
SEL	Studies in English Literature, 1500–1900
SLitI	Studies in the Literary Imagination
SMC	Studies in Medieval Culture (Western Michigan University)
SN	Studia Neophilologica
SP	Studies in Philology
SR	Sewanee Review
SoRA	Southern Review: An Australian Journal of Literary Studies (University of Adelaide)
TLS	(London) Times Literary Supplement
TSLL	Texas Studies in Literature and Language
UES	Unisa English Studies
UTQ	University of Toronto Quarterly

Introduction

That the section on Wyatt in this Reference Guide occupies more space
than the other two combined, and that the section on Surrey is briefer
than the one listing studies that compare him in one way or another
with Wyatt offer ample evidence of the fundamental reversal in critical judgment about the relative worth and significance of the two
poets that has taken place in the twentieth century. On a purely
quantitative level, this state of affairs is easily accounted for:
Wyatt has commanded more attention in the last five decades, when
literary criticism gradually emerged out of chambers and into the
academic marketplace; scholars publish more now than did their predecessors, and they prefer Wyatt. Other, similarly tangential but
significant factors also help to explain this phenomenon. For one,
Wyatt wrote more than Surrey did, thus providing students, quite
simply, with more to do; that we do not yet know how much more provides opportunities for investigations in print that do not accrue to
Surrey, whose canon is at present apparently well established.
Another reason for the modern preference is that today's readers iden-
tify more readily with the sensibility of Wyatt and his poetic personas: his well-documented problems with the amoral requirements of
court politics and his speakers' collective rejection of the behavior
patterns expected of the courtly lover sit well with a generation
that views the machinations of its own leaders with increasing irony
and questions not only the value, but the very reality, of amour
courtois. We are more fascinated by Wyatt's near executions than we
are by Surrey's actual one because one of Wyatt's brushes with the
block was reportedly instigated by the contrivances of his Machia-
vellian enemies, while the other might have been precipitated by his
relationship with the captivating Anne Boleyn, and thus part of real
rather than literary history; we are led to view Surrey's conflicts
with established authority, on the other hand, as part of the dyna-
mics of power politics, in which his own thoughtless hubris played a
significant part, and we long ago dismissed his relationship with
"Geraldine" as literary invention.

Thus the simple reality of numbers, together with the extraliterary preference for one kind of human being over another, helps
to provide at least surface reasons for the modern verdict in favor
of Wyatt: we prefer Hamlet to Hotspur and Touchstone to Valentine.

Introduction

More to the point, we prefer Measure for Measure to Romeo and Juliet, which is to say that we prefer the poetry of Wyatt to that of Surrey because it satisfies our requirements for a point of view and a style that reflect the complexity of human experience rather than those that mirror its antique coherence. In a more specific sense, the rise of Wyatt and the decline of Surrey are correspondent to the modern verdict in favor of Donne's violently yoked antitheses and wrenching accents over the amplified harmonies of the Spenserian poets and the simple lyric grace of the Sons of Ben. In short, the peregrinations of Wyatt and Surrey criticism clearly reflect an alteration in literary as well as human sensibility, one that involves more than the specific qualities of the poetry written by two early Tudor courtiers. While it is not my purpose to concentrate on the relationship of that poetry to such larger contexts, it is impossible to ignore it in a survey of the more significant developments in Wyatt and Surrey criticism.

The chronology documented in the bibliography that follows reveals three major periods, and the suggestion of a fourth. The first, roughly comprising the sixteenth and seventeenth centuries, generally sees Wyatt and Surrey as literary twins. The second, covering the better part of the eighteenth and nineteenth, records the emergence of Surrey as the dominant and favored figure. The third, beginning in the nineteenth and continuing virtually to the present, chronicles the gradual decline of Surrey in the wake of the unmistakable triumph of Wyatt. As of this writing, the momentum of Wyatt criticism seems to have reached its crest in the 1960s, for the recorded evidence of the criticism during the present decade seems to indicate the return to a more balanced, less competitive assessment of both poets, one that has its roots not in their literary kinship, as it had in the earliest criticism, but in the liberation of one from the other that has taken place during the Wyatt revival.

Much of the literary activity surrounding the two poets during the first period was not, of course, criticism in the modern sense at all, as Surrey's own comments on Wyatt illustrate. In his published elegy on his elder contemporary's death, An excellent Epitaffe of syr Thomas Wyat [W 1952.2], as well as in his two sonnets on the same occasion ("Dyvers thy death" and "In the rude age") Surrey occupies himself primarily with praising Wyatt's moral virtues rather than his literary ones; and in his poem praising Wyatt's Psalm translations ("The greate Macedon") he concentrates on their moral rather than their literary effects. John Hall's pious objections in The Court of Virtue [W 1565] to Wyatt's love poems in The Court of Venus [W 1955.1] are similarly tangential to criticism, as is Thomas Nashe's romantic and fictitious narrative about Surrey's love life in The Vnfortvnate Traveller [S 1594]. And the now infamous relegation of Wyatt to anonymous status on the title page of the Songes and Sonettes, written by the ryght honorable Lorde Henry Haward late Earle of Surrey, and other [WS 1557] is generally recognized to have been based on political rather than literary considerations.

Introduction

Early comments on their poetry that can be termed "critical" at least in a general sense reflect the dual role of the two poets in the development of the new literary humanism rather than their individual poetic accomplishments. John Leland, in his own elegy on Wyatt's death, published in the same year as the Epitaffe, compares him favorably with Chaucer, Dante, and Petrarch, and names Surrey as his literary disciple and heir [W 1542.1]. And George Puttenham, in The Arte of English Poesie [WS 1589], hails them together as "the first reformers of our English meetre and stile" and "the two chief lanternes of light to all others that haue since employde their pennes upon English poesie," finding "little difference" between them in his more wide-ranging enthusiasm for the beauties of the new eloquence. Puttenham's specific literary preoccupation is that of the rhetorical handbooks, and Wyatt and Surrey, among others, provide him with examples of the use of the figures he classifies in his treatise. The two poets, he tells us, travelled to Italy (Surrey was there only in Puttenham's--and Nashe's--imagination) and there discovered the iambic eloquence in the sonnets of "their Maister Francis Petrarcha," the quintessential humanist who taught them the techniques that they together put to use in forming the new poetic mode.

Puttenham's comments, in addition to stating the standard view of Wyatt and Surrey during the first period, provided the basis for a number of more recent studies. In his de facto literary marriage of the two, he set the tone for much of the material annotated in the third section of this bibliography, much of which corrects his lack of discrimination by insisting on Wyatt's superiority. And in linking the two poets with Petrarch, he opened another line of modern criticism: the study of the precise nature of their debt to the "Maister." His emphasis on the figures, moreover, foreshadowed the return of some recent criticism to the study of the relation of Renaissance poetry, including that of Wyatt and Surrey, to the prevailing literary methods of its own age.

The Songes and Sonettes, or "Tottel's Miscellany," also inadvertently initiated a significant body of modern studies related to the two poets. Not only does it provide one of the major texts of their work, but the editorial regularization of the meter in the poems it contains has been considered in this century even more outrageous than its omission of Wyatt from the title page; this has been particularly relevant to criticism of Wyatt, whose metrics have been a source of puzzlement for the better part of the history of both textual and interpretive criticism on him. Furthermore, the editors, probably without intending to, mark what later becomes an essential distinction between the two poets by singling out "the weightiness of the depe-witted Sir Thomas Wyatt the elders verse" and "the honorable stile of the noble earle of Surrey" as their characterizing terms.

That distinction, together with the editorial emasculation of Wyatt's metrics, prefaces the attitude of the second period of

Introduction

writing on the two poets. After an interregnum during which commentators maintain the uncritical and harmonious marriage performed by Puttenham, interest in their poetry revives in the eighteenth century, and when it does, it is clearly dominated by Surrey. This alteration in judgment, one that carried through the nineteenth century and into the early twentieth, is perhaps best understood in relation to the disapproval of the prosody and poetic of the Metaphysical Poets by eighteenth-century writers. Samuel Johnson's brilliant but less than enthusiastic observation of the essential nature of metaphysical wit as "discordia concors," wherein "the most heterogeneous ideas are yoked by violence together," betrays the critical sensibility that led to the decline of affection for Wyatt. And Pope's regularization of Donne's metrics in his revision of the poet's Satyre IV illustrates the same kind of attachment to the regular line that motivated the alterations performed by the Miscellany's editors:

                                        Under this pitch
            He would not fly; I chaffed him; but as itch
            Scratched into smart, and as blunt iron ground
            Into an edge, hurts worse: so, I (fool) found,
            Crossing hurt me...   (Donne, lines 87-91)

            Wild to get loose, his Patience I provoke,
            Mistake, confound, object, at all he spoke.
            But as coarse Iron, sharpen'd, mangles more,
            And Itch most hurts, when anger'd to a Sore;
            So when you plague a Fool, 'tis still the Curse,
            You only make the Matter worse and worse.
                              (Pope, lines 116-121)

It also helps to explain why Pope calls Surrey "the Granville of a former Age" in his galaxy of poets in Windsor-Forest (line 292).

     Pope's revisions of Donne and his praise of Surrey also inform the neoclassical bias that forms the basis for the most comprehensive discussion of Wyatt and Surrey in the century and a half following their deaths: that contained in Thomas Warton's The History of English Poetry [WS 1781]. Perhaps Warton's point of view is most apparent in his arrangement: he violates chronology by treating Surrey first, thus allowing himself the liberty of calling Surrey "the first English classical poet" despite his own professed admiration for the morality and polish of Wyatt's Horatian satires. Clearly, that judgment is based on stylistic criteria alone, an unavoidable conclusion considering Warton's emphases in the rest of his discussion of the two poets: he bases his distinctions between them principally on the values of smooth numbers, unconceited (and non-Petrarchan) intelligibility, and "elegance of sentiment,"

all qualities considered characteristic of Surrey or Pope but absent
in Wyatt or the Metaphysical Poets; indeed, echoing Johnson's sentiments, Warton opens his discussion of Surrey's sonnets by observing
with approval that they "have nothing of that metaphysical cast which
marks the Italian poets," and he makes unmistakable his meaning by
specifying that he is talking about the absence of the "elaborate
conceits" that he finds in both Petrarch and Wyatt. Obviously Warton's premises, like those of Johnson and Pope, reflect the changing
values of literary history, specifically the gradual metamorphosis
of humanism into neoclassicism, of the regard for eloquence in general into the particular equations between eloquence and rigidly
smooth and unconceited iambic pentameter.

It is perhaps of only incidental interest that both Warton and
Pope accept without reservation Nashe's mythical romance about Surrey, but it is a testimony to the staying power of neoclassical
critical values that the first writer to question that story, Alexander Chalmers, does not transfer his skepticism to Warton's criticism; in his sketches of Wyatt and Surrey in The Works of the English
Poets [WS 1810], Chalmers gives us the first fairly reliable biographies of the two poets, while in the same breath seconding the
unqualified verdict in favor of Surrey's poetry over Wyatt's--and in
terms strikingly similar to Warton's: Wyatt is inferior to Surrey
"in all respects," but particularly because his "versification and
language are deficient in harmony and perspicuity," and overburdened
with "puerile conceits and contrarieties"; with Warton, he specifically excepts Wyatt's satires from censure--again, in much the same
words: Wyatt "claims a place in the English series chiefly as being
the first moral satirist, and as having represented the vices and
follies of his time in the true spirit of the didactic muse." The
anti-Wyatt bias clearly becomes part of imitative literary criticism:
as various commentators echo the Miscellany, Puttenham, and Nashe,
and as Warton echoes the anti-metaphysical sensibility and Nashe, so
Chalmers, while rejecting Nashe, echoes Warton.

In his huge edition of Wyatt and Surrey, published shortly after
Chalmers' Works, George Frederick Nott [WS 1816.1] continues to give
credence to Nashe (despite Chalmers' reservations), and adds to the
applause for Surrey's smoothness and to the chastisement of Wyatt's
"rude and unformed" style, his rough versification, his archaic diction, and his overdone conceits. Nevertheless, despite finding
little originality or historical significance in Wyatt's verse, Nott
sounds the beginnings of renewed respect for Wyatt's "amatory odes":
they possess, he finds, "a certain earnestness of expression, and a
dignified simplicity of thought" that is lacking not only in Surrey
but in "every other writer in our language," a judgment that in its
overstated way echoes the recognition of "the weightiness of the
depe-witted Sir Thomas Wyatt the elders verse" in Tottel's Miscellany; more significantly, it is a perception that is repeated
numerous times and in numerous ways in the twentieth century.
However, Nott's most important contribution to modern Wyatt-Surrey

criticism lies in his editorial work: he was the first to edit the
poets from the available manuscripts, thus beginning the pioneer work
so necessary for a correct reading of them after the freewheeling
emendations by the editors of the Miscellany. The significance of
proper editorial work on early Tudor poetry, emphasized with some
heat by H. A. Mason only recently [W 1972.5], is with Nott fully
recognized for the first time.

But the depth to which Wyatt's star had fallen rendered Nott's
efforts meaningless to the anonymous author[s] of a very long response to his edition in the Edinburgh Review [WS 1816]. In a dia-
tribe that is startling even following the dismissal of Wyatt in the
eighteenth century, the anonymous reviewer spends a few brief paragraphs telling his readers why the volume devoted to Wyatt was a
waste of time, finishing the attack by observing that while Wyatt
"was a man of wit, a shrewd observer, a subtle politician..., in no
true sense of the word was he a poet," and spending the rest of his
time on what he considers the rather minimal virtues of Surrey.

The review's contempt for Wyatt and faint praise for Surrey did
not discourage further publication of their poems in the nineteenth
century, however. Both are published in the Aldine series [W 1831,
S 1831] and in Robert Bell's Annotated English Poets [W 1854.2,
S 1854], and while the Aldine editors provide no meaningful criticism, Bell advances significantly the movement toward the reappraisal
of Wyatt's individual merits that was to reach its fullest expression
and volume in the twentieth century. Although still tied to the now
traditional acceptance of Surrey's superiority, he is the first to
suggest that the differences between them resulted from differences
in kind rather than degree. Dismissing the odd coupling of the two
poets that had originated with Leland and Puttenham, Bell points out
the unlikelihood that they had ever met, and, more to the point, suggests that Wyatt's poetry was distinguished by qualities quite lacking in Surrey: his poetry is "more thoughtful," "more compressed
and weighty," and his diction less antiquated than originally thought.
Furthermore, Bell foreshadows another of the principal modern preoccupations by questioning the traditional dismissal of Wyatt's "harsh"
metrics ("his versification, incidentally harsh and refractory, is,
generally, regular and sonorous") and unintelligible conceits (his
poetry is "singularly free from conceits"). It is as if Bell had
read a different poet; despite the generalized and impressionistic
(even inaccurate) nature of his observations, he stands with Nott as
the first to see Wyatt as a separate, if not equal, poetic voice.

With the help of Nott, Bell, and the Aldine editors, then, Wyatt
survived the vitriol of the Edinburgh Review and, in fact, began once
again to be recognized for his contributions to English poetry in the
general surveys. And at the very end of the century W. J. Courthope,
in A History of English Poetry [WS 1897], states in more specific
terms some of the major observations of modern critics: Wyatt's best
poems are those in the simple native forms influenced not by foreign

models but by contemporary music; and even in his adaptations of
Continental originals, he is best when his own voice penetrates
through his sources. Courthope quite clearly redirects the emphasis
on Wyatt's artlessness in comparison to Surrey's art by pointing out
that the essential differences between them are based on different
categories of judgment: Surrey's style is his "predominant poetical
virtue," and his improvements on earlier metrical practices give
him the more significant place in literary history, whereas in
Wyatt's less artful poetry "matter prevails over form," an interesting contrast that at once looks forward to twentieth-century critics'
fascination with finding out exactly what is going on in some of his
more ambiguous poems and backward to that increasingly interesting
distinction between the "weightiness" of the "depe-witted" Wyatt and
the "honorable stile" of the "noble earle."

Another late nineteenth-century study, Edmond Bapst's biography
of Surrey [S 1891], requires comment for a number of reasons. For
one, Bapst buries once and for all the fictions about Surrey's Italian travels, his friendship with Wyatt, and his love for Geraldine.
Also, in contrast to the romances of previous biographies and the
sentimental and/or ax-grinding accounts of the twentieth century, he
provides a sober and evenhanded appraisal of Surrey's character,
without insisting on making connections between his life and his love
poetry. But Bapst is particularly interesting because his book sym-
bolizes the direction of modern comment on Surrey: the only book
written exclusively on the poet in the twentieth century, Edwin
Casady's Henry Howard, Earl of Surrey [S 1938] is a biography. Wyatt,
on the other hand, is the subject of a number of important book-length
studies, not one of which is a biography. The implications of these
facts are rather clear: the old fascination with Surrey the nobleman,
even deromanticized, is more interesting to modern readers than his
poetry, while the fascination with Wyatt the poet--or the persona--is
more interesting than either. And for the same reason that Hamlet the
man or Hamlet the play is more interesting than Shakespeare, Wyatt becomes the dominant figure in twentieth-century criticism of early
Tudor poetry, or, at worst, shares the laurel with Skelton.

The Wyatt revival begins to take on a more well-defined shape
early in the century with the publication of Agnes K. Foxwell's
A Study of Sir Thomas Wyatt's Poems and her two-volume edition, The
Poems of Sir Thomas Wiat [W 1911, W 1913]. The two works deal with
various topics, the most important of which look forward to later
criticism. Her discussion of the three major Wyatt manuscripts, the
Egerton (Wyatt's autograph, which Foxwell identifies as the most
important), the Devonshire (the oldest), and Add. MS. 28635, represents an early stage in the long and contentious debate about his
text and canon that has not yet been resolved. Her exhaustive, if
ill-advised, attempt to decipher his system of versification by
means of chronology and variations on a series of rules forms an important part of that long debate. And her attempt to establish
sources, both native and Continental, for his various poetic forms
becomes the basis for another very fruitful line of investigation in

later studies. But perhaps the most interesting of her observations, at least in retrospect, are her recognition of Wyatt's similarities to Donne and her perceptive conclusion that "the upholding of Truth in life, and the continual war waged against falseness, are the two dominant notes" in his poetry, the first of which leads to more mature investigations of his hard lines and the dramatic nature of his verse, the second of which becomes one in a long series of increasingly convincing efforts to articulate his (or his personas') fundamental attitude(s) toward existence. The absence of similar preoccupations in twentieth-century criticism of Surrey helps to explain the modern resurgence of Wyatt.

Other early twentieth-century studies add to the new interest in and respect for Wyatt generated by Nott, Bell, Courthope, and Foxwell. John Erskine, in The Elizabethan Lyric [WS 1903] finds him of real historical significance as "the earliest singer of the Elizabethan subjective lyric," and actually considers him more successful in the lyric genres than Surrey. George Saintsbury presents, in The History of English Prosody [WS 1906.2], an evenhanded and detailed account of his contributions to sonnet development and, instead of complaining about his versification, blames its capriciousness on the general problems of English pronunciation in the early sixteenth century. And in The Cambridge History of English Literature [WS 1909], Harold Child expresses appreciation for Wyatt's improvements on the "vague thought, loose expression and irregular metre" of the Chaucerians and, with Saintsbury, dismisses his metrical aberrations as the product of the unstable state of English pronunciation, going one step further by placing equal blame on the false text of the Miscellany. Child sounds several other modern chords as well, finding value in the unconventional "personal note" in Wyatt's love poems, recognizing the special excellence of the native lyrics, and noticing with others a harbinger of Donne in the "ruggedness" of Wyatt's versification. Frederick Morgan Padelford, on the other hand, steps backward by supplementing Foxwell's list of prosodic variants to further support her contention that Wyatt's departures from strict iambic pentameter were, in Padelford's words, "in accordance with a body of recognized prosodic variants" [W 1923].

The efforts of Foxwell and Padelford to prove that Wyatt was iambic and decasyllabic at heart remind us that the Wyatt revival was still very much in its early stages in the early part of the century. The standards of the Old Criticism, exemplified by its preference not only for uncomplicated metrics but for unconceited language and unambiguous statement--all qualities generally associated with Surrey since Warton and before--remain in force through most of the first three decades of this century. Despite their generally positive attitude toward Wyatt, both Saintsbury and Child, for example, still consider Surrey the more accomplished poet, and Padelford, in his edition of Early Sixteenth Century Lyrics [WS 1907], finds Surrey "in all respects a successful pupil of Petrarch" because of his "technique, care for form, clearness and compression, felicity of diction, and rhythmical ease," while judging most of Wyatt's Petrarchan poems as failures because of their subtle conceits, "artificial" antitheses, and "trite" metaphors. Specific studies of the sonnet forms of the two poets by Hanscom [WS 1901], Lathrop [WS 1905] and Bullock [WS 1923], while all concerned with formal sources, nevertheless assume in passing that Surrey's practice represented an improvement over Wyatt's.

Furthermore, textual studies of Surrey compete with Foxwell's on Wyatt during the early decades. The work of several German scholars [S 1881, 1902, 1903, 1905], together with that of Gladys D. Willcock [S 1919, 1920.2, 1922.1] on Surrey's translation of Book Four of the Aeneid provide the climate for Padelford's significant edition of The Poems of Henry Howard, Earl of Surrey [S 1920.1] which, in addition to providing the most accurate text of Surrey up to its time, reaffirms the traditional judgments of his merits and importance. While he gives Wyatt full credit for his own advances in prosody, Padelford quite naturally focuses his attention on Surrey's development of the English sonnet and blank verse, and on the virtues of his prosody (particularly his caesuras and run-on lines) and diction ("direct, firm, and muscular, but flexible and euphonious"). He also gives us another biography, "The Dramatic Career of Surrey," that, even without the defunct fictions of Nashe, et al., is unembarrassedly romantic and intimately related to the poems, which Padelford, consistent with the extraliterary nature of much of the old interest in Surrey's poetry, labels a "lyrical accompaniment" to an "impressive tragedy."

But the most significant--and essentially the last--vote in favor of Surrey over Wyatt is registered in a book that even today is considered one of the most important studies of the poetry of the early years of the sixteenth century, John M. Berdan's Early Tudor Poetry [S 1920, W 1920]. In its very arrangement Berdan's treatment of the two poets is a testimony to its time: while he discusses Wyatt in interspersed larger sections, he devotes a separate, titled, culminating chapter to Surrey. And his criticism of Wyatt is consistent with his organization: the poet's main appeal is not personal or autobiographical, but merely literary and intellectual; the bulk of his work consists of literary exercises in translation of Italian sources, most of which are inferior and characterized by that Petrarchan method "wherein a metaphor is...pursued to its last ramification"; except for the individual merits of those poems that deal with "the life around him" or that are meant to be sung, his technical virtues represent his main value to the Elizabethans. In Surrey's poetry, on the other hand, Berdan sees the maturity reached by the end of the early Tudor period, a maturity resulting from the combination of Italian, native, and classical sources with a well-tuned poetic sensibility. In short, Berdan finds nothing of the human interest in Wyatt that Padelford sees in Surrey's "lyrical accompaniment[s]," and he shares with Warton the old prejudice against Wyatt's curling metaphors. But it is important to keep in mind that his praise of Surrey is itself relatively faint in the context of his larger view of early Tudor poetry in general: it is essentially "'prentice work" for the greater accomplishments of the Elizabethans, a judgment similar to C. S. Lewis's later contrast between "drab" and "golden" thirty-four years later [WS 1954]. It is significant that the rehabilitation of that whole body of verse does not take place until after the complete exhumation of Wyatt's reputation.

The criticism generally regarded as the first real proclamation of the Wyatt revival is that contained in E. M. W. Tillyard's The Poetry of Sir Thomas Wyatt: A Selection and a Study [W 1929.2], a book that does for Wyatt's reputation what Grierson's Metaphysical Lyrics and Poems of the XVIIth Century does for Donne's. Tillyard bases the introductory comments to his selection on the premise that Wyatt's best poetry is the product not of fumbling imitations of more sophisticated foreign models but of conscious artistic decisions, and goes on from that to reassess his prosody, his relation to his sources, the relative merits of the various kinds of poems in his canon, and his relation to Donne and Surrey. From Tillyard's point of view the "roughness" of Wyatt's metrics is actually a deliberate and subtle type of irregularity that produces "extreme simplicity of language and an almost conversational cadence," qualities best seen not in his translations and adaptations of foreign models, but in his native songs, which achieve a "lyric spontaneity" that mirrors the revival of music in the medieval and Tudor English courts, and which thus merit more serious attention than his rondeaux, sonnets, epigrams, or even the Satires and Psalms. The qualities of those lyrics, moreover, produce in their conversational and spontaneous tone a dramatic effect similar to those of Donne, and distinguish Wyatt completely from Surrey, whose poems contain "no more drama, no more sense of the here and now than...most of the lyrics of Matthew Arnold."

It is necessary to recognize that Tillyard's reappraisal was neither entirely new nor immediately felt. His appreciation of Wyatt's prosody had been preceded by a gradual tempering of Warton's antipathy, and he was not the first to point out the virtues of Wyatt's native lyrics or the affinities between Wyatt and Donne. Nevertheless, his explicit rejection of Surrey and his reassessment of the motives and effects of Wyatt's irregular prosody, together with the fundamental change in the foundations of critical judgment implied in his statement that "Wyatt, by virtue of his profounder and more passionate temperament is a greater poet than Surrey" represent significant departures from the mainstream of previous critical opinion--and eventually become the basis for its redirection.

But not immediately. In the same year that Tillyard published his remarks, Hyder Rollins published the second volume, containing notes and introduction, of his edition of the Songes and Sonettes,

Introduction

entitled <u>Tottel's Miscellany (1557-1587)</u> [WS 1929]. While acknowledging Wyatt's historical importance, Rollins, perhaps influenced by the literary sensibility of the anthology's first editor[s], voices old and familiar reservations about his "elaborate conceits," "grotesque imagery," "strange pronunciation" and "rough movement," and credits Surrey with the correction of those faults. The virtually simultaneous publication of the opposing views of Tillyard and Rollins at the end of the third decade of the twentieth century, then, leaves unresolved the question of the comparative worth and significance of Wyatt and Surrey, and the scattered comments comparing them during the 1930s add little clarification to the debate.

However, publications treating the two poets separately during that period provide, in retrospect, a gauge of the momentum gathering in Wyatt's favor. Charles Read Baskervill's introduction to his edition of Wyatt's translation of Plutarch's <u>Quyete of Mynde</u> [W 1931] praises the "sinewy and vigorous prose style" and "moral earnestness" of the translation and specifically connects it with "a significant phase of the new Tudor poetry" that is to be distinguished from "the rigid conventions and far fetched conceits of lyric and sonnet." And E. K. Chambers, in <u>Sir Thomas Wyatt and Some Collected Studies</u> [W 1933] seconds Tillyard's preference for the poet's native songs over the translations as well as his recognition of the similarity between Wyatt and Donne: each poet reflects the point of view of the "psychologist, watching his own emotions in detachment." While both Tillyard and Chambers provide brief biographies of Wyatt, their interest is clearly centered on establishing the specific and peculiar qualities of his work. In this their studies differ markedly from the only extensive treatment of Surrey during the decade, Casady's biography [S 1938], which relegates "Surrey's Contribution to English Literature" to an appendix that, in the general opinion of its reviewers, adds nothing new to Surrey criticism [S 1939.1, 1939.2, 1939.3, 1939.4, 1939.6]. But perhaps the most influential assessment of the two poets in the 1930s is contained in Yvor Winters' series of articles on "The 16th Century Lyric in England" in <u>Poetry: A Magazine of Verse</u> [WS 1939], which add another more comprehensive dimension to the study of Renaissance poetry in general by distinguishing between the non-Petrarchan, "plain" school, characterized by its intellectual and complex depth, its restrained and direct style, and its "sombre and disillusioned" tone, and the eloquent/Petrarchan school, which is chiefly characterized by the absence of those qualities. Winters establishes a new set of categories, one that reflects an essential alteration of the old ones implied in the criticism of Warton and his followers; and in placing Wyatt's poetry in the first category and Surrey's principally in the second, he contributes another pattern that informs the resurrection of the former and the burial of the latter—one later reaffirmed explicitly by Douglas Peterson in <u>The English Lyric from Wyatt to Donne</u> [WS 1967.2].

Introduction

The next decade continues the trend established in the 1930s:
the bibliography does not record a single significant study exclusively devoted to Surrey, while Wyatt scholarship produces a concordance, a number of significant articles, and two new editions.
Eva Catherine Hangan's concordance of Wyatt's complete works [W 1941],
based on Foxwell's edition, establishes a basis for Josephine Miles'
comparisons between Wyatt's diction and Donne's [W 1945, WS 1948],
and two very well-known essays provide commonsense explanations for
his metrics and style: D. W. Harding, in "The Rhythmical Intention
in Wyatt's Poetry" [W 1946], suggests that we recognize that his
lines follow the natural rhythms of speech rather than the set system outlined originally by Foxwell, and that they also reflect both
the movement toward iambic pentameter and the survival of native al-
literative/accentual "pausing verse"; and Hallett Smith, in "The Art
of Sir Thomas Wyatt" [W 1946.1], advises us that Wyatt's poetic aims
were different from those of Surrey and Spenser, and that judging
his "roughness" by the standards of their "sweet and sonorous" lines
errs in failing to see that it comes from his desire to achieve the
peculiar effects characteristic of the plain style. An equally
reasonable, if less heralded, article, E. D. Mackerness' "The Transitional Nature of Wyatt's Poetry" [W 1948], offers a general commentary that ranges from Wyatt's relation to Chaucer, Donne, and music
to the virtues of his metrics and the dramatic nature of his verse.
The three essays are strikingly similar in their joint enthusiasm
for Wyatt's peculiar strengths, and important for later criticism
because of what they consider those strengths to be: his conversational metrics, his similarities to Chaucer and Donne, his "plain
style," his dramatic immediacy, his relation to music.

If the printing of a writer's work is an accurate gauge of his
reputation, then the year 1949 marks another plateau in Wyatt criticism. Alan Swallow's edition of Some Poems by Sir Thomas Wyatt
[W 1949.2] and Kenneth Muir's Collected Poems of Sir Thomas Wyatt
[W 1949.1], together with the reprinting of Tillyard's Selection
[W 1949.3], complete the first stage in the Wyatt revival that had
been tentatively approached in the nineteenth century and fully
initiated with the original publication of Tillyard in 1929. That
Surrey was not to be edited again until the 1960s is perhaps best
accounted for in Muir's dismissal of his significance as "one of the
most curious delusions in English literary history," a remark that
in its benign contempt marks the full turn of the wheel in modern
criticism of the two poets. Although Veré L. Rubel had examined
both poets with equal vigor in Poetic Diction in the English Renaissance [WS 1941], her concentration on the more traditional
approaches of rhetoric and diction perhaps itself signals the demise
of interest in the kind of poetry Surrey wrote.

The continued emphasis on Wyatt in the 1950s is perhaps most
accurately indicated by the fact that more essays were published on
"They fle from me" than on all of Surrey. The one significant study
of his poetry during the decade, Ants Oras' "Surrey's Technique of

Introduction

Phonetic Echoes" [S 1951], suggests, in a way, his departure from
the field, for it concentrates on his Aeneid translations, which
represent an activity not engaged in by Wyatt, and singles out for
comment the "grave stateliness" and clarity produced by his use of
assonance, consonance and rhyme, techniques that do not clash with
Wyatt's peculiarities. Furthermore, the major books published during
the decade are virtually unanimous in their verdict in favor of Wyatt.
The only full-length study of the poet, Sergio Baldi's La Poesia di
Sir Thomas Wyatt [W 1953], is naturally the most detailed one, covering Wyatt's life, texts, and chronology, as well as surveying
Wyatt criticism and providing a comprehensive discussion of his
metrics that relates them to Donne and Milton as well as to modern
poetry. (The only other book devoted exclusively to Wyatt, Russell
A. Fraser's edition of The Court of Venus [W 1955.1], is of historical importance because it records the presence of work by the poet
in England's first poetic anthology.) Books dealing with both Wyatt
and Surrey begin to sound familiar: Tillyard's The English Renaissance: Fact or Fiction? [WS 1952] finds that Wyatt's lyrics
transcend his age in their (Donne-like) dramatic and introspective
psychology, while labeling the less original Surrey as typically
Tudor in his classical "balance and harmony"; J. W. Lever, in The
Elizabethan Love Sonnet [WS 1956.2], finds Wyatt more faithful to
Petrarch and more effective than Surrey in the art of the sonnet;
and H. A. Mason, in Humanism and Poetry in the Early Tudor Period
[WS 1959], while differing substantially with the growing enthusiasm
for Wyatt's lyrics at the expense of his translations (the study of
the Devonshire lyrics "belongs to sociology rather than literature"),
recognizes Wyatt the "Grant Translateur" as "the only poet of the
first period of Humanism," his "isolated superiority" unchallenged
by Surrey; and while C. S. Lewis finds neither poet of sufficient
merit to climb out of the "Drab Age," he does recognize that Wyatt's
"fame is in the ascendent," an admission that at this point in the
history of Wyatt-Surrey criticism quivers with understatement
[WS 1954]. Only A. Lytton Sells, in The Italian Influence in English Poetry [WS 1955] remains interested in both poets.

The works of Baldi, Tillyard, Lever, Lewis, and Mason are probably the most important of the large number of publications on Wyatt
in the 1950s. But even a necessarily rigid selection of other
statements must include Swallow's "The Pentameter Lines in Skelton
and Wyatt" [W 1950.5], which returns to the long debate over Wyatt's
prosody, and Harding's "The Poetry of Wyatt" [W 1954.2], which re-
iterates his conclusions about Wyatt's "pausing rhythm" and enters
another theory about his love poems that continues to be important
in later criticism: the interesting view that the language of the
love tradition provided the poet with a vehicle for dealing with
more serious ideas. Harding's suggestion is an interesting example
of the merging of two separate traditions associated with Wyatt:
the old view of his moral and "depe-witted" character that goes back
to Surrey's Epitaffe and the preface to the Miscellany, and the
gradually increasing recognition of the dramatic nature of his poetry
in modern criticism.

Introduction

The growth of interest in Wyatt continues to gather force in the
1960s, and produces a still larger and more significant body of
criticism of all sorts and in all forms. In addition, interest in
Surrey undergoes its own minor revival after thirty years of relative silence. Predictably, the interest in both poets is accompanied by increased attention to their texts. Kenneth Muir continues his work on Wyatt by editing his letters for a partial biography, the Life and Letters of Sir Thomas Wyatt [W 1963.3], and by
bringing out two new editions of the poems: the first, Sir Thomas
Wyatt and His Circle: Unpublished Poems [W 1961.6], is based on a
manuscript of Tudor poetry, the Blage, which, in addition to con-
taing many Wyatt poems that appear in the other manuscripts, also
contains a significant number of heretofore unascribed poems that
Muir believes might be his as well; the second, which Muir edited
with Patricia Thomson, is a new Collected Poems [W 1969.3] that
combines the 1949 edition of the same title with the Blage poems.
Surrey is also represented in two editions: Emrys Jones' Henry
Howard, Earl of Surrey: Poems [S 1964] and Florence Ridley's edition of his Aeneid translations [S 1963.2]. Jones' principal
focus in his critical remarks is on Surrey's Latin neoclassicism,
and he thus concentrates, as did Oras, on the humanistic eloquence
in the translations of Virgil. Ridley attempts to demonstrate
Surrey's heavy debt in the translations to Gavin Douglas' Eneados,
and thus prints them with Douglasisms in italics. But the most
significant textual work published in the decade is Ruth Hughey's
meticulous edition of The Arundel Harington Manuscript of Tudor
Poetry [WS 1960.2], which provides the model for editorial work on
the poetry of Wyatt, Surrey and their contemporaries, one that becomes more clearly recognized in the next decade, when the shortcomings of much of the textual scholarship on the poets become the
subject of some debate.

The increasingly intimate relationship between Wyatt scholarship
and the principles of the New Criticism is clearly exemplified during
the 1960s by the many additional published attempts to clarify the
various types of ambiguity in "They fle from me" [see Index];
indeed, the emergence of that poem as the single most thoroughly
explicated Wyatt work provides the clearest and most specific mani-
festation of the modern revival of the poet. Nevertheless, the
two most significant studies of his work during the decade are both
at least partly historical in approach. Patricia Thomson's Sir
Thomas Wyatt and his Background [W 1964.13], as its title implies,
explores the various literary and extraliterary forces that went
into the definition of his individual poetic modes: his personal
experiences in life as well as his contemporary literary, social,
and political milieu; she thus investigates the traditions of
courtly love, classical and Tudor moral and political philosophy,
Renaissance humanism, Petrarch and his Italian commentators, Chaucer, Serafino, Horace. Raymond Southall, in The Courtly Maker
[W 1964.10], begins with essentially the same premise as Thomson--
that the poetry of Wyatt and his contemporaries must be examined

against the realities of Tudor court life--but he takes a giant step
away from that context by concentrating more specifically on the
individual psychological sensibility behind the poet's rejection of
his milieu. Southall's subject is not Wyatt, really, but Wyatt's
personas, because he is not convinced that the manuscripts betray
his identity. The result is a book that combines the methods of
historical and psychological criticism and one that, in addition to
its other contributions, provides a new and more complex view of the
Wyatt-Donne connection, finding the differences between the two poets
to lie in Wyatt's more intimate personal involvement with the courtly
world that they both reject.

The studies of Thomson and Southall signal the coming of age of
Wyatt criticism, and other works contemporary with theirs develop
further one's sense of that maturity. Otto Hietsch, in Die Petrarcaübersetzungen Sir Thomas Wyatts [W 1960], distinguishes between
Wyatt's literal renderings of Petrarch and those poems in which he
transcends his Italian master to deal with his own personal and literary circumstances. Sergio Baldi's second book on the poet
[W 1961] emphasizes the personal, as opposed to the Petrarchan,
source of his characteristic "sadness" and his unique poetic technique. Essays by Marco Pecoraro [W 1961.7], Donald Guss [W 1963.2,
1965.4], Michael McCanles [W 1968.5], and Donald M. Friedman
[W 1966.2, 1967, 1968.1] also redirect our attention away from his
sources toward more complex psychological and philosophical motives
that penetrate beneath them and alter them in significant ways.
Another essay by Southall betrays these new interests in its very
title: "The Personality of Sir Thomas Wyatt" [W 1964.12]; as does
another by Friedman: "Wyatt's Amoris Personae" [W 1966.3]. And
Karl P. Wentersdorf applies Caroline Spurgeon's method of studying
Shakespeare's Imagery to "The Imagery of Wyatt" [W 1965.16], illus-
trating further the relevance of modern critical methods to Wyatt's
poetry, and helping to explain further the gradual resurgence of his
reputation during the course of the last four or five decades.

The liberation of Wyatt's poetry from its traditional associa-
tions with his sources also reminds us of his latter-day divorce
from Surrey. But liberation works two ways, and the rebirth of
emphasis on Surrey's "neoclassicism," together with the related revival of interest in his Aeneid, indicates that the parting between
the two poets has been mutually beneficial. Hallet Smith's reminder
[W 1946.1] that Wyatt's aims and methods should be distinguished
from those of Surrey and Spenser was one of the most important
catalysts in the Wyatt revival; similarly William O. Harris, in a
study of the two poets' very different renderings of Petrarch's
"Amor, che nel penser mio vive e regna," concludes that the differences between their translations result not from Surrey's inferior
abilities but from "quite different, but equally valid purposes"
[S 1969]. More comprehensive studies that include discussions of
both poets suggest, implicitly or explicitly, the same point.
Peterson's more detailed development of Winters' categories

in The English Lyric from Wyatt to Donne [WS 1967.2], while clearly favoring Wyatt's "plain" to Surrey's "eloquent" style, nevertheless contrasts the two poets on the basis of generic, rather than merely personal, differences, as does Maurice Evans in English Poetry in the Sixteenth Century [WS 1967.1]. And John Buxton, in A Tradition of Poetry [WS 1967], accounts for the twentieth-century rejection of Surrey in terms of the difference between his classical and stylistic poetic detachment as opposed to the more personal involvement in their poetry of Gavin Douglas and Wyatt. John Thompson, in The Founding of English Metre [WS 1961.1], however, is more "traditional" --which, ironically, means that at this point in the history of Wyatt and Surrey criticism he extols Wyatt at the expense of Surrey on the basis of a single category of judgment.

As of this writing, it is beginning to appear that the 1960s represented the crest of the Wyatt revival. The present decade has not yet produced critical work on his poetry that is equal in quality, significance or abundance to the work of the last one. Nor has it yet fulfilled the promise of the minor resurgence of Surrey that seemed to be gathering force during the same period of time. While the apparent loss of momentum in both camps is no doubt the result of a complex of forces still in the process of formation, and thus undecipherable at this moment, one pattern seems to have emerged so far: much recent work on the two poets has been involved, in one way or another, with that done in the recent past.

This pattern is particularly apparent in recent discussions of Wyatt's texts. Both H. A. Mason and Joost Daalder articulate harsh reservations about the Muir and Muir-Thomson editions of the previous decade, although they express their dissatisfaction in different ways: Mason writes Editing Wyatt [W 1972.5], an unusual monograph that corrects "the many hundreds of errors" in the Muir-Thomson edition and follows that with an interesting proposal for a community scholarly effort aimed at producing a definitive Wyatt text; Daalder edits his own version of the Collected Poems [W 1975]. However, the controversy does not end there, for Mason finds other faults with Daalder's edition, and finally voices his own exasperated preference for the old editions of Nott and Swallow [W 1976.2]. Richard Harrier has recently published The Canon of Sir Thomas Wyatt's Poetry [W 1975.1], an exhaustive study of all the major manuscripts and printed sources, but that too has drawn criticism from Mason [W 1976.2]. All of which suggests that work on Wyatt's text and canon has not yet ended, or even begun to end.

Some of the other recent work done on both poets also looks backward. This decade has seen the publication of "A Wyatt Bibliography" [W 1970.4], a bibliography of "Recent Studies in Wyatt and Surrey" [WS 1971], and a book-length collection of extracts from major Wyatt criticism [W 1974.9]; this reference guide provides another summation. In addition, many critical essays simply echo previous statements about Wyatt's sources, metrics, multifaceted

personas, socio-literary milieu and ambiquities while others continue
the discussions about Surrey's neoclassical metrics and style.

Despite the reflexive nature of much recent scholarship, however,
some of it points in other directions that have not been fully ex-
plored. Robert G. Twombly focuses fresh attention on Wyatt's Psalms
[W 1970.6], and Mason and Michael Rudick examine Surrey's [S 1971,
1975]. A. N. Brilliant looks more closely at Wyatt's prose style
in The Quyete of Mynde [W 1971.2], while Daalder reexamines the
relationship of Tottel's Miscellany and Wyatt from a substantive
rather than a metrical point of view [W 1972.2]. And Walter R. Davis
and David A. Richardson explore in more significant detail the effects of Surrey's classical humanism [S 1974.1, 1976.1] If there is
a trend in the most recent criticism of the two poets, it may have to
do with a look backward not to the 1960s but to the sixteenth century,
that is, to the practice of Tudor composition and its effect not so
much on the style as on the structure of their verse. Thomas Hannen's essay on Wyatt's rhetorical structures in The Rhetoric of
Renaissance Poetry from Wyatt to Milton [W 1974.5] takes just such
an approach, as do recent essays on Surrey by myself and Leonard
Nathan [S 1973, 1976, 1977]. Indeed, Alastair Fowler, in Conceitful
Thought [WS 1975], argues by means of close explication of ambiguous
poems by both poets that they might very well be better understood
and appreciated by modern readers who have informed themselves of
the principles behind the actual writing of Tudor verse. It is
interesting that Mason articulates a somewhat similar position about
the study of Tudor texts in Editing Wyatt.

From one point of view, then, the history of Wyatt-Surrey criticism has come full circle. From another, it has simply involved
increasingly complex approaches to the same set of concerns: the
relationship of their poetry to native and Continental sources, its
place in the development of English prosody and style, its illumina-
tion of the problem of determining the legitimacy of early English
texts, and its place in the development of the modern critical sensibility. As part of such larger matters, the profound differences
between the two poets help us to understand in microcosm the dynam-
ics of English literary history and criticism in general, and in so
doing justifies our continuing attention. And as the recognition of
their particular contributions to those processes becomes increasingly clear through the methods of modern explication, it becomes
more and more apparent that historical significance and individual
gifts form an inevitably complementary whole.

Writings about Wyatt

1542

BECON, THOMAS. [Dedication], in The New Pollecye of Warre.
   London: printed by J. Maylerre for J. Gough, sig. B4v.
      Dedicatory praises of Wyatt's "perfect knowledge of the
   diuersitie of Languages" and his "graue exercise of diuine
   litterature." [Cited in, quoted from W 1968.]

1 LELAND, JOHN. Naeniae in mortem Thomae Viati equitis incomparabilis. London: R. Wolfius [STC 15446].
      A collection of Latin poetic tributes to Wyatt.

2 SURREY, HENRY HOWARD, EARL OF. An excellent Epitaffe of syr
   Thomas Wyat, With two other compendious dytties, wherin
   are touchyd, and set furth the state of mannes lyfe.
   London: printed by Iohn Herforde for Robert Toye [STC
   26054].
      Contains "Wyat resteth here." The other two poems are
   neither on Wyatt nor by Surrey.

1544

BETHAM, PETER. [Dedication], in his translation of Preceptes
   of Warre, Set forth by James the erle of Purlila. London:
   Edward Whytchurche, sig. A6r.
      Praises Wyatt for remaining in the tradition of Chaucer
   rather than affecting inkhorn terms and foreign words.
   [Cited in W 1968.]

1545

LELAND, JOHN. Cygnea cantio. London: J. Herford [STC
   15444].
      Praises Wyatt's contributions to Britain's naval
   defense. [From W 1974.9.]

1

1550

SHERRY, RICHARD. <u>A Treatise of Schemes and Tropes</u>. London:
John Day.
Praises Wyatt's eloquence. [From the facsimile ed.,
Herbert W. Hildebrandt. Gainesville, Florida: Scholars'
Facsimiles & Reprints, 1969.]

1557

SURREY, HENRY HOWARD, Earl of. "Dyvers thy death," "In the
rude age," and "The great Macedon," in <u>Songes and Sonettes</u>
[WS 1557].
Poems on Wyatt, the first two lamenting his death and
attacking his enemies, the third praising his Psalms.

1565

HALL, JOHN. <u>The Couurte of Vertue Contaynynge Many holy or</u>
<u>spretuall songes Sonettes psalmes ballettes shorte senten-</u>
<u>ces as well of holy scriptures as others &c</u>. London:
printed by Thomas Marshe [STC 12632].
Transforms secular poems by Wyatt ("My penne take payne,"
"Blame not my lute," "My lute awake") into moralizing
pieces as part of a general attack on secular poetry.
[From W 1961.1.]

1831

ANON. "Memoir of Sir Thomas Wyatt," in <u>The Poetical Works of</u>
<u>Sir Thomas Wyatt</u>. The Aldine Edition of the British Poets.
London: Bell and Daldy, pp. ix-lxi.
Brief biography. [Dated 1830 in <u>BM Catalogue</u>. Re-
printed: W 1854, 1870.]

1848

ANON. "Anne Boleyn and Sir Thomas Wyatt." <u>Bentley's Miscel-</u>
<u>lany</u>, 23:233-238.
Tells the story of Wyatt's leading role in the removal
of Anne's body from its grave in St. Peter's Church in the
Tower to her family estate at Blickling, and eventually to
the family tomb at Salle.

1850

BRUCE, JOHN. "Recovery of the Lost Accusation of Sir Thomas
Wyatt, the Poet, by Bishop Bonner." Gentlemen's Magazine,
32 (June), 563-570.
  Provides a transcript of the letter (from Petyt Ms. no.
47, fo. 9), together with introduction and commentary on
the accusations.

1 _____. "Unpublished Anecdotes of Sir Thomas Wyatt the Poet,
and of Other Members of That Family." Gentlemen's Magazine, 32 (September), 235-241.
  Relates incidents about Wyatt's parents, his capture
and ransom in Italy, and his first imprisonment in the
Tower. [Includes transcripts of letters relating to the
imprisonment.]

1854

ANON. "Memoir of Sir Thomas Wyatt," in The Poetical Works of
Sir Thomas Wyatt. The Aldine Edition of the British Poets.
London: Bell and Daldy, pp. ix-lxi.
  Reprint of W 1931.

1 ANON. "Memoir of Sir Thomas Wyatt," in The Poetical Works of
Sir Thomas Wyatt. With a Memoir. Boston: Little, Brown
and Co.; New York: Evans and Dickerson; Philadelphia:
Lippincott, Grambo and Co., pp. xi-xlvii.
  Slightly revised version of W 1854.

2 BELL, ROBERT. "Sir Thomas Wyatt. 1503-1542," in his edition
of Poetical Works of Sir Thomas Wyatt. The Annotated Edition of the English Poets, edited by Robert Bell. London:
John W. Parker and Son, pp. 11-60.
  Nott's assertion that Surrey influenced Wyatt's adoption of the iambic form [WS 1816.1] is contradicted by the
evidence: Wyatt was older, and it is unlikely that the
two ever met. Wyatt's poetry, while generally inferior to
Surrey's, is nevertheless "more thoughtful" and "more compressed and weighty." His diction is less antiquated than
heretofore thought; his vocabulary is large; "his versification, incidentally harsh and refractory, is, generally,
regular and sonorous," its deficiencies due to problems
with foreign models. While he lacks originality, his
reading in foreign authors gave his poetry "scope and
variety," and he is freer of conceit than they. [Includes
biography.]

3

1868

CLARKE, CHARLES COWDEN. "The Life of Sir Thomas Wyatt," in
his edition of The Poetical Works of Sir Thomas Wyatt.
With a Memoir and Critical Dissertation. Edinburgh:
William P. Nimmo, pp. v-xvii.
Biography and brief commentary on the poetry.

1870

ANON. "Memoir of Sir Thomas Wyatt," in The Poetical Works of
Sir Thomas Wyatt. The Aldine Edition of the British Poets.
London: Bell and Daldy, pp. ix-xcvi.
Reprint of W 1831.

1871

BOND, EDWARD A. "Wyatt's Poems." The Athenaeum, no. 2274
(May 27), pp. 654-655.
Describes contents of the Devonshire Manuscript (BM Add.
MS. 17492), locating Wyatt poems, and providing evidence
relating to its ownership and date.

1877

*ANON. "Sir Thomas Wyatt the Elder." Dublin University Maga-
zine, 89, p. 161.
Cited in W 1970.4.

1886

ALSCHER, RUDOLF. Sir Thomas Wyatt und Seine Stellung in der
Entwickelungageschichte der Englischen Literatur und Ver-
kunst. Weiner Beitrage zur Deutschen und Englischen
Philologie, edited by R. Heinzel, J. Minor, and J. Schip-
per. Wien: Wilhelm Braumuller, 151 pp.
Discusses Wyatt's life, works (sonnets, rondeaux, odes,
"sinngedichte," Psalms, Satires, letters), and versification (rhythm, prosody, word accent/stress, rhyme, verse
[stanza] structure). [In German.]

1889

SIMONDS, WILLIAM EDWARD. Sir Thomas Wyatt and His Poems.
   Boston: D. C. Heath & Co., 156 pp.
      Classifies Wyatt's poems into six chronological groups,
   subdividing each by form and content, for the purpose of
   relating his poetic development to his life. These groups,
   in turn, are subordinated to the two "grand divisions" of
   his poetic activity and his life: the "Court Period"
   (1521-1522 to 1536), which includes most of the love poems,
   and the later period (1536 to 1542), characterized by "a
   deeper insight, a more earnest view of life; the expression
   of religious feeling; an inclination to philosophize," and
   comprising mainly the Satires and the Psalm paraphrases.
   [Includes biography, discussion of texts, tables, indices.]

1890

BROWNLOW, E. B. "Sir Thomas Wyatt." The Nation, 51 (September 11), 211.
      Asks for information on possible sources for "Like unto
   these unmeasurable mountains" and identifies the source of
   "Avising the bright beams" as Petrarch's "Mirando '1 Sol
   de begli occhi sereno." Recommends further investigation
   of sources for Wyatt's poetry.

1891

_____. "Sonnets of Sir Thomas Wyatt." Poet-Lore, 3, no. 1,
   44-45.
      The source for "Avising the bright beams" is Petrarch's
   "Mirando '1 Sol de' begli occhi sereno." The source for
   "I abide, and abide" is Marot's "J'attends secours de ma
   seule pensée."

1   _____. "Wyatt's Sonnets and Their Sources." Poet-Lore, 3,
   no. 3, 127-134.
      Evidence indicates that Wyatt, rather than Surrey, in-
   troduced the sonnet to England. [Includes a list of
   twenty of Wyatt's sonnets with their sources and twelve
   whose sources have not been identified.]

2   COOK, ALBERT S. "The Original of Wyatt's 'Unmeasurable
   Mountains.'" Poet-Lore, 3, no. 2, 97-98.
      The source for the poem is St. Gelais' sonnet "Voyant
   ces monts de veue ainsi lointaine."

1891

3   KOEPPEL, E[MIL]. "Sir Thomas Wyatt und Melin de Saint-Gelais."
        Anglia, 13:77-78.
            Compares "Lyke vnto these vnmeasurable mountaines" to
        St. Gelais' "Voyant ces monts de veue ainsi lointaine" and
        "The enmy of life, decayer of all kinde" to St. Gelais'
        "Pres du sercueil d'une morte gisante." [In German.]

4   WADDINGTON, SAMUEL. "The Sonnets of Sir Thomas Wyatt."
        Athenaeum, 97 (May 23), 667.
            Prints Wyatt's "Like unto these unmeasurable mountains"
        with Austin Dobson's "When from afar these mountain tops I
        view," both of which are translations of St. Gelais' "Voy-
        ant ces monts de veue aussi lointaine." Prefers Dobson's
        version.

                                1895

De MARCHI, LUIGI. "L'Influenza della Lirica Italiana sulla
    Lirica Inglese nel Secolo XVI (Sir Tommaso Wyatt)." NA,
    ser. 3, 50, 136-155.
        Wyatt brought back to England lyric forms and traditions
    that were not fundamentally Petrarchan, partly because of
    his argumentative, as opposed to lyric, sensibility, partly
    because he found in Italy the hybrid form of the sonnet
    produced by its association with the strambotto in the
    fifteenth century. Wyatt was not a poet in the true sense
    of the term, but rather a collector of poetry for music;
    unfortunately he tried unsuccessfully to make the musical
    lyric a vehicle for thoughts that were too serious for its
    light form. Thus the great Italian tradition of the tre-
    cento was brought to England in a rather flimsy form.
    [In Italian.]

                                1896

FLÜGEL, EWALD. "Die Handschriftliche Überlieferung der
    Gedichte von Sir Thomas Wyatt." Anglia, 18: 263-290.
        Discusses Egerton MS. 2711, Devonshire MS. 17492 and
    BM Add. MS. 28635, quoting liberally from Nott's discus-
    sion of the Wyatt texts [WS 1816.1]. Provides transcrip-
    tions of the Egerton MS. [In German.]

1897

_____. "Die Handschriftliche Überlieferung der Gedichte von
Sir Thomas Wyatt." Anglia, 19:175-210, 413-450.
    Continuation of W 1896: transcriptions from the
Egerton MS. [In German.]

1902

TILEY, ARTHUR. "Wyatt and Sannazaro." MLQ, 5, 149 [?].
    Cited in W 1970.4.

1908

BERDAN, JOHN M. "The Migrations of a Sonnet." MLN, 23,
    no. 2 (February), 33-36.
    Internal and external evidence indicates that Wyatt's
"Like to these unmesurable montayns" is a translation of
Sannazaro's "Simile a questi smisurati monti," and that
St. Gelais' "Voyant ces monts de veue ainsi lointaine"
is actually a translation of Wyatt's sonnet. [See also
W 1891.2, 1891.3, 1891.4]

1   KASTNER, L. E. "The Elizabethan Sonneteers and the French
    Poets." MLR, 3, no. 3 (April), 273-274.
    Wyatt's "Like unto these unmeasurable mountains" is "an
almost verbatim translation" of Sannazaro's "Simile a
questi smisurati monti." Berdan's contention [W 1908]
that St. Gelais' "Voyant ces monts de veue ainsi lointaine"
is derived from Wyatt's sonnet is unconvincing."

1909

BERDAN, JOHN M. and L. E. KASTNER. "Wyatt and the French
    Sonneteers." MLR, 4, no. 2 (January), 240-253.
    Berdan replies to Kastner [W 1908.1], reaffirming his
contention that St. Gelais translated "Like to these unmesurable montayns" [W 1908]; Kastner again disagrees.

1910

BERDAN, JOHN M. "Professor Kastner's Hypothesis." MLN, 25,
    no. 1 (January), 1-4.

1910

Reaffirms his conviction that Wyatt's "Like to these
unmesurable montayns" is the source for, rather than a
translation of, St. Gelais' "Voyant ces monts de veue
ainsi lointaine." [See also W 1890, 1891.2, 1891.3, 1891.4,
1908, 1908.1, 1909.]

1911

FOXWELL, A. K. A Study of Sir Thomas Wyatt's Poems. London:
University of London Press, 168 pp.
Comparison of the three major Wyatt manuscripts--Eger-
ton, Devonshire and Harrington no. 2 (Add. MS. 28635)--
confirms that the Devonshire is the earliest, that the
Harrington shows signs of moving toward the "corrected"
versions in Tottel's Miscellany, and that the Egerton,
Wyatt's autograph copy containing emendations of Devonshire in his own hand, is the most important because it
provides a record of his system of versification and a
clearly outlined order of stylistic development that records "the history in progressive order of his struggles
with, and his subsequent victory over, the five-stressed
line." In this process he was influenced particularly by
Pynson's 1526 Chaucer, which provided him not only with
models for his entire system of versification, but for his
rhyming system, his spelling, his grammatical endings, and
his archaisms. The Pynson edition also served as a guide,
with Trissino's Poetica, for Wyatt's translations of
Petrarch, which initiated the period (1527-1540) of Italian
influence on his work. That period, marked by his introduction into English of the sonnet, terza rima, and ottava
rima, shows a gradual development from derivative Petrarchism to the mature accomplishment of the Psalms which,
with the Satires, comprise his best poetry. French and
classical influences on his poetry are clear but less important. The Devonshire lyrics, the epigrams, and the
poems in poulter's measure demonstrate that even while he
was "groping" toward the decasyllabic line in his more
"rugged" and important poems, he "had an ear for harmony,
and an eye for correct form." [Includes description of
major manuscripts, and appendices providing a history of
the Devonshire manuscript, "specimen sheets of poems,"
tables of variants, a glossary of archaic words, and a
bibliography. Reprinted: W 1964.3.]

8

1913

FOXWELL, A. K. "Introduction" and "Commentary," in her edition of The Poems of Sir Thomas Wiat. Vol. 2. London: University of London Press, pp. v-xxii, 1-181.

"The upholding of Truth in life, and the continual war waged against falseness, are the two dominant notes in Wiat's poetry," and are expressed particularly in his "belief in the equal distribution of moral right and wrong" and in the distinction he makes between passion and love.

Evidence from the Egerton MS. suggests that "Wiat did not study verse systematically until after his first visit to Italy in 1527," when he began developing the five-foot line from Italian hendasyllables with the help of Trissino's Poetica, Petrarch, and Pynson's Chaucer; he later came under the influence of Thynne's Chaucer. It was during those early years that he wrote his rondeaux and early sonnets, but the sonnets "extend over the whole range" of his career, and indicate the permanence of Italian influence on his verse in contrast to the brevity of the French. His epigrams, inspired by Marot and St. Gelais but modeled stylistically on Serafino's strambotti, "mark his return to Court." The "miscellaneous poems" can be divided into two groups, those written between 1528 and 1536, and those written after 1536; most of them are native lyrics whose development shows a gradually increasing "maturity of thought and elegance of expression." The Satires also show the combined influence of the Italians (Alamanni) and Chaucer ("The Knight's Tale" and Troilus). The source for the Psalms was the much-inferior paraphrase of Aretino, but they were also influenced by Marot and, later, the Great Bible and the 1530 Psalter; of particular importance was Wyatt's choice of terza rima for his version.

An earlier manuscript, the Devonshire, does not provide a chronological order for its Wyatt poems; it consists mainly of court songs, with scattered sonnets, epigrams and parts of two of the Satires. Other sources for Wyatt's poetry include Tottel's Miscellany, the Court of Venus and other, minor, manuscripts. [Includes appendices.]

1920

BERDAN, JOHN M. Early Tudor Poetry. New York: Macmillan, pp. 344-345, 445-486, 518-523, passim.

Wyatt's poems show little classical or French influence. The major source of his poetry is Italian, the major appeal strictly literary. His sonnets, far from

being autobiographical or personal, are literary exercises
in translation and imitation of those "purely intellectual"
Petrarchan sonnets "wherein a metaphor is first selected
and then pursued to its last ramification." The same is
true of his use of Serafino, Alamanni, and Aretino: in
each case Wyatt, as he does with Petrarch, chooses inferior
examples of their work and treats those examples in a
purely intellectual and literary way. Yet it is in such
practice that his "great contribution to literature" lies:
the Elizabethans found in his work "examples of a large
variety of verse forms [rondeau, sonnet, terza rima, ottava
rima, monorime, triplets, refrains, quatrains, douzaines,
trezaines, Poulter's measure] coldly but carefully worked
out." On the other hand he shows intrinsic merit (as opposed to technical usefulness) in those poems which observe
"the life around him" ("They fle from me") and in "those
written to be sung." [Includes some biography, mainly re-
butting the evidence of the purported affair between Wyatt
and Anne Boleyn. See also S 1920.]

1922

HAMMOND, ELEANOR PRESCOTT. "Poems 'Signed' by Sir Thomas
Wyatt." MLN, 37, no. 7 (November), 505-506.
Evidence that Wyatt sometimes "signed" poems by creating
anagrams on his name at the beginnings of stanzas suggests
the possibility of assigning poems to him which have previously been attributed to Surrey or to the "Uncertain
Authors" of Tottel's Miscellany.

1 STARNES, D. T. "An Erroneous Ascription to Wyatt." MLN, 37,
no. 3 (March), 188.
The poem entitled An Epitaph of Sir Thomas Gravenor,
Knight, by Wyatt's editors could not have been written by
Wyatt because Gravenor outlived him by seven or eight
years.

1923

PADELFORD, FREDERICK MORGAN. "The Scansion of Wyatt's Early
Sonnets." SP, 20, no. 2 (April), 137-152.
The regularity of meter in Wyatt's later sonnets, the
regular use of the romance accent during the sixteenth
century, and the prosody of Chaucer, Lydgate, Hawes,
Barclay, and Skelton all testify to the likelihood that
the iambic decasyllabic line was the basis of Wyatt's

early sonnets. Further evidence supporting this conclusion comes from a "rearranged" and "supplemented" list of
prosodic variants from Foxwell's Study [W 1911], which
suggests that Wyatt departed from strict iambic pentameter
only when such a departure was "in accordance with a body
of recognized prosodic variants" established by past theory
and practice.

1925

LARBAUD, VALERY. "Sir Thomas Wyatt." Commerce, 4 (Prin-
temps), 127-145.
  A twentieth-century Frenchman, inspired by the lines
"But I am here in Kent and Christendom/ Among the Muses,
where I read and rhyme" (from "Myne owne John Poyntz"), is
prompted to think of Wyatt's life and poetry, specifically
the relation of his poetry to French and Italian sources.
He sees Wyatt as the only poet of his time who possessed
the means of direct contact with the Continent, and finds
in his verse the meeting of the English, Italian, and
French muses, with the Italian influence dominant (because
of "l'italomanie du temps") and the French often intermediate between the Italian model and Wyatt. More specifically, he finds the more Italianate St. Gelais a more
direct influence on Wyatt than Marot, but also finds Wyatt
influenced more fundamentally by the Lyonnais school, as
represented by Maurice Scève, than by the earlier, Parisian
school. Finally, however, he suggests that Wyatt was an
original poet in the best sense of the term, introducing
into the clichés and abstractions of his themes the passion of personal experience. But while he finds Wyatt
superior to St. Gelais, he finds him less a poet than Marot
or Scève. [In French.]

1 PARRY, G. A. "A French Rondeau and a Rondeau of Wyatt's."
MLR, 20, no. 4 (October), 461-462.
  MS. 5447 fonds francais (Bibliothèque Nationale) con-
tains an anonymous poem that resembles closely Wyatt's
"Ye old mule."

2 WALKER, HUGH. English Satire and Satirists. London: J. M.
Dent and Sons, pp. 59-62.
  Wyatt "takes the first step in that evolution of satiric
verse which culminates in Dryden and Pope." He is distinguished from his contemporaries because he went back to
Horace and made "the classic spirit his own" and because
he recognized the nature of the English tongue sufficiently

1925

to adopt <u>terza rima</u> as his metrical form. He is influenced
mainly by Horace and Alamanni, with only echoes from Juve-
nal and Persius.

1928

GRIFFITH, R. H. "A Lost 'Boke of Balettes' (?1550-1600)."
<u>TLS</u>, no. 1,379 (July 5), p. 504.
Reports the discovery of a fragment of a printed work
with the running title "A Boke of Balettes," which contains
Wyatt's "My penne take payne" and a fragment of an unidentified poem. [Includes transcriptions.]

1   ROSSITER, A. P. "Tottel's Miscellany and Wyatt." <u>TLS</u>, no. 1,
397 (November 8), p. 834.
Points out differences between readings in Tottel's and
in the Egerton MS., and suggests that, while Wyatt's sonnets "stump along on wooden legs," his songs indicate his
prosodic value.

2   TILLYARD, E. M. W. "A Lost 'Boke of Balettes.'" <u>TLS</u>, no. 1,
380 (July 12), p. 520.
The unidentified fragment discovered and transcribed by
Griffith [W 1928] is from Wyatt's "If fansy would favor."

1929

ANON. "Wyatt and Ralegh" [Review of E. M. W. Tillyard, <u>The
Poetry of Sir Thomas Wyatt</u> (W 1929.2)]. <u>TLS</u>, no. 1,442
(September 19), pp. 709-710.
Tillyard's book is more valuable than <u>Poetry of The
English Renaissance</u> (eds. Hebel and Hudson) because of his
careful modernization of the old spelling and his better
choice of examples, and because he uses Foxwell's edition
[W 1913] rather than Tottel's Miscellany, thus reproduc-
ing more faithfully Wyatt's original prosodic technique.
But Tillyard's most valuable contribution lies in his em-
phasis on Wyatt's connection to earlier English poetry and
song (rather than to Continental models), a connection
that may explain his influence on Ralegh and the other
Elizabethans.

*1   LAW, ROBERT ADGER. "More about the 'Boke of Balettes.'" <u>TLS</u>,
December 26, p. 1097[?].
Cited in W 1970.4.

2 TILLYARD, E. M. W. "Introduction," in his The Poetry of Sir
Thomas Wyatt: A Selection and a Study. London: Scholartis Press, pp. 3-56.
Wyatt's poetry was influenced by both native and foreign sources. His native songs represent his best work
because they reflect not only the "lyric spontaneity and
the intimate connection of words and tune" inherited from
the revival of music in the medieval and Renaissance English courts, but also because they communicate on some
occasions a "touch of drama" and a deliberate "roughness"
that distinguish him from his predecessors and contemporaries and look forward to Donne; at other times they
possess a "free and varied lyrical movement" that marks
Wyatt as the first of the Elizabethans. The most dominant
foreign influence on his poetry was Italian: the conceited style and ottava rima of Serafino, the terza rima of
Alamanni, the sonnets of Petrarch. From the French he
learned the rondeau and, perhaps, the varied use of refrain and stanza form. "There is little classical influence" except for Horace's satires and, perhaps, his odes
and sapphics. However, "in neither the rondeau, the
sonnet, nor the eight-lined epigram was Wyatt really at
home," and his satires and Psalms are, for the most part,
failures. [Includes a brief biography, a short discussion
of manuscript and printed sources, and a short survey of
Wyatt criticism from the sixteenth to the early twentieth
centuries. Reprinted: W 1949.3, 1978.5.]

1930

E. C. B. Review of E. M. W. Tillyard, The Poetry of Sir
Thomas Wyatt [W 1929.2]. MLR, 25, no. 3 (July), 383-384.
Quarrels with Tillyard's positive view of Wyatt's de-
fense against Bonner's accusations: the defense "appears
to have been composed merely to relieve the feelings of
Wyatt, who then submitted himself to the King's mercy with
the distressing meekness of any other Tudor Englishman."
The rest of the review is positive.

1 GRIFFITH, REGINALD HARVEY and ROBERT ADGER LAW. "'A Boke of
Balettes' and 'The Courte of Venus.'" Studies in English,
no. 10, The University of Texas Bulletin, no. 3026
(July 8), pp. 5-12.
Reviews the scholarship on the relationship of the two
texts and prints the possible Wyatt poems from both in
parallel transcriptions, with notes. Concludes that the
Stark fragment of the "Boke" suggests the existence of a

1930

"collection of lyric poems possibly earlier than Tottel's Miscellany" and "new readings of the text of at least two of Wyatt's poems and possibly four stanzas of a third poem." [See also W 1928, 1928.2, 1929.1.]

2   PADELFORD, FREDERICK MORGAN. Review of E. M. W. Tillyard, The Poems [sic] of Sir Thomas Wyatt [W 1929.2]. MLN, 45, no. 5 (May), 333-334.
      Contrary to Tillyard's belief, the iambic line as practiced by Hawes and Barclay did indeed have a "unifying pattern."

*3   SHEPHARD, OSCAR H. "Sir Thomas Wyatt." Papers of the Manchester Literary Club, 56:30-52.
      Cited in W 1970.4.

1931

BASKERVILL, CHARLES READ. "Introduction," in his facsimile edition of Plutarch's Quyete of Mynde Translated by Thomas Wyat. Huntington Library Publications. Cambridge, Massachusetts: Harvard University Press, pp. v-xv.
      Wyatt's translation, based on William Budé's Latin rendering of Plutarch, is difficult to read because of its loose constructions, but it is of interest to literary historians because it exemplifies his interest in native English diction and his "sinewy and vigorous prose style." It is of further significance because it represents "the first English translation of a classical treatise on philosophy" in over forty years, because it is an early (1527) example of the "vein of seriousness" and Stoicism seen in Wyatt's later work, and because it demonstrates "a significant phase of the new Tudor poetry": "the moral earnestness and sanity that went hand in hand with the rigid conventions and farfetched conceits of lyric and sonnet."

1   HEALING, A. C. Review of E. M. W. Tillyard, The Poetry of Sir Thomas Wyatt [W 1929.2]. RES, 7, no. 25 (January), 93-94.
      Tillyard's attitude was influenced by Courthope [WS 1897]. The book is particularly valuable for pointing out the regularizing of Wyatt's metrics in Tottel's Miscellany and for emphasizing Wyatt's songs.

2   PRAZ, MARIO. "Donne's Relation to the Poetry of His Time," in A Garland for John Donne. Edited by Theodore Spencer. Cambridge, Massachusetts: Harvard University Press, pp. 63-65.

Wyatt was the first English poet to write in the "dialectical style" that was to become characteristic of Donne.
But Wyatt's anticipation of Donne was itself the product
of the earlier influence of Petrarch.

1932

C. J. S. Review of Charles Read Baskervill, ed., Plutarch's
Quyete of Mynd [W 1931]. MLR, 27, no. 1 (January), 115.
The "admirable" introduction points out the signifi-
cance of Wyatt's translation.

1933

CHAMBERS, E. K. "Sir Thomas Wyatt," in his Sir Thomas Wyatt
and Some Collected Studies. London: Sidgwick & Jackson,
pp. 98-145.
Wyatt's best poetry is found in the "lyrical 'balettes,'" many of which were probably set to music. In
approximately 120 examples of the genre written by Wyatt
are found "more than seventy distinct stanza-forms," all
basically iambic, but with varying meters, rhyme schemes,
and refrains. Originating as they do from medieval neo-
Latin and vernacular poetry, they show Wyatt "at the end
rather than the beginning of a tradition." They also
demonstrate a "facility of rhythmical accomplishment"
rarely matched by the Elizabethans.
Compared with the balettes, Wyatt's other metrical
forms--ottava rima, terza rima, rondeau, rhyme-royal,
poulter's measure, and especially the sonnet--are "stiff
and difficult to scan" or "simply unmetrical." Their
inferiority has not yet been explained adequately, "but
it is noticeable...that [their] awkwardness is at its
height in those which most closely follow their [foreign]
originals," suggesting that they are translation exercises
intended for later revision.
In the balettes, Wyatt often adopts the medieval/
Petrarchan convention of the lover's bondage, but he also
frequently exhibits "the Tudor mood," which rebels against
it. He displays little affinity with either the visual
imagery and metaphorical range of Petrarch or the "lavish-
ness" and "passion for visible things" of the Elizabethans;
rather, he shares with Donne the point of view of the
"psychologist, watching his own emotions in detachment."
[Provides a biography, an account of the major manuscript

1933

and printed sources, and a discussion of the relation of
Anne Boleyn and Elizabeth Darrell to the love poems.]

1934

*CHINI, EMMA. "Il sorgere del Petrarchismo in Inghilterra e
la Poesia di Sir Thomas Wyatt." Estr. da Civilta Moderna,
6:92-101, 203-216.
Cited in W 1970.4.

1   HAYES, ALBERT McHARG. "Wyatt's Letters to His Son." MLN,
49, no. 6 (November), 446-449.
BM Add. MS. 33271 contains texts of Wyatt's two letters
to Thomas Wyatt the Younger that provide information not
included in Foxwell's transcripts from the Egerton MS.
[W 1913]: a specific date and place for the first letter
(April 15, Paris); the suggestion that Wyatt had a daughter; and evidence in Wyatt's own words of his difficulties
with his wife.

1935

CHADBURN, PAUL. "Sir Thomas Wyatt 1503-1542," in The Great
Tudors. Edited by Katharine Garvin. London: Ivor Nich-
olson & Watson, pp. 145-161.
The "keynote of Wyatt's life and poetry" is the lament
for the death of the chivalric past, specifically for the
violations of the "ideal of service" he observes in both
the love situation and the political one. The true musical quality of his poetry, ruined by the editor of
Tottel's Miscellany, comes from the "sinewy contention
between the intellect and...the ideal, which often breaks
the surface rhythm...of [his] courtly love songs" (e.g.,
"They fle from me," "Fforget not yet"). His best poems
were written between 1537 and 1540, when the distance
between the ideal and the actual became most pronounced in
his conflict with Bonner; these later years are documented
in his prose Defence, in the Satires (where his disap-
pointment with the court combines with Reformation disil-
lusionment with Catholicism), and in the Psalms (where
"the conception of service is shifted from King and
country to God"). His struggle to simplify the idea of
love links him with Donne and Shakespeare, but he differs
from them in holding to the context of the chivalric
ideal. [Finds Surrey similar to Wyatt in his laments for
the chivalric past, particularly in "So crewell prison."]

1   PADELFORD, FREDERICK MORGAN. Review of E. K. Chambers, Sir
     Thomas Wyatt and Some Collected Studies [W 1933]. MLN, 50,
     no. 3 (March), 207.
         Chambers provides an interesting explanation for Wyatt's
     metrical irregularity and convincing evidence of his in-
     timacy with Anne Boleyn and Elizabeth Darrell.

2   PRAZ, MARIO. Review of E. K. Chambers, Sir Thomas Wyatt and
     Some Collected Studies [W 1933]. ES, 17:184.
         Wyatt's affinity with Donne was earlier pointed out in
     Praz's essay in A Garland for John Donne [W 1931.2].

                             1936

     STARNES, D. T. "Sir Thomas Gravener." TLS, no. 1,803
     (August 22), p. 680.
         The Gravener who has been identified as the subject of
     Wyatt's epitaph from Harleian MS. no. 78 died seven years
     after Wyatt. [See also W 1922.1.]

                             1939

     HALSTEAD, W. L. "Note on the Text of The Famous History of
     Sir Thomas Wyatt." MLN, 54, no. 8 (December), 585-589.
         Discusses problems of text, authorship, and history of
     the performances of the play, printed in 1607.

1   PARKER, WILLIAM R. "The Sonnets in Tottel's Miscellany."
     PMLA, 54, no. 3 (September), 669-677.
         Wyatt, whose greater variety of rhyme patterns show him
     to be the most experimental of the contributors to the
     Miscellany, might have been the author of three sonnets
     not previously ascribed to him: "O Petrarke hed and
     prince of poets all," written in the enclosed five-rhyme
     pattern that "for many years seems to have been Wyatt's
     and Wyatt's alone"; "With petrarke to compare there may
     no wight," which follows his practice of employing the
     couplet rhyme without the couplet construction at the end;
     and "For loue Appollo (his God head set aside)," which is
     "the earliest known example of the typical Petrarchian
     sonnet," but with the "turn" at the seventh line that
     suggests Wyatt's unconventional structure.

1941

1941

HANGEN, EVA CATHERINE. A Concordance to the Complete Poetical
Works of Sir Thomas Wyatt. Chicago: University of Chicago
Press, 545 pp.
Based on Foxwell's edition [W 1913], but "so arranged
that all words listed may be located readily in any
edition...or in anthologies." Poems are entered by short
titles, lines are quoted in full "except those exceeding
pentameter length," and head words are in modernized spelling. Includes cross references, parenthetical explanatory
insertions, a list of words omitted, Wyatt editions, collections, and manuscripts, and a short-title index.

1 PADELFORD, FREDERICK M[ORGAN]. Review of Eva Catherine
Hangen, A Concordance to the Complete Poetical Works of
Sir Thomas Wyatt [W 1941]. MLQ, 2, no. 3 (September), 506.
"Cursory examination" of the Concordance reveals that
"by the third decade of the sixteenth century the language
had acquired a stabilized and flexible vocabulary," that
"Wyatt used practically no poetical words," and that his
vocabulary is less obsolete today than Spenser's.

1942

BALDWIN, T. W. Review of Eva Catherine Hangen, A Concordance
to the Complete Poetical Works of Sir Thomas Wyatt
[W 1941]. JEGP, 41, no. 1 (January), 123.
Hangen does not include substantive or accidental
variants.

1 KENNEDY, ARTHUR G. "The Making and Use of a Concordance"
[Review of Eva Catherine Hangen, A Concordance to the
Complete Poetical Works of Sir Thomas Wyatt (W 1941)].
AS, 17, no. 4 (December), 255-259.
Measures Hangen's Concordance according to several
general criteria, finding it unsatisfactory on several
counts: the number of different editions of Wyatt's poems;
confusion over the use of Foxwell's edition; lack of detail
in the bibliography; various problems with individual entries; and omissions, typographical errors, improper
alphabetization, inconsistent punctuation and capitaliza-
tion.

1943

TUVE, ROSEMOND. "A Critical Survey of Scholarship in the
Field of English Literature of the Renaissance." SP, 40,
no. 2 (April), 248.
   Predicts a "revaluation of Wyatt" as part of the larger
shift in interest away from "authors unracked by doubts"
(like Spenser) toward works "which present the excitement
or the irony of obscurity" (like those of Chapman,
Greville, and the Metaphysical Poets).

1945

MILES, JOSEPHINE. "From Good to Bright: A Note on Poetic
History," PMLA, 60, no. 3 (September), 766-774.
   Evidence shows that Wyatt, like many other poets, preferred "the standards epithets good and bad to the qualities epithets bright and dark." This choice of adjectives
indicates "how peripheral was the notion of sensory modification to Wyatt and how central...was the poetic function
of verifying and evaluating human relationship."

1 UTLEY, FRANCIS LEE. "Wyatt as a Scottish Poet." MLN, 60,
   no. 2 (February), 106-111.
      The Scottish Bannatyne Manuscript (1568) contains
   transcriptions of two Wyatt poems, "I as as I am" and "Lo
   quhat it is to lufe," both of which show "how an English
   poem could be transmogrified into Scots." Collation of
   the first with Foxwell's edition [W 1913] shows clearly
   that "some of the best poetry in Wyatt has been destroyed
   in the Scottish copy"; the second, ascribed for no apparent reason to Alexander Scott, is garbled and error-prone
   to the point of nonsense.

1946

HARDING, D. W. "The Rhythmical Intention in Wyatt's Poetry."
Scrutiny, 14, no. 2 (December), 90-102.
   Wyatt's verse exemplifies the error of assuming that
the post-Chaucerian English poets somehow "lost the art of
metrical writing." There exists no evidence to support
the contention that his departures from flowing metrical
verse were the result either of bungling or of special
rules for such deviations. On the contrary, the logical
explanation for his prosodic practice is that he was following "speech rhythms" and grouping words in "rhythm

1946

units suggested partly by the sense and partly by conven-
ience in forming the sounds of the words"--in short, that
in many of his poems he was intentionally writing "pausing
verse" rather than "flowing verse." Thus while at times
he reflects the movement toward regular iambic pentameter,
at other times he reflects the revival of native
alliterative-accentual verse.

1   SMITH, HALLETT. "The Art of Sir Thomas Wyatt." HLQ, 9,
    no. 4 (August), 323-355.
        A sound estimate of Wyatt's poetry can best be achieved
    by recognizing "the nature of his poetry and what it is
    trying to do." From this point of view, it becomes ap-
    parent that the differences between his poetry and that of
    his contemporaries result not from his failure to achieve
    the "sweet and sonorous" manner characteristic of English
    poetry from Surrey to Spenser, but from very different
    poetic values and aims. Examination of the manuscript
    versions of his epigrams, for example, indicates that
    their metrical "roughness" comes from the desire to
    achieve compression, to improve rhetorical and logical
    strategy, and to modify tone and attitude in order to give
    the impression of dramatic immediacy. Comparison of his
    translation of Petrarch's "Amor che nel pensier mio vivo e
    regna" with Surrey's shows that, in taking the sonnet's
    conceit more seriously, Wyatt makes the imagery more vivid
    and meaningful than that in Surrey's more conventional and
    smooth version. In his three Satires, Wyatt combines the
    attitude and theme of Horace with the ironic humor of
    Chaucer, eschewing the aureate style to achieve satire
    which combines rhetorical and dramatic vigor with conver-
    sational plain English. In his songs and lyrics--forms
    which by their nature are metrically smooth--he adapts his
    metrical schemes (particularly his refrains) to make them
    more responsive to shifts in tone, in the speaker's role,
    and in rhetorical organization, thus improving consider-
    ably on his more "primitive and naive material." Finally,
    his complex diction is informed by an awareness of conno-
    tation that illustrates again his ability to "use a plain
    language...and yet achieve a richness that makes poetry."

1947

JOHNSON, S. F. and WILLIAM R. ORWEN. "Wyatt's 'The Lover
    Compareth his State.'" Explicator, 5, no. 6 (April),
    item 40.

Explication of Wyatt's poems "begins with distrust of Tottel," as evidenced by comparison of the versions of "My galley charged with forgetfulness" in the Miscellany, Foxwell [W 1913], and Tillyard [W 1929.2]. Comparison with Petrarch's original clarifies Wyatt's ambiguities and demonstrates that "in several instances Wyatt's renderings are not very faithful."

1   MUIR, KENNETH. "Unpublished Poems in the Devonshire MS." Proceedings of the Leeds Philosophical and Literary Society (Literary and Historical Section), 6, parts 1-4 [1944-1947], 253-282.
    Classifies groups in the MS. that contain poems that are or may be Wyatt's. Provides transcripts of unpublished poems, some of which may be Wyatt's.

2   RADFORD, W. LOCKE. "Sir Thomas Wyatt: A Memorial in Sherborne Abbey." N&Q, 192 (April 19), 171.
    There is a tablet inscribed in Wyatt's memory in the floor of Wickham Chapel.

3   ZANDVOORT, R. W. "On Literary Echoes." ES, 28, 1979-1980.
    Reports the use of Wyatt's phrase "stalkying within my chamber" from "They fle from me" in a TLS review of Gunther's Inside U.S.A., pointing out that the phrase is that of Tottel's Miscellany rather than a manuscript source and commenting on the use of the word "stalk."

1948

MACKERNESS, E. D. "The Transitional Nature of Wyatt's Poetry." English, 7, no. 39, 120-124.
    Wyatt's verse shows the influence of Chaucer in its sometimes archaic diction and of Skelton in its often traditional metrical schemes. Objections to his metrical roughness are "unreasonable," and objections to his unstressed end-rhymes do not take into account the way such rhymes move his rhythm forward. Among his substantive innovations are a change in the lover-persona's attitude from Petrarchan despair to one of frustration and its attendant "degree of detachment, and therefore of comprehension" and the dramatic nature of the persona's development, which is characterized by "the formation of attitudes within the framework of the poem itself" that is so characteristic of Donne. But that which accounts most particularly for the "'transitional'" nature of Wyatt's verse is its relationship to music.

1948

1   MUIR, KENNETH. "The Text of Wyatt." <u>N&Q</u>, 193 (March 20),
      124-125.
          Lists errors in Foxwell's [W 1913] reading of the Wyatt
      manuscripts.

2   _____. "Wyatt's Poems in Add. MS. 17492." <u>N&Q</u>, 193 (Febru-
      ary 7), 53-54.
          Lists errors in Foxwell's [W 1913] reading of the Dev-
      onshire MS.

3   PATTISON, BRUCE. <u>Music and Poetry of the English Renaissance</u>.
      London: Methuen & Co., passim.
          Wyatt is mentioned briefly in discussions of the carol,
      the madrigal, the use of refrain, court music, and the
      relation of poetry to Renaissance music.

<u>1949</u>

HILLYER, ROBERT. "Elizabethan Lyrics" [Review of Alan Swal-
      low, ed., <u>Some Poems of Sir Thomas Wyatt</u> (W 1949.2)].
      <u>New York Times Book Review</u>, May 22, p. 7.
          Swallow passes too lightly over Wyatt's role in the
      development of the sonnet, and his treatment of metrics is
      "too generalized," but his treatment of Wyatt's attitude
      toward love and his stanzaic structure are "sound."

1   MUIR, KENNETH. "Introduction," in his edition of <u>Collected</u>
      <u>Poems of Sir Thomas Wyatt</u>. London: Routledge and Kegan
      Paul, pp. ix-xxx.
          Wyatt's poetry has been underestimated because of
      earlier critical preference for Surrey ("one of the most
      curious delusions in English literary history"), over-
      emphasis on his historical role as importer of the sonnet
      and as precursor of the Elizabethans, and misunderstand-
      ing of his metrics. Actually, his translations and
      sonnets are inferior to, and of less importance than, his
      lyrics, "some fifty" of which are "the best lyrics written
      in English before the great Elizabethans"; they are
      written in "an astonishing variety of stanza forms," and,
      unlike those of his contemporaries, they do not need
      musical accompaniment to be fully effective. It is on
      these poems that his "reputation...should rest": their
      "rugged versification...conveys the force and subtlety of
      his emotion, while preserving the illusion of a man talk-
      ing to men," a quality he shares with Donne. Finally, it
      is Wyatt's "individual voice" that characterizes these
      poems, and separates him from the anonymous lyric poets

of earlier centuries. [Includes a brief biography, and a characterization of Wyatt based on his letters. Reprinted: W 1950.3.]

2   SWALLOW, ALAN. "Preface," in his edition of Some Poems of Sir Thomas Wyatt. Books of the Renaissance. New York: The Swallow Press and William Morrow & Co., pp. vii-x.
    The variety of Wyatt's technical experiments in metrics and poetic forms led to "the establishment of a poetic tradition in which we count most of the great English poetry." Among his more significant contributions were his "dramatic structure" and "conversational movement," his use of metaphor, conceit, and wordplay in "giving tension to the language of the poem," his control of tone and attitude, his establishment of "accentual-syllabic metrics," the "great flexibility" of his lines and stanza patterns, his "use of the line and stanza forms...in exact relationship with the grammar and thought forms of the language," and, finally, his bold departure from Petrarchan convention in voicing "concern with the appropriate action, with justice due lover, man, citizen, even God."

3   TILLYARD, E. M. W. "Introduction," in his The Poetry of Sir Thomas Wyatt: A Selection and a Study. London: Chatto & Windus.
    Reprint of W 1929.2.

1950

BATESON, F. W. "Sir Thomas Wyatt and the Renaissance," in his English Poetry: A Critical Introduction. London, New York and Toronto: Longmans, Green and Co., pp. 140-148.
    The hunting metaphors in "Whoso list to hunt" and "They flee from me" illustrate the relationship between the "unpredictable universe" of the Renaissance and "the Renaissance man who believed in himself and in his luck, not really on rational grounds...but simply because he was himself." In this Wyatt's two poems epitomize the shift from the harmonious connection between physical and spiritual in the medieval world to the separation between the two realms of experience in the new England of the Renaissance.

1   DALEY, A. STUART. "The Uncertain Author of Poem 225, Tottel's Miscellany." SP, 47, no. 3 (July), 485-493.
    "To my mishap alas I fynde" was probably written by Sir Francis Bryan.

1950

2   MASON, H. A. "Wyatt and the Scholars" [Reviews of Kenneth
        Muir, ed., Collected Poems (W 1949.1), E. M. W. Tillyard,
        The Poetry of Sir Thomas Wyatt (W 1949.3) and Gerald
        Bullett, ed., Silver Poets of the Sixteenth Century
        (WS 1947)]. Scrutiny, 17, no. 1 (Spring), 72–80.
           Muir's edition is valuable for its texts, but not its
        criticism. Tillyard's criticism is too prescriptive.
        Wyatt criticism needs now to assess his relation to the
        native tradition ("as measured by...[his] resistance to
        foreign influence") and to his cultural and social back-
        ground.

3   MUIR, KENNETH. "Introduction," in his edition of Collected
        Poems of Sir Thomas Wyatt. Cambridge, Massachusetts:
        Harvard University Press.
        Reprint of W 1949.1.

4   NOSWORTHY, J. M. Reviews of E. M. W. Tillyard, The Poetry of
        Sir Thomas Wyatt [W 1949.3] and Kenneth Muir, ed.,
        Collected Poems [W 1949.1]. Life and Letters, 65 (April
        to June), 62–66.
           If, as the publication of the two editions suggests,
        a "Wyatt cult" is beginning, it will be of more value if
        it also brings attention to Surrey, Skelton, Hawes and
        Barclay. Wyatt scholarship needs to examine his medieval
        heritage, decipher the obscurity in his poetry, relate
        the poetry to its background and conventions, and solve
        the mysteries of its versification, particularly the re-
        lation of its metrics to Tudor music. Despite such unre-
        solved problems, it is clear that Wyatt was "a master of
        his craft," though less so than Surrey.

5   SWALLOW, ALAN. "The Pentameter Lines in Skelton and Wyatt."
        MP, 48, no. 1 (August), 1–11.
           Attempts to account for the apparent inconsistencies
        in the accentuation of the iambic pentameter line by
        Wyatt and Skelton have heretofore been inconclusive or
        self-contradictory. The following suggestions provide
        more comprehensive explanations for their metrical method:
        (1) both syllabification and accentuation might, at the
        time, have been "naturally so pronounced that some of the
        lines which we now find 'rough' were read as regular pen-
        tameters"; (2) in his translations, Wyatt was more
        concerned with providing close renderings of his originals
        than with polishing his metrics; (3) perhaps both poets
        adhered to the tradition that "maintained a sharp dis-
        tinction between lyrical and nonlyrical poetry," reserving

iambic pentameter for their lyrics and the longer, "broken-back" line for their more serious verse. Finally, however, one must conclude that the metrical tradition in which the poets wrote was such that "they would have felt no compulsion...to make the lines fit a single pattern," although it is clear that both do represent a movement toward the iambic pattern.

6   WEST, BILL COVODE. 'Sir Thomas Wyatt,' in "Anti-Petrarchism: A Study of the Reaction against the Courtly Tradition in English Love-Poetry from Wyatt to Donne." Ph.D. dissertation, Northwestern, pp. 209-243.
      Wyatt's reputation as a Petrarchan poet is contradicted by evidence that shows he rejected Petrarch's ideology, conventions, etiquette, and even "the most conspicuous and vulnerable aspects of Petrarchan conceit and rhetoric." The sources of his anti-Petrarchism were the medieval lyric, Chaucer, and his own "personal bent."

1951

HARDING, D. W. Review of Kenneth Muir, ed., Collected Poems of Sir Thomas Wyatt [W 1949.1]. RES, n.s. 2, no. 6 (April), 162-164.
      Muir does not treat Wyatt's "themes and values," but he does correct "the main misconceptions...and prejudices" in previous Wyatt criticism.

1   STEIN, ARNOLD. "The Criticism of Wyatt" [Review of Kenneth Muir, ed., Collected Poems (W 1949.1)]. KR, 13, no. 4 (Autumn), 703-709.
      Wyatt's reputation has suffered because of misleading comparisons with Surrey and criticism based on eighteenth- and nineteenth-century standards. Modern scholarship should correct the earlier misapprehensions, as pointed out in the recent studies by Hallet Smith [W 1946.1], F. W. Bateson [W 1950], Alan Swallow [W 1950.5], D. W. Harding [W 1946], and Muir.

2   TILLEMANS, TH[OMAS]. King and Courtier: A Cultural Reconnaissance into an Age of Transition With Illustrations Drawn from the Poetry of Sir Thomas Wyatt and other Sources. Haarlem: Joh. Enschedé en Zonen, 62 pp.
      Includes eighteen poems by Wyatt that illustrate the changing social and cultural milieu of the English Renaissance. Suggests that an assessment of his poetry must take into account sixteenth-century changes in

1951

punctuation, music in the court of Henry VIII, Wyatt's
deliberate and accidental "roughness," and the patriotic
motive behind his imitations of Continental models. [Also
contains a brief bibliography and notes. Reprinted:
W 1977.3, 1978.4.]

1952

HARRIER, RICHARD CHARLES. 'Introduction,' in his edition of
"The Poetry of Sir Thomas Wyatt." Ph.D. dissertation,
Harvard, pp. 1-82.
Discusses Wyatt's poems relating to his life, particularly those possibly alluding to Anne Boleyn. Also examines both his native and continental lyrics: the native
poems represent the search for "an individual tone of
voice rather than mere metrical experiments," and are
characterized by the gradually increasing sense of frustration at the artificial formulas of courtly love; his
adaptations of Petrarch are characterized by a rejection
of Petrarchan amplification and the reinterpretation of
Petrarchan content that leads to an uncourtly "revolt of
the lover"; other continental writers (Serafino, Marot,
Alamanni) had little effect on Wyatt's tone. [Includes a
discussion of the manuscripts and notes to the poems.]

1 MOORE, ARTHUR K. "The Design of Wyatt's 'They flee from me.'"
Anglia, 71:102-111.
The poem "exhibits certain affinities" with the order
prescribed for the judicial oration: the first stanza,
the general arraignment of women, corresponds to the second of the seven parts, the narration; the second stanza,
which specifies a particular woman, "functions as an
integral part of the presentation of the iudicialis causa,
specifically furnishing a vehicle for the confirmation,"
which itself is presented in the third stanza. Further
explication indicates that the animal image of the first
stanza is meant to represent a falcon. But it is necessary to understand that both the rhetorical arrangement
and the animal imagery "have been subordinated to the
complex experience which is the essence of the poem."

2 WIATT, WILLIAM H. "Sir Thomas Wyatt and 'Sephame.'" *N&Q*,
197 (June 7), 244.
The "Sephame" alluded to in "You that in love" may have
been Edward Sepham, a court astrologer. His prediction of
ill fortune for Wyatt in May probably alludes both to the

imprisonment in 1534 and the one in 1536. "The composition of the poem may therefore be dated after May 1536, and Sephame's prediction to May 1534."

1953

BALDI, SERGIO. <u>La Poesia di Sir Thomas Wyatt[,] Il Primo Petrarchista Inglese</u>. Florence: Felice Le Monnier, 262 pp.
   Discusses Wyatt's life (Chapter 1), texts, chronology, criticism (2), metrics ("La Struttura del Verso," 3), and the content of the poetry (4). Chapter 3 finds the modern critical revaluation of Wyatt useful in surmounting earlier objections to the harshness of his metrics, but considers it mistaken in relating his verse historically to either the broken-back line of Lydgate or the development of iambic pentameter, concluding that we must measure his lines by their own internal rhythms, which inform not only the <u>ballatelle</u> (songs) but the sonnets and Satires as well. Chapter 4 provides chronological classification of approximately one-fourth of Wyatt's poems, dating one group of twenty at 1527, another group of thirty after 1536, the Psalms at 1541; observes that the moral/didactic quality of his verse belongs to the second part of his life, but that the love poems are even then dependent on the same Petrarchan models; finds further that our understanding of his love poetry, contrary to romantic criticism that focuses on his female object(s) or on his biography, must come from a concentration on the emotional attitude of the poet, the emotional content of the poem; suggests that the females in the love poems are only pretexts or concrete representations of one single emotion, common to the Satires and Psalms as well as the love poems, and that the emotion revealed is one of sadness, as expressed most clearly in "Forget not yet," "Blame not my lute," and "With serving still." [Includes appendices on sources, interpretations; textual notes; bibliography. Chapters 3 and 4 appear to be related to Baldi's <u>Sir Thomas Wyatt</u>, trans. F. T. Prince (W 1961). In Italian.]

1   DUNCAN-JONES, E. E. "Wyatt's <u>They Flee From Me</u>." Explicator, 12 (November), item 9.
   Disagrees with Johnson's [W 1953.3] reading of "naked" and his belief that "they" refers to courtiers: the poem is about a single lady.

1953

2 HARRIER, RICHARD C. and KENNETH MUIR. "Notes on the Text and
Interpretation of Sir Thomas Wyatt's Poetry." N&Q, 198
(June), 234-236.
Although Muir's Collected Poems [W 1949.1] corrects
many of the textual errors in Foxwell's edition [W 1913],
his edition nevertheless contains errors in spelling and
wording, some of which result in substantive misreadings.
It is also "deficient in glosses" and mistaken in ignoring
evidence of emendations in punctuation by later hands in
Egerton MS. 2711--particularly those of Nicholas Grimald--,
and it reproduces at least one important error in Tottel's
Miscellany.
In his response, Muir [p. 236] points out that he was
using modern punctuation, some of which may coincide with
Grimald's; he also comments on the other corrections and
suggestions.

3 JOHNSON, S. F. "Wyatt's 'They flee from me.'" Explicator,
11, no. 6 (April), item 39.
The poem is best understood by distinguishing between
"latent" and "manifest" metaphorical meaning in the first
two stanzas. In the first, "they" are birds, while the
"latent content of the metaphor" suggests that they are
perhaps mistresses, but more probably courtiers, in the
pejorative sense. In the second, the "manifest content"
suggests a single mistress while the "latent" meaning
suggests Fortune. Analysis on the basis of these dis-
tinctions, then, suggests that the poem echoes the theme
of de contemptu mundi.

4 MASON, H. A. "Wyatt and the Psalms--I." TLS, no. 2,665
(February 27), p. 144.
Wyatt's rendering of Psalm 37 is "a fairly close verse
translation" of Ioannes Campensis' 1532 Latin version, and
his Penitential Psalms show evidence that he supplemented
his use of Aretino's prose paraphrase with help from the
rival versions of Campensis and Zwingli and a sermon by
Fisher. Such evidence demonstrates the creative quality
of Wyatt's translations: he alternates between close
adherence to his models and "free flights" away from them
toward autobiographical expression, and in his best passages succeeds in transforming "translation...into
dramatic self-presentation." [Companion article:
WS 1953.1].

28

5   MAXWELL, J. C. "Notes on the Text and Interpretation of Sir
       Thomas Wyatt's Poetry." N&Q, 198 (August), 361.
          Congratulates Harrier [W 1953.2] for correcting a Muir
       reading [W 1949.1] of the idiom "in hid."

6   WATSON, MELVIN R. "Wyatt, Chaucer, and Terza Rima." MLN,
       68, no. 2 (February), 124-125.
          Wyatt has been mistakenly credited with introducing
       terza rima into English when, in fact, Chaucer's "The
       Complaint to his Lady" contains a passage with the first
       English use of the form. Wyatt, however, was the first
       to use it for a whole poem.

                               1954

    EVANS, ROBERT O. "Some Aspects of Wyatt's Metrical Tech-
       nique." JEGP, 53, no. 2 (April), 197-213.
          The impression of irregularity, or roughness, in Wyatt's
       verse is largely a result of our failure to recognize that
       he was applying to his lines a system of metrical elision,
       especially in the case of -eth and -es inflections, one
       that goes back to Chaucer and is used extensively by poets
       from Henryson to Milton. Other difficulties observed in
       his verse--inversion, short lines, rhyming of masculine
       and feminine syllables--are less significant then hereto-
       fore recognized, and are also part of common practice.
       It is, finally, correct to assume that Wyatt intended to
       write pentameter lines more consistently than, for example,
       Swallow [W 1950.5] suggests.

1   GOTTFRIED, RUDOLF. "Sir Thomas Wyatt and Pietro Bembo."
       N&Q, 199, n.s. 1 (July), 278-280.
          Wyatt's "At last withdrawe yowre cruelltie" is a para-
       phrase of Bembo's "Voi mi poneste in foco." Mechanical
       and substantive differences between the two poems show
       Wyatt's to be "heavier," less witty, and misogynist, and
       thus ambigouous in pronoun reference and logic in the
       final stanza. In a larger sense, these differences indi-
       cate "a certain backwardness in early Tudor poetry, which,
       though it felt the need to imitate, could hardly reproduce
       the technical dexterity of foreign models yet."

2   HARDING, D. W. "The Poetry of Wyatt," in The Age of Chaucer.
       Edited by Boris Ford. The Pelican Guide to English Lit-
       erature, Vol. I. Baltimore: Penguin Books, pp. 197-212.
          Full appreciation of Wyatt's poetry requires that we
       confront misunderstandings about his rhythm and about the

relation of his verse to conventional love poetry. Both
of these obstacles can be circumvented by the preliminary
recognition of the "conversational quality" of much of his
verse, which produces a fusion of "'musical' qualities"
and the "usages of speech" and which also unites the conventional vocabulary of love with "everyday experience and
everyday words." Specifically, his rhythmic skill is
exemplified in his use of the refrain as part of the thematic and rhythmical structure of many of his lyrics, and
in his practice of combining in single lines both the
regular meters of the carol tradition and the "pausing
verse" of fifteenth-century discursive poetry. More importantly, it is necessary to recognize that the love
tradition provided him with a vehicle for "serious communication with his friends" and for more general statements
about universal human experience.

3   HARRIER, RICHARD C. "Notes on Wyatt and Anne Boleyn." <u>JEGP</u>,
    53, no. 4 (October), 581-584.
        Despite the arguments of Foxwell [W 1911] and Chambers
    [W 1933], there is no meaningful evidence of an affair
    between Wyatt and Anne, and therefore no reason to see her
    as the target of his antifeminist poems.

4   LONG, JOHN H. "Blame Not Wyatt's Lute." <u>RN</u>, 7, no. 4 (Win-
    ter), 127-130.
        A late sixteenth-century commonplace book residing in
    the Folger Shakespeare Library (MS. 448.16) includes a
    lute tablature entitled "Blame not my lute." It might
    have been written to accompany Wyatt's poem of that name,
    although it provides only the necessary chords. Recon-
    struction of the syllabic setting with Wyatt's text
    reveals that the discords in the original chord setting
    might have been purposeful, thus suggesting a relationship
    between words and music that is consistent with the theory
    of Renaissance English composers. The reconstruction also
    indicates that, as Tudor lyric poetry is better understood
    in relation to its musical settings, the settings them-
    selves "may require their texts for better comprehension."

5   PURVES, JOHN. Review of Sergio Baldi, <u>La Poesia di Sir
    Thomas Wyatt</u> [W 1953]. <u>RES</u>, n.s. 5, no. 19, 279-282.
        Baldi's analysis of Wyatt's prosody, which includes the
    related matters of pronunciation and phonology, is "the
    true <u>raison d'etre</u>" of the book.

1955

6   SPENCER, TERENCE.   Review of Sergio Baldi, <u>La Poesia di Sir</u>
    <u>Thomas Wyatt</u> [W 1953]. <u>MLR</u>, 49, no. 2 (April), 269-270.
        Baldi's study shows an awareness of modern criticism,
    and relies on both Muir's <u>Collected Poems</u> [W 1949.1] and a
    reexamination of the manuscripts. It is particularly
    valuable for pointing out the source in Petrarch for
    "Lament my loss," and for commenting on Wyatt's prosody
    from an Italian point of view.

1955

BUKOFZER, MANFRED F. "'Blame Not My Lute.'" <u>RN</u>, 8, no. 1
    (Spring), 12.
        Long's explanation for the relation of discords to
    words in the setting of Wyatt's poem [W 1954.4] is "more
    ingenious than convincing," because it results from a
    misreading of the crucial letters in the original notation.

1   FRASER, RUSSELL A. "Introduction," in his edition of <u>The</u>
    <u>Court of Venus</u>. Durham, North Carolina: Duke University
    Press, pp. 3-77.
        Contemporary allusions, historical, biographical, and
    textual evidence, together with stylistic and thematic
    parallels suggest the connection of Wyatt's poetry with
    <u>The Court</u>. More specifically, five of the fourteen court
    poems surviving in its three extant fragments are defi-
    nitely Wyatt's, three are probably his, and of the seven
    of uncertain authorship, "some or all" may also be his.

2   FREEDMAN, LILA HERMANN. 'Thomas Wyatt,' in her "Satiric
    Personae: A Study of Point of View in Formal Verse Satire
    in the English Renaissance from Wyatt to Marston."
    Ph.D. dissertation, University of Wisconsin, pp. 190-198.
        Wyatt's three Satires, the first in the sixteenth cen-
    tury to be "deliberately modelled on classical examples,"
    differ from later English examples of the genre in their
    relaxed tone and in the generalizing nature of their point
    of view, which can perhaps be attributed to the emphasis
    on satiric personality, poetic structure, and "the moral
    universal" in the attitude toward satire in the sixteenth
    century, emphases observable in the glosses to English
    editions of the Roman satirists in the latter half of the
    century.

1955

3   GOMBOSI, OTTO. "Blame not Wyatt." RN, 8, no. 1 (Spring),
    12-14.
        In addition to the error pointed out by Bukofzer
    [W 1955], Long [W 1954.4] fails to recognize that the
    music he considers a setting for "Blame not my lute" was
    "adapted from a much older pattern that had served before
    as a neatly elastic formula for singing and playing of
    poetry of various kinds."

4   REES, D. G. "Sir Thomas Wyatt's Translations from Petrarch."
    CL, 7, no. 1 (Winter), 15-24.
        Those sonnets from the Canzoniere translated most
    closely by Wyatt are principally intellectual and techni-
    cal in appeal, and are "among the more artificial, elab-
    orate, and conceited" in Petrarch, each of them consisting
    mainly of "an intellectual exposition of some psychological
    situation in terms of a single image, or in the logical
    working out in detail of some basic conceit." Comparisons
    show that Wyatt turns Petrarch's "economy, clarity, and
    neatness" into "obscurity," "meaningless padding," and
    "jerkiness" of rhythm. Nevertheless, Wyatt sometimes
    succeeds in bringing to the more "mannered and literary"
    of the originals a "vivid" and "realistic" vigor, as in
    "My galy charged with forgetfulness." Finally, however,
    it is in his less literal adaptations of Petrarch, par-
    ticularly in the traditionally English short-lined ballets
    ("Perdye I saide it not" and "O goodely hand"), where he
    renders Petrarch's technical complexity with extreme
    native simplicity, that Wyatt is at his best.

1956

FUCILLA, JOSEPH G. "The Direct Source of Wyatt's Epigram:
    'In Dowtfull Brest...'" RN, 9, no. 4 (Winter), 187-188.
        The poem is a "virtually literal" translation of an
    Italian epigram, "Mentre nel duro petto e dispietato,"
    found recently in the Biblioteca Nacional of Madrid.

1   LAW, ROBERT ADGAR. "More About A Boke of Balettes, 1547-
    1549." LCUT, 5, no. 4 (Spring), 3-5.
        Reviews the scholarship done on the fragment, reaffirm-
    ing its important connection with The Court of Venus and
    the Wyatt canon.

2 MUMFORD, IVY L. "Musical Settings to the Poems of Sir Thomas
     Wyatt." M&L, 37, no. 4 (October), 315-322.
        Evidence of the relation of Wyatt's poems to music,
     heretofore provided only by the existence of the musical
     setting for "A Robyn, joly Robyn," is strengthened by the
     recent discovery of lute settings to "Hevyn and erth and
     all that here me plain" and "Blame not my lute" (located
     in B. M. Royal App. 58 and Folger MS. 448.16, respective-
     ly). In addition, BM Add. MS. 31992 contains musical
     settings that might relate to "I find no peace" and "What
     vaileth truth?" Also, "If ever man myght him avaunt" is
     known to have been accompanied by a lute tablature. [See
     also W 1958.2.]

3 YOUNG, JAMES DEAN. "The Possibility of Form: A Study of the
     Prosody of Sir Thomas Wyatt." Ph.D. dissertation, Rice,
     414 pp.
        Provides "an objective description of Wyatt's prosodi-
     cal practices in an attempt to formulate the rules he used
     in composition," but concludes that his technique indi-
     cates "an unwillingness to be committed to a rigid
     prosody" and that such an examination cannot answer ques-
     tions about his procedure. Nevertheless, the evidence
     does show that Wyatt used various devices that gave him
     greater freedom, resulting in a "metrical treatment of
     syllables [that]...is considerably looser than that al-
     lowed most English poets"; further evidence indicates a
     relationship between that looseness and his diction, his
     conception of the poetic line, and his stanza structures,
     and results in the general conclusion that his prosody is
     comprised of variations on the accentual and syllabic
     systems. [Includes tables, glossary, and index of rhymes.]

1957

HAINSWORTH, J. D. "Sir Thomas Wyatt's Use of the Love Con-
     vention." EIC, 7, no. 1 (January), 90-95.
        Most of Wyatt's poems can be categorized as either (1)
     love poems, (2) autobiographical poems, or (3) poems not
     easily recognized as either (1) or (2), possibly because of
     his desire to obscure personal allusions through the love
     convention, or simply because of the availability of the
     "Petrarchan mould." "They fle from me" belongs to the
     third category; more significantly, its ambiguity, par-
     ticularly in the second and third stanzas, contributes to
     the dramatic effect of the poem, "since it gives expres-
     sion to the tension between the poet's experience and the

1957

love convention which is absorbing it" and "points to what
is happening in the mind of the poet as he composes the
poem." Thus the poem documents Wyatt's "readjustment" to
personal circumstance through his entry into, then rejection of, the conventional lover's role, and provides a
psychological explanation for "those 'dramatic' and 'manly'
qualities so often noted in the love poetry of Wyatt."

1 HOENIGER, J. D. "A Wyatt Manuscript." N&Q, 202, n.s. 4
(March), 103-104.
    A sixteenth-century commonplace book in University Col-
lege, Cambridge, contains versions of "Venemous Thorns"
and "Mine Own John Poyns," both of which differ from all
other versions.

2 NEWMAN, JOEL. "An Italian Source for Wyatt's 'Madame, with-
outen many wordes.'" RN, 10, no. 1 (Spring), 13-15.
    The likely source for the poem is "Madonna, non so dir
tante parole," by Dragonetto Bonifacio, Marchese d'Oria,
an early sixteenth-century Italian poet and madrigalist.

3 PETERSON, DOUGLAS LEE. 'Sir Thomas Wyatt,' in "The Development of the English Lyric in the Sixteenth Century: A
Study of Styles and Structure." Ph.D. dissertation,
Stanford, pp. 147-191.
    Wyatt, "constitutionally at odds with courtly society"
as well as with its literary attitudes and language, preferred the "plain" to the "eloquent" style. In both his
Petrarchan adaptations and his original poems there is
observable a development away from the use of fashionable
ornament and established rhetorical structures for their
own sake toward an interest in ideas, and in the psychological analysis of "the ethical implications of courtly
love doctrine." His verse thus "marks the beginning of
the lyric of self-analysis" and establishes his place
"among the best and most original poets of his century."
[See also WS 1967.2.]

4 REES, D. G. "Wyatt and Petrarch." MLR, 52, no. 3 (July),
389-391.
    Those who read Wyatt's "Was I never yet of your love
greved" as a rejection of its source, Petrarch's "Io non
fu' d'amor voi lassato unqu' anco," fail to recognize that
the Italian sonnet is as defiant as the English, and that
Wyatt's version is a faithful rendering of it.

1958

EVANS, ROBERT O.   "Some Autobiographical Aspects of Wyatt's
    Verse." N&Q, 203, n.s. 5 (Feburary), 48-52.
       The general inclination to deny the likelihood of an
    intimate relationship between Wyatt and Anne Boleyn, begun
    in the nineteenth century and continued in the twentieth,
    is undercut somewhat by the evidence of sixteenth-century
    accounts, which generally agree that they had been lovers.
    Thus it is likely that Wyatt was indeed referring to Anne
    in poems like "They fle from me" and "What word is that."

1   MARTIN, MARY FORSTER.   "Stow's 'Annals' and 'The Famous His-
    torie of Sir Thomas Wyatt.'" MLR, 53, no. 1 (January),
    75-77.
       The chief sources for the play were Stow's Annals (1600,
    1601) and Holinshead (1587).

2   MUMFORD, IVY L.   "Sir Thomas Wyatt's Songs: A Trio of Prob-
    lems in Manuscript Sources." M&L, 39, no. 3 (July),
    262-264.
       BM Add. MS. 31992 contains two pieces for lute that
    have titles similar to Wyatt's "I fynde no peace" and
    "What vaileth trouth?" BM Add. MS. 31392 contains one
    that recalls "A Robyn, joly Robyn." There is not yet
    sufficient evidence proving the relationship of those
    pieces to the poems. [See also W 1956.2.].

3   WIATT, WILLIAM H.   "A Source for Wyatt's 'What menythe thys?'"
    RN, 11, no. 4 (Winter), 251-252.
       A close parallel to the poem's first three stanzas is
    found in Ovid's Amores, I, ii, 1-4.

1959

COMBELLACK, FREDERICK M.   "Wyatt's 'They flee from me.'"
    Explicator, 17, no. 5 (February), item 36.
       The creatures referred to in the opening stanza are the
    doves of Venus; Wyatt is there suggesting the favorable
    position he once held with the Goddess of Love. "'Naked
    feet'" are appropriate to birds, and they provide a "meta-
    phorical counterpart" to the lady's nakedness in the
    second stanza. Both stanzas thus "describe, metaphorically
    and literally, the same event, the visit of the lady to
    the poet's room."

1959

1   HARRIER, RICHARD C. "A New Biographical Criticism of Wyatt."
    N&Q, 204, n.s. 6, no. 1 (January), 189.
        Evans' argument that Wyatt is alluding to Anne Boleyn
    in several poems [W 1958] "misses the obvious, ignores
    evidence," and exemplifies the type of argument that "gave
    the New Criticism its power to reduce biographical study
    in American Universities."

2   SCHMUTZLER, KARL E. "Harington's Metrical Paraphrases of the
    Seven Penitential Psalms: Three Manuscript Versions."
    PBSA, 53 (Third Quarter), 241.
        Suggests that Harington's paraphrases were inspired by
    Wyatt's.

3   STEIN, ARNOLD. "Wyatt's 'They flee from me.'" SR, 67, no. 1
    (January-March), 28-44.
        The poem progresses on an ascending scale of imagery
    from animality (stanza 1) to sexuality (2) to "'new
    fangilnes'" (3), which is "the self-awareness of human
    consciousness." All three stages are measured, success-
    ively and simultaneously, against the language and behavior
    of the code of courtly love, thus creating complex dramatic
    tension between animal and human on the one hand, and be-
    tween both those levels and the higher ideal on the other.
    The result is a "modern" poem that communicates its theme
    by means of the rich and ambiguous connotations of old-
    world diction and the dramatic conflicts among the various
    sides of human nature and human love.

4   THOMSON, PATRICIA. "Wyatt and the Petrarchan Commentators."
    RES, n.s. 10, no. 39, 225-233.
        Wyatt's departures from Petrarch's sensibility--his
    worldliness and realism, his rebellious unorthodoxy and
    egotism--might have been influenced by those Italian com-
    mentaries on Petrarch published before or during his
    "Italian" period (1527-1541). The commentaries interpret
    the Canzoniere in various ways--"as a philosophical treat-
    ise or a biography, as a manual of love or of style"--and
    interpretations of individual sonnets are colored by the
    different points of view of the commentators themselves.
    [See also W 1964.13.]

5   WYATT, STANLEY CHARLES. "Sir Thomas Wyatt the Elder," in his
    Cheneys and Wyatts: A Brief History in Two Parts. Chel-
    sea: Carey & Claridge, pp. 102-108.
        Brief biography of Wyatt.

1960

HIETSCH, OTTO. Die Petrarcaübersetzungen Sir Thomas Wyatts:
Eine Sprachvergleichende Studie. Weiner Beitrage Zur
Englischen Philologie, Vol. 57, edited by Friedrich Wild.
Stuttgart: Wilhelm Braumuller, 231 pp.
    A study of Wyatt's poetry divided into two sections.
The first ["Wyatts Sprache und Ubersetzungstil"] is a general discussion of Wyatt's language and style of translation, including a section on "Wyatt and Surrey" and
comments on native influences on his poems and the relation
of the poems to his experiences; suggests that modern commentators err in underestimating Petrarch's influence on
Wyatt, and says that Wyatt translated the Italian poet
because they shared a similar sensibility. The second
section ["A. Ubersetzungen" and "B. Um- und Nachdichtungen
(in verschiendenen versformen")] juxtaposes poems by
Petrarch and Wyatt's versions of them: twelve sonnets and
two canzone that Wyatt translates with relative faithful-
ness (A) and ten that are more freely translated adaptations (B); each poem and its translation/adaptation are
accompanied by general comparative discussion and commentary on individual lines. [Includes bibliography of
Petrarch and Wyatt texts, Renaissance translation, anthologies, literary history and criticism; no index.] [In German.]

1   MORRIS, HARRY. "Birds, Does and Manliness in 'They fle from
me.'" EIC, 10, no. 4 (October), 484-492.
    The lady referred to in the final couplet, contrary to
earlier interpretations, might be a different woman from
the cruel mistress of the previous stanzas. If so, the
poem belongs to the last of the three categories of
Wyatt's love poems--(1) lover's lament, (2) lover's assertion of independence, and (3) "the lover's finding a
substitute for the lost mistress." This suggests humor-
ous, rather than bitter, irony in the poem. Also, critics
have erred in attempting to assign to the "they" of the
first stanza a specific animal identity; the animal
imagery is traditional.

2   MUIR, KENNETH. "An Unpublished Wyatt Poem." EIC, 10, no. 2
(April), 229-230.
    Presents "Quondam was I in my Lady's gras" as an
excerpt from a manuscript at Trinity College, Dublin
(D.2.7), which contains "more than thirty of Wyatt's known
poems and two others which are ascribed him in the MS."
Suggests that "many of the other poems in the MS. are also
his." [See also W 1960.3, 1960.4, 1960.5, 1961.6.]

37

Writings about Wyatt

3 _____. "An Unrecorded Wyatt Manuscript." TLS, no. 3,038
(May 20), p. 328.
    The Blage manuscript in Trinity College Library, Dublin,
heretofore unexamined by Wyatt's editors, is "second only
to E[gerton] in reliability." It contains thirty-three
poems by Wyatt and two by Surrey, as well as "more than
seventy unpublished poems," two of which are identified as
Wyatt's and many of which are "in his characteristic
styles." [See also W 1960.2, 1960.4, 1960.5, 1961.6.]

4 _____. "Unpublished Poems of Sir Thomas Wyatt." London
Magazine, 7, no. 3 (March), 11-17.
    Announces existence of the Blage manuscript and forth-
coming edition based on it [W 1961.6], and prints six
Wyatt poems from it. [See also W 1960.2, 1960.3, 1960.5]

5 _____. "Wyatt Poems in a Dublin Manuscript." REL, 1, no. 4
(October), 51-65.
    The Blage manuscript in Trinity College Library, Dublin,
contains thirty-three Wyatt poems in texts often "greatly
superior" to previously-known readings, as well as seventy
other poems written between 1530 and 1550, some of which
appear also to be Wyatt's on the basis of style and biographical allusions. The compiler of the collection was
probably Sir George Blage, a Renaissance gentleman-poet
who knew both Wyatt and Surrey. The thirty-three Wyatt
poems are written in three different hands, "and many of
the other poems in the same three hands can...be ascribed
to him or to a brilliant imitator of his work." [Includes
transcripts of six poems Muir considers to be Wyatt's;
see also W 1960.2-1960.4, 1961.6]

6 _____. "An Unrecorded Wyatt Manuscript." TLS, no. 3,040
(June 3), p. 353.
    Southall [W 1960.8] errs in saying that Nott [WS 1816.1]
was the source for the text of Certayn Psalmes in Collected Poems [W 1949.1]. The copy-text for the edition
was "the manuscript of the Psalms in Wyatt's own handwriting" [i.e., the Egerton].

7 MUMFORD, IVY L. "The Canzone in Sixteenth Century English
Verse With Particular Reference to Wyatt's Renderings
from Petrarch's Canzoniere." EM, 11:21-32.
    Wyatt translated three canzoni from the Canzoniere and
one from Bembo's Gli Asolani, in each case translating
the subject matter but not the form, and in each case
choosing English meters related to song. This indicates
that the translation of canzone subject matter ends with

Wyatt, that he was aware of the form's relation to music, and that he was interested in "verses written to be sung."

8　SOUTHALL, RAYMOND.　"An Unrecorded Wyatt Manuscript."　TLS, no. 3,039 (May 27), p. 337.

Wyatt editors have not indicated an awareness of the existence of another printed source of his poetry: "Certayn Psalmes chosen out the Psalter of David commonlye called the vii Penytentiall Psalmes, drawen into englysche meter by Sir T. Wyat Knight, published by Thomas Raynald and John Haryngton, December 31, 1549."

Muir, probably accepting the information that the source was destroyed, used Nott [WS 1816.1] for his edition [W 1949.1].

9　_____.　"An Unrecorded Wyatt Manuscript."　TLS, no. 3,041 (June 10), p. 369.

Apologizes to Muir [W 1960.6], but points out that the observation was "justified by Muir's edition" [W 1949.1].

10　WHITING, GEORGE W.　"Fortune in Wyatt's 'They flee from me.'"　EIC, 10, no. 2 (April), 220–222.

The poem is about Fortune: "'she' is Fortune, which had once favoured him (stanza two), has deserted him (stanza one) and is inconsistent and unfaithful (stanza three)." Thus the poem provides, under the guise of a love complaint, an expression of a more universal and human experience.

11　WIATT, WILLIAM H.　"Sir Thomas Wyatt's Wordplay."　AnM, 1: 96–101.

The sixteenth-century concept of poetic wit identified it with "skill in the use of language, or rhetorical ability," and its appeal was essentially intellectual. Selected examples from Wyatt's poetry and prose of three types of rhetorical wordplay--adnominatio, traductio, and significatio--illustrate the importance of such devices in any study of his work.

1961

BALDI, SERGIO.　Sir Thomas Wyatt.　Translated by F. T. Prince. Writers and Their Work, no. 139, edited by Bonamy Dobrée. London:　Longmans, Green, and Co., 42 pp.

The characteristic "sadness" of Wyatt's poetry comes from "an innate melancholy of temperament" that cannot be adequately accounted for in his biography or in poetic

tradition. That it manifests itself primarily in his love
poetry indicates only that it was in that genre that he
"found the best means of expressing his poetic self." His
attitude toward love throughout the poetry is consistently
unhappy: it is marked by bitterness about both the woman
and himself; by exaggerated celebration of the freedom
that comes with not being in love--which is contradicted
by his propensity to recall past sufferings; and by the
paradoxically similar frustration that accompanies both
being in and out of love (which is punctuated repeatedly
by the theme of Fortune's hostility). There is, further,
a "sense of wonder" at the traditional Petrarchan situations that produces in the poetry a direct and simple
realism of treatment, and a legalistic attitude toward the
love situation that results in pathetic recriminations
rather than "noble disdain."

Wyatt's poetic technique combines the traditions of the
French ballade, native song, and Petrarch. While he is
best with the simple meters of the song ("ballette"), the
complexity of his poetic sensibility led him to "compositions which are intermediate in character between the
'ballette' and the 'ballade,'" and which result in the
harmonic fusion of rhythm and syntax. His Petrarchan
poems are generally written in the accentual "'broken-
backed'" line, and display "the same feeling for rhythm
and syntax" as the ballades and ballettes. But while he
deals successfully with Petrarchan technique, he does not
duplicate Petrarchan substance, replacing Petrarch's
spiritual renunciation of unrequited love with "self-pity,
pleading and argument," and ignoring Petrarch's emotional
shades and pictorial images. Nevertheless, Petrarch
taught him "a discipline in poetic composition and style,"
as well as a means of mastering poetic emotion. He was
also influenced by Serafino and Alamanni, finding authority for his sarcasm in the former, and learning to moderate
his violent tone from the latter. [Includes brief biography.]

1   FRASER, RUSSELL A. "Introduction," in his edition of <u>John
     Hall: The Court of Virtue (1565)</u>. New Brunswick, New
     Jersey: Rutgers University Press, pp. xii, xvi, xvii.
         Several Wyatt poems ("My penne take payne," "Blame not
     my lute," "My lute awake") "undergo an enfeebling trans-
     formation" as part of Hall's attack on secular, courtly
     poetry.

2   GERARD, ALBERT S. and J. D. HAINSWORTH. "Wyatt's 'They Flee
     From Me.'" <u>EIC</u>, 11, no. 3 (July), 359-368.
          The many recent readings of the poem miss the point in
     attempting to identify the images represented by "they"
     and "she" because the poem focuses not on them but on the
     general theme of the inconstancy of women and Fortune, and,
     more significantly, on "the mood of the deserted poet him-
     self." The poem's time scheme reflects the progression of
     the persona's mood from bitterness to ironic speculation;
     "the ending of the poem is Pyrrhonic and anticipates in
     its own way the serene scepticism of...the Counter-
     Renaissance." [Hainsworth reviews some of the recent
     criticism of the poem, including Gerard's.]

3   HOLLANDER, JOHN. <u>The Untuning of the Sky: Ideas of Music
     in English Poetry, 1500-1700.</u> Princeton, New Jersey:
     Princeton University Press, pp. 128-132, 157.
          Discusses "My lute, awake" and "Blame not my lute" as
     the earliest English Poems that identify the lute with the
     poetic muse or the poet's own voice. Also mentions the
     use of Wyatt's "A robyn, joly robyn" in <u>Twelfth Night</u>.

4   MAXWELL, J. C. Review of Kenneth Muir, ed., <u>Sir Thomas
     Wyatt and His Circle: Unpublished Poems</u> [W 1961.6].
     <u>N&Q</u>, 206, n.s. 8, no. 8 (August), 317-318.
          Muir is "pretty certainly right" in seeing "a fair
     amount of completely new Wyatt" in the Blage MS.

5   MUIR, KENNETH. "Blundeville, Wyatt and Shakespeare." <u>N&Q</u>,
     206, n.s. 8, no. 8 (August), 293-294.
          A book entitled <u>Three morall Treatises</u>, translated from
     Plutarch's <u>Moralia</u> by Thomas Blundeville, may have been
     influenced by Wyatt's <u>Quyete of Mynde</u>. The phrase
     "plesaunt remembraunce of thinges past" occurs in both,
     as well as in Shakespeare's sonnet.

6   _____. "Introduction," in his edition of <u>Sir Thomas Wyatt
     and His Circle: Unpublished Poems</u>. English Reprints
     Series, No. 18, edited by Kenneth Muir. Liverpool:
     Liverpool University Press, pp. ix-xviii.
          This edition is a selection of fifty-one poems from
     the "Blage" MS., part or all of which once belonged to
     Sir George Blage, an acquaintance of Wyatt and Surrey.
     The MS. contains thirty-four known Wyatt poems, and at
     least one of Surrey's, plus more than seventy others,
     many of which are very good, and many of which (handwrit-
     ing indicates) may be Wyatt's. [Includes appendices

containing sixteen previously published poems by Wyatt in
the MS., variants, and a list of poems from the MS. not
included in the edition.]

7 PECORARO, MARCO. "Un Nuovo Contributo sulla Prima Experienza
    Petrarchesca in Inghilterra." Italica, 38, no. 1 (March),
    91-98.
        Wyatt began translating Petrarch in 1527 to offer him
    as a model for imitation, and also because he found in the
    Canzoniere a model for voicing his own melancholy response
    to domestic and political disappointment. As shown by
    Hietsch [W 1960], these poems fall into two categories:
    (1) relatively literal translations characterized by pro-
    saic renderings of Petrarch's images and sounds in homely,
    archaic, and more concrete native English; and (2) poems
    that imitate Petrarch only in certain expressions and
    images and are subordinated to the expression of Wyatt's
    own poetic world, his own literary context. The latter
    type demonstrate that Wyatt's Petrarchism is fundamentally
    original, an attempt at "una nuova intonazione ed espres-
    sione poetica." [In Italian.]

8 REES, D. G. Review of Otto Hietsch, Die Petrarcaübersetzungen
    Sir Thomas Wyatts [W 1960]. MLR, 56, no. 3 (July), 467.
        The line by line comparison of Wyatt poems with their
    Petrarchan originals in the second section is useful, but
    it uncovers no new sources. The first section, an attempt
    to defend the translations, is fragmented and "shadowy,"
    and not as useful as Baldi's "recent book" [W 1953, 1961].

9 STEVENS, JOHN. Music and Poetry in the Early Tudor Court.
    London: Methuen and Co., pp. 134-138, 147-150, passim.
        There exists no significant evidence, in either con-
    temporary accounts of Wyatt or in his poetry itself, that
    he intentionally wrote songs for musical accompaniment--
    or, indeed, that he had any interest in music beyond the
    conventional. On the contrary, his "balets" are to be
    understood in the context of the conventions of the social-
    literary "'game'" of courtly love. It is the quality of
    that tradition, rather than any connection with music,
    that explains the trite superficiality of most of his
    lyrics.

10 THOMSON, PATRICIA. "Wyatt and the School of Serafino." CL,
    13, no. 4 (Fall), 289-315.
        The influence on Wyatt of fifteenth-century Charitean
    Petrarchanism, particularly Serafino's strambotti, is

indicated by the approximately thirty examples of the strambotto he wrote. These poems show that Wyatt found both its form and attitude more congenial than the Petarchan sonnet. Its distich unit, interwoven rhyming, couplet ending, and similarity to rhyme royal made the form easier to translate than the sonnet. And the characteristics of the form as Serafino used it--its "inventiveness, wit, and gallantry," its tight logical structure, its ties with music, its epigrammatic brevity and point, its ingenuity--were those which appealed to him in general. Furthermore, Wyatt also shared Serafino's satirical, sardonic attitude toward love, and it is that attitude that distinguishes Wyatt from Petrarch. He is most successful with Serafino's less serious poems, and his original attempts at the strambotti get better as they become less derivative. [See also W 1964.13.]

11   TYDEMAN, WILLIAM M. "Biographical Data on Sir Thomas Wyatt."
     N&Q, 206, n.s. 8, no. 11 (November), 414-415.
        Evidence establishes that Wyatt's father, Sir Henry
     Wyatt, died on November 10, 1536, not 1537, as reported
     in the D.N.B.

12   WIATT, WILLIAM H. "On the Date of Sir Thomas Wyatt's Knight-
     hood." JEGP, 60:268-272.
        Wyatt was knighted on Easter Day, March 28, 1535, not,
     as previously thought, on the same day in 1536 or 1537.

                              1962

     BIRENBAUM, HARVEY. "Convention and Self: A Study in the
        Poetry of Sir Thomas Wyatt." Ph.D. dissertation, Yale,
        281 pp.
           Wyatt is "a significant transitional poet" because
        his lyrics bring together the conventionalism and indivi-
        dualism of both the English Middle Ages and the Renais-
        sance. He responds to convention mainly by extending it
        from within and "broadening its range of perception";
        more specifically, he combines typical love conventions
        with Stoic attitudes, and in so doing expresses a more
        complex combination of attitudes than either tradition
        can carry alone. This results in a new and "dynamic
        sense of personal immediacy" in his poetry.

1   THOMSON, PATRICIA. "A Note on Wyatt's Prose Style in Quyete
     of Mynde." HLQ, 25, no. 2 (February), 147-156.

1962

Wyatt's prose in the translation demonstrates not only
the primitive state of English prose theory at the time,
but also his "deliberate adoption of a hard, short manner,"
designed, perhaps, to render the Latin into the fewest
possible English words. Comparison of a passage from
Wyatt's version with the same passage from Thomas Blundeville's (1561) shows that Wyatt's "hardness" results
partly from his brevity and partly from his attempt to
follow too closely the Latin of their common original,
Guillaume Budé's version of Plutarch. This results in
unemphatic sentence structure, faulty logic, "muddled"
grammar, monotonous description, and, in general, a style
which is "overloaded, unbalanced, and obscure" in contrast
to Blundeville's better planned and better executed version. Nevertheless, Wyatt's plain style is more effective
than Blundeville's Elizabethan fullness in its directness
and simplicity. Furthermore, his diction, if limited,
"represents the best in the tradition of plain prose in
England," and looks forward to the mature prose of his
Defence, where he is concerned not with literary Latin
but "the realities of his day." [See also W 1964.13].

2   ____. "Sir Thomas Wyatt: Classical Philosophy and English
Humanism." HLQ, 25, no. 2 (February), 79-96.
Wyatt's Quyete of Mynde is a "pioneer work" that "gives
Wyatt a place, albeit a humble one, in the humanist movement," and articulates and explains the serious tone of
much of his other writings. Originally commanded by
Katherine of Aragon to translate Book II of Petrarch's
De remediis utriusque fortunae, Wyatt translated Plutarch's essay instead because of the difficulty of turning
the eloquent diversity of Petrarch's Latin into English,
because of Petrarch's repetitiousness, and because the
contents of both originals are essentially the same.
Wyatt's literal and plain English, the result of his concern for matter over manner, links him with the didactic,
rather than the eloquent, tradition of early humanism, and
looks forward to the practical plainness of the letters to
his son, the moral tone of his translations and imitations
of Latin poems, the outlook of his anti-court Satires, and
even the philosophical attitude frequently expressed in
his Petrarchan poems. All of which indicates that the
"total complex" of Wyatt's work includes the values and
attitudes of classical moral philosophy and English
Christian humanism. [See also W 1964.13.]

1963

BERTHOFF, ANN. "The Falconer's Dream of Trust: Wyatt's
  'They fle from me.'" SR, 71, no. 1 (Winter), 477-494.
      Allegorical readings that interpret the poem as a
  statement on courtly/neoplatonic love or hunting fail to
  recognize its larger theme, one that "represents the whole
  range of Wyatt's attitudes towards the conditions of life."
  The poem is not about infidelity, but about "Man's inevitable and necessary foolhardiness," as expressed through
  the more specific theme of service and courtly hire. The
  double imagery of falconry and love in the first stanza
  leads to the "completely human" encounter of the second,
  which is not a description of ideal love, but of love
  that is impossible because it is, like everything else,
  subject to Fortune. But the poem does not end with
  ironic acceptance and quiet retirement; instead it suggests continuation of the struggle despite the recognition
  of the truth, an attitude consistent with the events and
  decisions of Wyatt's life.

1 CANDELARIA, FREDERICK H. "The Necklace of Wyatt's 'Diere.'"
     ELN, 1, no. 1 (September), 4-5.
         Two possible analogues to "Noli me tangere, for Cesars
     1 ame" (from "Who so list to hount"), one from the
     Bible (John 20: 17), the other from the Greek Anthology
     (V: 158), suggest that Wyatt's wording may have been in-
     fluenced by "the appeal to his wit of a sacred-profane
     parody."

2 GUSS, DONALD. "Wyatt, Alamanni, and Literary Imitation."
     JRUL, 26, no. 1 (December), 6-13.
         The very subtle differences between "Myne owne John
     Poynz" and its source, Alamanni's tenth satire, illuminate
     both the moral seriousness of Wyatt's vision and the
     fundamental originality of Renaissance literary imitation.
     Although Wyatt generally follows Alamanni's contrast
     between public and private life "tercet for tercet," he
     changes its spirit, through minor alterations in diction,
     rhetoric and structure, from cultivated Horation cynicism
     to "an indignant attack upon the world's corruption, and
     a dramatic presentation of his own proud integrity."

3 MUIR, KENNETH. "Wyatt's Poetry," in his Life and Letters of
     Sir Thomas Wyatt. Liverpool: Liverpool University Press,
     pp. 222-260.
         Canon. In addition to the Psalms and Satires, the
     Wyatt canon includes the 101 shorter poems in the Egerton
     MS., "at least 28 of the poems in the Blage MS.," "at

least 23" from the Devonshire MS. that are not included
in the Egerton or Blage, eight poems from other MSS., and
the sixteen poems "ascribed to him by Tottel, of which no
MS. copy has survived." Of the remaining 75 poems vari-
ously ascribed to him, many are probably his also.
Translations. While the "imperfect rhymes" of Wyatt's
Petrarchan translations are bothersome, it is clear that
his rough rhythms and his departures from Petrarch's meaning and tone are deliberate and effective. Lyrics.
Criticism of the conventionality of his lyrics overlooks
the way in which his "poetic individuality shines through
the conventions," but those who see similarity between
Wyatt and Donne fail to notice "the complete absence in
Wyatt's poetry of metaphysical wit" or the fact that "the
majority of his poems were written in a convention...
against which Donne was in reaction." Satires. Wyatt was
"the first English writer of formal satire," and superior
in the genre to Hall, Marston, Lodge, and Donne. Penitential Psalms. The Psalms, with their prologues, "are
essentially a single poem," but are not original in phrasing or imagery. [Major portion (pp. 1-221) is biography,
with the texts of letters, documents, and the Defence,
and including letters by others; also includes appendices.]

4   MUMFORD, IVY L. "Sir Thomas Wyatt's Verse and Italian
    Musical Sources." EM, 14: 9-26.
        Although none of the musical settings for Italian poems
    adapted or translated by Wyatt is extant, it is likely
    that he chose certain poems by Serafino, Petrarch, and
    other Italian poets because they had already been set to
    music in Italy. Sixteen Wyatt poems--sonnets, strambotti,
    and frottole--have sources in Serafino's poesia per
    musica, and of the 27 poems he took from the Canzoniere,
    three sonnets, two canzoni, and one madrigal have musical
    sources as well. The evidence indicates the influence of
    these sources on Wyatt's stanza forms, and points out "a
    unique contribution to English verse," one apparently not
    shared in by the other contributors to Tottel's Miscellany.

5   NELSON, C. E. "A Note on Wyatt and Ovid." MLR, 58, no. 1
    (January), 60-63.
        The probable influence of Ovid's Amores on "What
    menythe thys?" and "They fle from me"--especially the
    second, where there are similarities not only in situation
    but in imagery and "sexual detail"--indicates that Wyatt
    was perhaps influenced by classical sources more than has
    heretofore been acknowledged. The source for the first
    poem is conventional, and so is Wyatt's version, but

because the source for the second is Ovid's "most sensual lyric," Wyatt finds it necessary to adapt it to "a convention that stresses the painfulness of a situation" and thus obscures its debt to Ovid.

6   SCHWARTZ, ELIAS. "The Meter of Some Poems of Wyatt." SP, 60, no. 2, part 1 (April), 155-165.
    Much of the difficulty encountered in dealing with Wyatt's metrical "roughness" can be eliminated if one assumes that he was consciously writing a four-stressed accentual line rather than deliberately or unconsciously violating the movement of iambic pentameter. Scansion of "Who so list to hount" and "They fle from me" illustrates that, by paying attention to mid-line pauses, "accent-pointing alliteration," progressive vowel coloring and echoing, natural accentuation and word grouping, and to the suggestion of sprung rhythm, the reader will observe a four-stress accentual pattern that results in "an organic metrical and rhythmical whole" consistent with the rhetorical emphases of the poems. On the basis of this kind of examination, Wyatt's poetry recalls Anglo-Saxon accentual verse and looks forward to modern free verse. The scansion also demonstrates that the "double audition," by which the reader is aware of the ideal norm set against the actual rhythm of a poem in iambic pentameter, functions in reverse with accentual verse, where natural speech patterns become the ideal against which is set the rhetorical emphasis of the four-stressed line.

7   SCOTT, DAVID. "Wyatt's Worst Poem." TLS, no. 3,211 (September 13), p. 696.
    The source for "When Dido festid first the wandryng Trojan knyght" was the De Sphaera of Joannes de Sacrobosco, "the foremost textbook of elementary astronomy" at the time. The poem, written to welcome the newly-crowned Anne of Cleves, was left unfinished because of Wyatt's return to the court of Charles V in November, 1539. This dating of the poem also indicates the possibility that the 1541 date traditionally given for the Psalms is wrong because they precede the poem in the Egerton MS. It is likely that Wyatt wrote the Psalms after Anne Boleyn's execution in 1536.

8   THOMSON, PATRICIA. Review of Kenneth Muir, ed., Sir Thomas Wyatt and His Circle: Unpublished Poems [W 1961.6]. RES, n.s. 14, no. 53, 101.
    This edition, if Muir's surmises about Wyatt authorship of unascribed poems are correct, proves that the Blage MS.

1963

contains "the most important contribution to the Wyatt canon since Nott [WS 1816.1] edited the Egerton and Devonshire MSS." It is superior to the Devonshire, and while it contains "a good deal of run-of-the-mill Tudor writing," it also includes "a handful of outstandingly beautiful poems."

9   TYDEMAN, WILLIAM M. "Wyatt's Poems and the Blage Manuscript: Verbal Resemblances." N&Q, 208, n.s. 10, no. 8 (August), 293–294.

     Many of the verbal parallels observed by Muir between the poems in the Blage MS. [W 1961.6] and those in his Collected Poems [W 1949.1] "derive ultimately from the large stock of clichés universally employed in courtly love poetry of the period." Tydeman offers other parallels that he considers more helpful in determining Wyatt authorship.

10   ZANDVOORT, R. W. Review of Sergio Baldi, Sir Thomas Wyatt [W 1961] and Kenneth Muir, ed., Sir Thomas Wyatt and His Circle: Unpublished Poems [W 1961.6]. ES, 44: 397–398.

     Baldi does not mention the regularization of Wyatt's metrics in Tottel's Miscellany. Muir furnishes "no definite proof" that the unascribed poems in the Blage MS. are Wyatt's.

1964

ANON. "Poetry at Court" [Review of Raymond Southall, The Courtly Maker (W 1964.10)]. TLS, no. 3,266 (October 1), p. 895.

     Southall's reexamination of the Egerton and Devonshire MSS. has given him "a fresh understanding both of the social circumstances and of the metrical forms" of the poetry in them. Although his enthusiasm for Wyatt has led him to underrate Surrey and the Elizabethans, his study is important for its verification of the "vivid actuality" beneath the social and literary conventions of courtly love, for its clarification of the problems of prosodic vocabulary, copyists' conventions, and punctuation inherent in the editing of early Tudor poets, and for his insistence on "the importance of understanding the conditions in which these poems were written and preserved." "He makes a strong case for a new edition of Wyatt's poems."

Writings about Wyatt

1964

1   ANON. "The Cultivated Courtier: Italian Forms in an English Tradition" [Review of Kenneth Muir, Life and Letters of Sir Thomas Wyatt (W 1963.3)]. TLS, no. 3,237 (March 12), p. 214.

       Wyatt retains a "North country forthrightness" that is observable in his prose and poetry, in his native works and translations. He consistently employs "proverbs, epitomes of traditional wisdom or observation that derive from the common sort," and adapts his foreign models to his own English manner. His poetry is best "where it comes closest to his manner of speaking," and while music is clearly an influence on much of his best work, he often uses a "prose order of words" that does not rely on it at all, and achieves the kind of "plain style" seen in Jonson. While he was never happy with Italian forms, they "helped him to correct the irregularity and diffuseness... of his earlier poetry."

2   ENDICOTT, ANNABEL M. "A Note on Wyatt and Serafino D'Aquilano." RN, 17, no. 4 (Winter), 301-303.

       An octave from the Blage MS., "Thou slepest ffast," previously unascribed, is very likely Wyatt's for two reasons: he was "the only early Tudor poet who thoroughly explored the possibilities of the Italian ottava," and the poem is, like many of his epigrams, a translation from Serafino. Comparison of the original with Wyatt's version, moreover, provides an "elementary study in construction" that illustrates Wyatt's method of composition and shows him moving toward the independence of the ottava rima prologues to the Penitential Psalms.

3   FOXWELL, A. K. A Study of Sir Thomas Wyatt's Poems. New York: Russell & Russell.

       Reprint of W 1911.

4   FULLER, JEAN OVERTON and RAYMOND SOUTHALL. "Wyatt and Petrarch." EIC, 14, no. 3 (July), 324-327.

       Fuller points out that "Who list to hcount" is a worldly, rather than courtly, translation; Southall agrees, but suggests that courtly love was itself a social, rather than literary, phenomenon.

5   GARDNER, HELEN. Review of Kenneth Muir, Life and Letters of Sir Thomas Wyatt [W 1963.3]. The Listener, 71, no. 1827 (April 2), 564.

       "The volume is really 'materials towards a life of Sir Thomas Wyatt,' not a true 'Life and Letters.'"

1964

6   GREENE, RICHARD LEIGHTON. "Wyatt's 'I am as I am' in Carol-
     Form." RES, n.s. 15, 175-180.
        A medieval carol on the fly-leaf of a collection of
     fifteenth-century sermons is a variant of Wyatt's poem.
     Evidence suggests that it is an earlier version that Wyatt
     expanded; if so, it provides "an excellent example of
     Wyatt's use of a medieval and native...tradition of poetry
     and of his adapting it to a new influence."

7   _____. "Wyatt's 'They fle from me' and the Busily Seeking
     Critics." BuR, 12, no. 3 (December), 17-30.
        The many misleading interpretations of the poem, par-
     ticularly those that identify "they" as falcons or deer
     and "she" as Fortune, miss the point that "the poem can
     be read (and memorized) as an elegantly erotic song, a
     dramatic lyric of a lover and his changing hap in his
     affairs with completely real and breathing human women."

8   HOWARTH, HERBERT. "Wyatt, Spenser and the Canzone."
     Italica, 41, no. 1 (March), 79-90.
        Spenser reproduced Petrarch's neo-Platonism, pictorial-
     ism and intermittent shifts in line length; Wyatt replaced
     those elements in his canzones with realism, skepticism,
     and Chaucer's rhyme royal. Petrarch's influence on Wyatt
     is evident, however, in the autobiographical cast of
     Wyatt's verse, as well as in its oxymorons, circumlocu-
     tions, and abstract grammatical figures, the last of
     which were a significant part of Shakespeare's repertoire.

9   SIMONS, ERIC N. The Queen and the Rebel: Mary Tudor and
     Wyatt the Younger. London: Frederick Muller, pp. 20-30.
        Brief biographical sketch of Wyatt in a book on his
     son.

10   SOUTHALL, RAYMOND. The Courtly Maker: An Essay on the Poetry
     of Wyatt and His Contemporaries. New York: Barnes and
     Noble, 188 pp.
        Because the identity of the writer of much of the
     poetry ascribed to Wyatt has not yet been clearly estab-
     lished, it is necessary to define its qualities by examin-
     ing it against the realities of Tudor court life. Such an
     examination reveals the possibility that, despite the
     anonymous and conventional nature of both the native
     lyrics and the translations included in the Devonshire and
     Egerton MSS., there seems to have been "at least one poet"
     who, rather than merely reflecting the conventions of
     courtly love, reinterpreted and redefined them in light
     of the political and moral realities of life in Court.

1964

This poet, influenced more fundamentally by Chaucer's
Troilus and Criseyde than by Continental sources, reproduced all the conventional situations and sentiments of
courtly love included in that poem, but focused on its
negative implications--"undeclared love, rejection, separation and betrayal"--and applied those to the expression
of "conflicting states of mind," in which the emotional
instability of the conventional courtly lover is made to
reflect the real instability of a world governed by Sin
and Fortune rather than the Divine Order reflected in
noncourtly Renaissance literature. The result of this
juxtaposition of ritual and reality was a body of poetry
that reflected a "psychological drama of inner perturba-
tion and distress" in which Love, Fortune, and Sin "are
made to appear simply as precipitants of various states
of consciousness" and whose rhythms mirror the specific
reality of human insecurity and isolation and the desire
for its opposite, the security of courtly patronage,
faithful friends, and true love. Eventually this "crisis
of consciousness" is tenuously resolved in the confident
and restrained Satires and in the Psalms, where Wyatt
achieves a point of view that reflects the forces of the
Reformation.

It is Wyatt's consistent contact with the specific
personal reality of the courtly world that marks the difference between his poetry and Donne's. The latter re-
volts against a dead courtly tradition, and thus maintains
a stability of spirit that finds expression in logical and
analogical conceits; Wyatt, immersed in the concrete
realities of court life, reflects the instability of a
real conflict whose expression is principally psychological and mirrored not in conceits but in rhythms, specifically, in phrasal units that suggest his personas'
instability. This method was unfortunately replaced by
the regularized metrics and conventional abstractions of
Surrey and the Elizabethans. [Includes appendices describ-
ing the Egerton and Devonshire MSS. and one dealing
briefly with Wyatt and Anne Boleyn.]

11   ____. "The Devonshire Manuscript Collection of Early Tudor
        Poetry, 1532-41." RES, n.s. 15, 142-150.
        When read in the context of social history and the
history of the manuscript itself, the Devonshire poems
can be seen to reflect not merely the literary conventions
of courtly love, but the "real danger of impolitic love,
disloyalty, and breaches of secrecy" made necessary in the
Tudor court. Such conditions made necessary the "essential

anonymity" of the poems, particularly those "currently, and
for no good reason, attributed to...Wyatt." [Provides
general description and brief account of the provenance of
the Devonshire. See also W 1964.10.]

12 _____. "The Personality of Sir Thomas Wyatt." EIC, 14,
no. 1 (January), 43-64.
      The "characteristic inwardness" of Wyatt's mind assimi-
lates the conventions of his poetry and makes them a
framework for the articulation of "various states of consciousness" that reflect the movement of his mind. His
rhythms reflect the turmoil, while his paradoxes impose on
them the stability of art. Wyatt resembles Surrey only in
those poems that do not reflect this "'crisis of consciousness.'" [See also W 1964.10.]

13 THOMSON, PATRICIA. Sir Thomas Wyatt and His Background.
Stanford, California: Stanford University Press; London:
Routledge and Kegan Paul, 312 pp.
      The records of Wyatt's public and private lives testify
to the continuing relevance of the code and idiom of
courtly love, as exemplified by the career of Anne Boleyn,
and the equal importance of both moral wisdom, represented
by Catherine of Aragon, and political wisdom, exemplified
by Cromwell. The significant roles played by all three in
Wyatt's career also suggest that his prose and poetry
reflected real experience.
      His Latin translations (Quyete of Mynde and poems), in-
fluenced by Catherine's humanistic wisdom, reveal Wyatt as
a minor Erasmian humanist: didactic and nonliterary in
approach, ethical, practical and unmystical in attitude,
and utilitarian and plain in style. His satires, though
similar in attitude, are more classical in form and style
than in subject matter. His Petrarchan poems also reflect
the blend of classical and Christian philosophy in their
dramatic conflict between "rational ideal" and "irrational
reality" that results in fictional stances similar to
those in Petrarch, Donne, and Yeats.
      The English lyrics are derivative, expressing the com-
monplaces of courtly love and the indirect guidance of
Chaucer, who exemplified the "narrative strength" necessary
to deal with the relationship between experience and convention. But in concentrating on the subjective relevance
of experience and image, Wyatt is more like Donne, although
he does not, like Donne, explore "a new and more complex
truth" or a new philosophy of love.
      The Petrarchan poems are more significant than Surrey's
because Wyatt takes Petrarch more seriously and translates

him more faithfully, rendering his "metaphysical manner" in a way that anticipates Donne, and remaining closer to his prosody and structure. Surrey, on the other hand, is more English in structure, more picturesque in imagery, more confident in assertion, and more regular in rhythm than either Petrarch or Wyatt; in addition, he is less interested in "the value of love" and "the experience of loving" than is Wyatt. And while Wyatt shows no interest in Petrarchan transcendentalism, and does not translate so closely the Petrarchan madrigal or canzone, these departures do not mark him as a rebel, for many of them--his worldliness, realism, rebellious unorthodoxy and egotism-- have precedents in Italian commentators on Petrarch. Another influence, that of fifteenth-century Chariten Petrarchanism, particularly Serafino's strambotti, provided Wyatt with a form, tone, structure, and attitude more congenial to him than Petrarch's.

The Satires are "Wyatt's greatest achievement in the poetry of insight and knowledge," and they represent his major original accomplishment, "the naturalization of classical satire." They show finally that for Wyatt "courtly wisdom was a richer source of inspiration than courtly love."

[Includes a brief biography, and appendices on the following: manuscripts, Wyatt's daughter, Sir Francis Bryan, the "May Day Sonnet," Anne Boleyn, the influence of Boethius, Chaucer, and Ariosto, "clichés in the Medieval Lyric," and Italian sonnet theory.]

14   ____. "Wyatt's Boethian Ballade." RES, n.s. 15, 262-267.
    Evidence suggests that Wyatt's "If thou wilt mighty be" was an independent translation from De Consolatione, uninfluenced by Chaucer's Boece. Furthermore, his departures from Boethius indicate that he was aiming at "a self-contained, consistent, compact, and personal statement" reflective of Stoicism. Nevertheless, the poem is Chaucerian in form if not substance, for it is a "formal imitation of a Chaucerian ballade," possibly the "Balade de Bon Conseyl," and as such a reflection of the "compatibility between Chaucerian and early Tudor moral lyric." [See also W 1964.13.]

15   ____. "Wyatt's Debt to Dante and Ariosto." EM, 15: 47-59.
    Puttenham's statement suggesting the influence of Dante and Ariosto on Wyatt (and Surrey) is "largely, if not entirely" a "red herring." The relationship is only a general one, buffered by the more specific influence of Petrarch and Serafino. [See also W 1964.13.]

1965

ANON. "Courting a Style" [Review of Patricia Thomson, <u>Sir Thomas Wyatt and His Background</u> (W 1964.13)]. <u>TLS</u>, no. 3, 296 (April 29), p. 332.
      Agrees generally with Thomson, but suggests that Wyatt was less influenced by Alamanni than she claims.

1   CUTLER, EDWARD J. Review of Patricia Thomson, <u>Sir Thomas Wyatt and His Background</u> [W 1964.13]. <u>Library Journal</u>, 90, no. 5 (March 1), 1120.
      Despite the "arbitrary cleavage" between life and letters, a "scholarly and impressive study."

2   FRASER, RUSSELL A. Review of Raymond Southall, <u>The Courtly Maker</u> [W 1964.10]. <u>ELN</u>, 3, no. 1 (September), 60-69.
      Southall's attempt "to acquit Wyatt's poetry of the charge of conventionality, to associate it to real life, and to represent the prosody as reflecting that association" leads him mistakenly to dismiss Italian influence and to overemphasize "reality as a touchstone of value," to commit the error of seeing poetry as imitation rather than ordering. Furthermore, he fails to recognize that Wyatt sometimes simply fails to follow the metrical pattern he sets up for a poem.

3   GRIFFIN, ALICE BRADLEY. "The Language of Sir Thomas Wyatt." Ph.D. dissertation, University of Pennsylvania, 160 pp.
      Statistical tabulations of Wyatt's native and foreign vocabulary sources and linguistic innovations, together with examination of the "internal nature" of his language, reveal that, contrary to expectation, he "did not evolve anything that might be regarded, however loosely, as a new poetic diction." On the contrary, the evidence suggests that he was "entirely representative of [his] age" in the "reactionary" and generally undistinguished quality of his imagery, diction, grammatical structure, and expression in general, in the abstract nature of his language, and in his "general tendency toward amplification instead of concentration and compression." The study implies, finally, that he was unsympathetic toward, and unsuited for, his subject matter. [Includes appendices on native and foreign words and sources, sound patterns, and Chaucer's influence.]

4   GUSS, DONALD L. "Wyatt's Petrarchism: An Instance of Creative Imitation in the Renaissance." <u>HLQ</u>, 29, no. 1 (November), 1-15.

The problem of understanding Wyatt's use of Petrarchan forms to express an un-Petrarchan attitude is best confronted by recognizing in his poetry the basic mode of Renaissance composition: imitation of "authorized rhetorical forms" as a means of expressing "authorized moral views," as exemplified particularly in his Satires. The process is repeated in the Petrarchan lyrics, where he transforms the conventional love situation into an examination of distributive justice, wherein the behavior of the lady is condemned through the persona's righteous indignation or Stoic disdain. The same process and attitude characterizes his "manly" non-Petrarchan lyrics as well, though in those he was probably anticipated by English and Continental courtly lyrics.

5   HARDISON, O. B.   Review of Patricia Thomson, Sir Thomas Wyatt and His Background [W 1964.13].   South Atlantic Quarterly, 64, no. 4 (Autumn), 570-571.
    Despite its virtues, the book is "a disappointment" because it ignores Platonic and humanistic ideas in Wyatt's background, because it does not deal with the aesthetic qualities of the poems, and because of its arbitrary compartmentalization of aspects of the poet's life and the literary traditions that influenced him.

6   HARRIER, RICHARD, [C.].   Review of Patricia Thomson, Sir Thomas Wyatt and His Background [W 1964.13].   MLQ, 26, no. 4 (December), 612-614.
    The chapters on background are "indispensable," those on biography and the English lyric weak, and that on humanism "of limited value." The book does not deal with Wyatt's meter.

7   HUTTAR, CHARLES A.   "'Forsake me neuer for no new': A Note on Wyatt's Poetic Diction."   N&Q, 210, n.s. 12, no. 5 (May), 170-172.
    Wyatt used the phrase "no new" at least four times, which indicates that it belongs to the "stockpile of poetic clichés" freely drawn upon by all the courtly makers.

8   KÖKERITZ, HELGE.   "Dialectical Traits in Sir Thomas Wyatt's Poetry," in Franciplegius: Medieval and Linguistic Studies in Honor of Francis Peabody Magoun, Jr.   Edited by Jess B. Bessinger, Jr. and Robert P. Creed.   New York: New York University Press, pp. 294-303.
    Wyatt, like most of those who left the country for a university and later went into government service, shed

1965

the linguistic habits of his youth and adopted the edu-
cated and courtly speech of London. Nevertheless, his
poems reveal the survival of "certain Kenticisms," principally phonological, in his diction.

9   LEA, K. M. Review of Kenneth Muir, Life and Letters of Sir
     Thomas Wyatt [W 1963.3]. RES, n.s. 16, no. 62, 190.
          The chief impression that comes from the letters is
     Wyatt's honesty. Muir's interpretation of the relation-
     ship of Wyatt and Anne Boleyn suggests that it was "more
     than Platonic"; and his comments on the poetry indicate
     that he has modified some of his positions in light of
     recent criticism.

10   L. V. R. Review of Patricia Thomson, Sir Thomas Wyatt and
     His Background [W 1964.13]. Neo-Latin News, 11, no. 4,
     in SCN, 23, no. 4 (Winter), 61.
          Wyatt's use of Budé's Latin version of Plutarch's De
     tranquillitate et securitate animi is "an excellent exam-
     ple of the interdependence of Neo-Latin and vernacular
     writing in the Renaissance," even though Budé's version is
     inferior to that of Erasmus.

11   MAYNARD, WINIFRED. "The Lyrics of Wyatt: Poems or Songs?"
     RES, n.s. 16, 1-13.
          Despite the absence of conclusive evidence linking
     Wyatt's lyrics with specific musical settings, both exter-
     nal and internal circumstances suggest the connection.
     Early Tudor court songbooks, especially the one containing
     the songs of Henry VIII (B.M. Add. MS. 31922) provide
     likely settings for some of Wyatt's verse, particularly
     for his divided fourteeners and other short-lined measures.
     There is less likelihood that he wrote for dance tunes.
     All in all, there are a "handful" of Wyatt's lyrics that
     resemble specific songs, but it is possible that he might
     have written many others with the knowledge that they
     would be put to music. Internal evidence also suggests
     the connection: some of his refrains, for example, are
     repeated while others are used as opening phrases that
     invite such repetition; furthermore, some of his cadences
     resolve "naturally into melodic shape," and over twenty
     of his lyrics contain some reference to music. The cumu-
     lative effect of the evidence suggests that "about fifty
     lyrics were consciously framed by Wyatt in such ways that
     they invite or are amenable to song."

12 NATHAN, LEONARD E. "Tradition and Newfangleness in Wyatt's
    'They Fle From Me.'" ELH, 32, no. 1 (March), 1-16.
        The poem belongs to the genre of fifteenth-century
    courtly love poems based on the conventions established
    by The Romaunt of the Rose and Troilus and Criseyde,
    specifically the passage in The Romaunt that describes
    the consolation available to the suffering lover through
    the exercise of "Swete-Thought," "the mental process by
    which the servant summons to mind the image of his absent
    mistress." This rhetorical description (efficatio), as
    seen, for example, in a "Ballade" and "Roundel" by Charles
    d'Orleans, was easily detached from the narrative context
    of The Romaunt, and turned into the mechanical expression
    of the love code characteristic of fifteenth-century
    lyrics. Without the narrative behind them, such poems
    became "sub-literary exercises in sentimental courtliness"
    that have nothing to do with real human behavior. "They
    fle from me" differs from those because of the stance of
    its speaker: the description of the lady is not a cata-
    logue but a dramatic scene, and it brings not consolation
    but further anguish; furthermore, the animal metaphor, the
    denial by the speaker that the experience was a dream, the
    refusal to rely on allegorical personification, and the
    subdued, confused irony at the end of the poem all suggest
    that Wyatt's purpose was to take seriously the real im-
    plications of a conventional situation. The poem thus
    provides an example of his "originality and power" as a
    poet as it expresses his "recurring poetic topic"--"the
    failure of human relationships to live up to their best
    possibilities." It also exemplifies the problem of un-
    certainty characteristic of his endings and the difficulty
    involved in interpreting them.

13 SMITH, HALLETT. Review of Patricia Thomson, Sir Thomas Wyatt
    and His Background [W 1964.13]. RN, 18, no. 4 (Winter),
    327-329.
        The book is "essential in the study of Wyatt," and
    particularly valuable because it "demolishes" the view of
    Mason [WS 1959] and Stevens [W 1961.9] that Wyatt's
    lyrics are only of sociological interest.

14 THOMSON, PATRICIA. Review of Kenneth Muir, Life and Letters
    of Sir Thomas Wyatt [W 1963.3]. N&Q, 210, n.s. 12,
    no. 10 (October), 390-391.
        An important volume because it provides "a complete
    and authentic text of all the known letters, memoranda,
    and speeches" of Wyatt and because it corrects some
    errors in previous biographies (although it contains some

errors of its own). The letters show Wyatt to be a "highly
skilled journalist" and the Defence is "one of the finest"
examples of prose rhetoric from the period.

15   TWOMBLY, ROBERT G. "Thomas Wyatt and the Rhetoric of Address."
      Ph.D. dissertation, Yale, 266 pp.
         That which connects Wyatt with English tradition and
      separates him from Petrarch is the presence in his poetry
      of a "dramatically involved audience." Sidney, "the real
      link between Petrarch and England," illustrates that the
      movement of much sixteenth-century poetry lies in the
      development of drama from "tonal nuances" and "the mind's
      own dialogue with...conceit." Wyatt departs from that
      tradition--as well as from the formulas of Chaucerian
      diction and courtly sensibility--by abandoning metaphor in
      favor of a dramatic voice and by departing from "dramatic
      dialogue" to achieve a single, isolated sensibility. This
      personal isolation is particularly apparent in the Satires,
      where he achieves "a sense of interior control challenging
      an exterior social and moral 'perplexity'"; in those son-
      nets "organized not conceptually through imagery but simply
      according to the dynamics of dialogue"; and in the Psalms,
      "a prolonged exercise in 'dialogue' thinking" through a
      "dramatic persona of sufficient power or importance or
      authority not to become hidden in the complexities of his
      alienation." [See also W 1969.4, 1970.6.]

16   WENTERSDORF, KARL P. "The Imagery of Wyatt." SN, 37: 161-
      173.
         Classification of Wyatt's imagery according to the
      model provided by Caroline Spurgeon's Shakespeare's
      Imagery indicates that "the vigor which may be regarded
      as the most characteristic trait of his work" comes more
      clearly from his tough, harsh, sometimes grotesque imagery
      than his rugged prosody or masculine themes. Analysis of
      the Wyatt canon (which contains fewer than four hundred
      images) groups the images according to five major sub-
      jects--(1) "Domestic and bodily action," (2) "Nature,"
      (3) "Daily Life," (4) "Learning and Arts," and (5) "Imagi-
      nation"--each of which contains a number of subdivisions.
      (1) contains the largest number of images among the major
      divisions, and "Bodily Movement and Action," grouped under
      (1), includes the largest number among the subdivisions.
      In all, "practically one-third of Wyatt's imagery is made
      up of concepts of movement and action," suggesting not
      only the relation of his imagery to his "vigor," but also
      the possible influence of his active experiences as cour-
      tier, soldier, and diplomat on his poetry. In addition,

his preoccupation with the substantive concept of freedom
complements his imagery of movement, suggesting that those
two elements provide the keynote to his poetry.

1966

*BALDI, SERGIO. "Sir Thomas Wyatt and Vellutello," in English
   Studies Today, 4th ser., eds. Alva Cellini and Georgio
   Melchoir. Rome: Edizioni di Storia e Letteratura,
   pp. 121-128.
      Cited in MHRA bibliography, vol. 41. See W 1966.1.

1   _____. "Una Fonte Petrarchesca Di Sir Thomas Wyatt," in
   Friendship's Garland: Essays Presented to Mario Praz on
   his Seventieth Birthday. Vol. 1. Edited by Vittorio
   Gabrielli. Storia e Letteratura: Raccolta di Studi e
   Testi, no. 106. Rome: Edizioni di Storia e Letteratura,
   pp. 87-93.
      Wyatt's "Though I my self be bridilled of my mynde,"
   heretofore considered an original poem, is a translation
   of Petrarch's "Orso al uostro destrier si po ben porre."
   Comparison of the two shows that Wyatt, as was his custom,
   translated by adapting the sonnet to his own circumstances,
   and suggests specifically the possibility that he wrote it
   while abroad, and that the "maisteres" of line 13 should
   be read as "master's." The comparison also indicates that
   Wyatt's obscurity is unintentional, the result of translating problems. Other differences between the two can
   be traced to Wyatt's use of Vellutello's 1525 commentary
   on Petrarch and to another Petrarchan sonnet," "Quando
   'l uoler, che con duo sproni ardenti." The influence of
   Vellutello is also observable in the translations "Auysing
   the bright bemes" and "Caesar, when that the traytor of
   Egipt"; in fact, the difference between the Devonshire and
   Egerton readings of the latter shows the influence of
   Vellutello on the (earlier) Devonshire version and the influence of Petrarch's "Et Hanibal, quand' a l'imperio
   afflito" on the (later) Egerton one. This suggests that
   Wyatt first used Vellutello as a schoolboy would, but
   later revised the translation because of a better understanding of Italian and Petrarch. [In Italian.]

2   FRIEDMAN, DONALD M. "The 'Thing' in Wyatt's Mind." EIC, 16,
   no. 4 (October), 375-381.
      The "thing" referred to most clearly in "My mothers
   maydes" is not, as Southall suggests [W 1964.10], a remem-
   bered experience, but rather the condition of inner

1966

stability Wyatt desires to maintain in the face of life's
vicissitudes. Inspired by Stoicism, he expresses his desire for this "quiet of mind" in much of his work, expanding its meaning to include such realities as "'spirit,'"
"'consciousness,'" and "'soul.'" In his love lyrics this
condition is set up against the assaults of passion and the
rituals of courtly love. Of particular interest here is
that he also incorporates this essentially secular doctrine into his Psalm translations, where "the health and
wholeness of the mind are...held to be of comparable importance to the heart's purification and the rejuvenation
of the repentant spirit." Thus it becomes clear that the
issues Wyatt deals with in his religious poems "are consistent with the major preoccupations of his secular
poetry."

3   _____. "Wyatt's Amoris Personae." MLQ, 27, no. 2 (June),
136-146.
The "distinctive mark of Wyatt's love poetry" is his
interest in "examining the mind of the courtly lover" as
it confronts the discrepancy between the postures of
rhetoric and language and the true motives underlying them.
This interest leads not to simple cynicism or outrage, but
to dramatic presentations of various personae who express
their recognition of the discrepancy in "a multitude of
differing, often contradictory stances" that objectify,
for example, their recognition of the shortcomings of
conventional diction in confronting complex feelings, or
that present the lover "using courtly rhetoric with ironic
intent." It also leads to oblique moral comment on the
dissociation of language from court behavior and the
courtly love situation. "Eche man me telleth" and "It may
be good" provide clear examples of this "repertory method."

4   GUSS, DONALD L. "Petrarchism in England: Wyatt and Gascoigne," in his John Donne, Petrarchist: Italian Conceits
and Love Theory in The Songs and Sonnets. Detroit: Wayne
State University Press, pp. 34-40.
"Wyatt represents strict imitation and humanistic Pet-
archism, Gascoigne free imitation and social Petrarchism."
Wyatt's Italiante poetry, though fundamentally Petrarchan
and neo-Stoic, is nevertheless "truly original," often
departing from the structural and rhetorical patterns of
its Petrarchan models, and ultimately transforming Petarch
into his own un-Petrarchan attitudes. He thus shows that
"integrity and individuality are not foreign even to humanistic Petrarchism."

5 _____. Reviews of Raymond Southall, The Courtly Maker and
    Patricia Thomson, Sir Thomas Wyatt and His Background
    [W 1964.10, 1964.13]. Criticism, 8, no. 1 (Winter),
    103-106.
        Southall is strong in discussing canon, political con-
    text, meter and psychology, but his historical theories
    are "suspect," and he overemphasizes the poetry's rela-
    tionship to Wyatt's life and times, failing to see them as
    literary imitation and failing also to prove his "major
    thesis": "that Wyatt climaxes a great English tradition,
    and that the later Renaissance lyric is degenerate."
    Thomson is "sensitive," "judicious," and "exhaustive," but
    sometimes too exhaustive, and she ignores the relationship
    between the English lyrics and Continental poetry and
    Wyatt's principles of imitation. Her book is of encyclo-
    pedic value because of the index.

6 HUTTAR, CHARLES A. "Wyatt and the Several Editions of The
    Court of Venus." SB, 19: 181-195.
        Fraser's belief [W 1955.1] in the likelihood that poems
    by Wyatt were included in the earliest extant fragment of
    The Court (1536-1539) cannot be either proven or disproven
    by available evidence.

7 MAYNARD, WINIFRED. Reviews of Patricia Thomson, Sir Thomas
    Wyatt and His Background and Raymond Southall, The Courtly
    Maker [W 1964.13, 1964.10]. RES, n.s. 17, no. 66, 191-194.
        Thomson's is a valuable and useful study of Wyatt's
    Italian models and sources, and its index is particularly
    helpful. However, she ignores the original sonnets.
    Southall's treatment of the pausing line carries on the
    work of C. S. Lewis and Harding [W 1946], and he demon-
    strates the need for the retention of manuscript punctua-
    tion in editorial work on Wyatt. But he overemphasizes
    rhythmic clues in identifying authorship, and his emphasis
    on psychology leads to "even more strained exegesis."

8 MUIR, KENNETH. Review of Otto Hietsch, Die Petrarcaüber-
    tzungen Sir Thomas Wyatts [W 1960]. ES, 47: 62-63.
        "One of the best" recent studies of Wyatt. Although
    primarily interested in Wyatt's translations of Petrarch,
    Hietsch also provides comment on other matters: Wyatt as
    "initiator" rather than "imitator," the poems as reflective
    of personal experience, and native influences. The book
    has no index.

1966

9   _____ . Review of Patricia Thomson, <u>Sir Thomas Wyatt and His</u>
       <u>Background</u> [W 1964.13]. <u>MLR</u>, 61, no. 2 (April), 272.
            "The best general criticism of Wyatt's poetry," but weak
       on the English lyric.

10   NORTON-SMITH, J. Review of Patricia Thomson, <u>Sir Thomas Wyatt</u>
       <u>and His Background</u> [W 1964.13]. <u>Critical Quarterly</u>, 8,
       no. 2 (Summer), 190-192.
            The book is "essential reading," although it over-
       emphasizes social conventions and political wisdom, and
       thus ignores the "unattractive kind of hard, personal logic-
       ality in Wyatt." Thomson also is mistaken in finding Wyatt
       superior to Serafino and in failing to recognize that the
       first Horatian satiric epistles in English are not Wyatt's,
       but Chaucer's <u>Envois</u> to Scogan and Bukton.

11   THOMAS, R. GEORGE. Review of Raymond Southall, <u>The Courtly</u>
       <u>Maker</u> [W 1964.10]. <u>MLR</u>, 61, no. 1 (January), 101-102.
            "The first full-scale attempt in English to assess
       Thomas Wyatt's poetry"; it should lead to a reappraisal
       not only of Wyatt but of "the aims and methods of early-
       Tudor poetry."

12   WIATT, WILLIAM H. "Sir Thomas Wyatt's Astrologer." <u>ELN</u>, 4,
       no. 2 (December) 89-92.
            Evidence reaffirms the identity of "Sephame" in Wyatt's
       sonnet "You that in love" as Edward Sepham.

<u>1967</u>

FRIEDMAN, DONALD M. "The Mind in the Poem: Wyatt's 'They
     Fle From Me.'" <u>SEL</u>, 7, no. 1 (Winter), 1-13.
          Critics who have noticed Wyatt's "instinct for drama in
     the lyric" have failed to see the extent to which his
     separation of speaker and poet, and the moral judgment
     implied in that separation, informs "They fle from me,"
     whose speaker "is a more fully imagined <u>persona</u> than any
     of Wyatt's other 'voices.'" He is a narrator/character
     whose ironic criticism of disdainful mistresses is itself
     open to moral censure; his self-pity, disbelief, and nos-
     talgia in the first stanza document his failure to recog-
     nize his own hypocritical cultivation of courtly "'gentil-
     nes'" for the purpose of sexual gratification, as does his

happy memory of the specific sexual encounter described in
the second. Similarly, his vengeful irony in the closing
lines is itself ironic because it ignores his own exercise
of the courtly rules for his own rapacious ends.

1   LINDSAY, DAVID W. "Wyatt's 'They Fle From Me': A Prosodic
      Note." FMLS, 3, no. 3 (July), 288-289.
         Scanning the poem as iambic pentameter is less satis-
      factory than observing the "more natural" pattern of four
      stresses divided by a central pause.

2   MACLEAN, HUGH. "Wyatt and Sidney" [Review of Patricia Thom-
      son, Sir Thomas Wyatt and His Background (W 1964.13)].
      UTQ, 36, no. 2 (January), 193-197.
         Thomson, unlike Southall [W 1964.10], successfully re-
      futes the "Mason-Stevens case" [WS 1959, W 1961.9] against
      the significance of Wyatt's English lyrics, and also re-
      sponds to Baldi's claim [W 1953 or 1961?] that Wyatt's
      Petrarchism is superficial.

3   MAYNARD, WINIFRED. "'To Smithe of Camden.'" RES, n.s. 18,
      no. 70 (May), 162-163.
         The phrase, written at the end of Wyatt's "Now all of
      chaunge" in the Arundel Harington Manuscript, refers to
      Henry Smith, a Protestant-turned-Papist whose suicide is
      described in Foxe's Book of Martyrs.

4   MUIR, KENNETH. "The Texts of Wyatt's Penitential Psalms."
      N&Q, 212, n.s. 14, no. 12 (December), 442-444.
         The authentic text is Egerton MS. 2711. [Includes
      selected variants and a diagram representing the relation-
      ship among the texts.]

*5 PLASBERG, ELAINE. "Covert Drama in Wyatt's 'They flee from
      me.'" CEJ, 3, no. 3, 19-23.
         Cited in W 1970.4.

6   PRAZ, MARIO. Review of Patricia Thomson, Sir Thomas Wyatt
      and His Background [W 1964.13]. CL, 19, no. 3 (Summer),
      285-286.
         The book is thorough, and particularly valuable in its
      comparisons between Wyatt and his sources because of
      Thomson's knowledge of Italian.

7   SOUTHALL, RAYMOND. "Wyatt's 'Ye Old Mule.'" ELN, 5, no. 1
      (September), 5-11.
         A close reading of the poem's syntax and diction,
      together with an examination of the Egerton MS. version,

1967

> reveals that the poem is a more vicious--and therefore
> more successful--example of its kind than has heretofore
> been realized.

1968

FIERO, JOHN WESLEY. "The Bright Transparent Glass: A Critical Study of the Poetry of Sir Thomas Wyatt." Ph.D.
dissertation, Florida State, 321 pp.
   Examination of "about fifty" of Wyatt's 190 poems
reveals individual and intrinsic poetic qualities "that
transcend the tastes of any particular age." The various
attempts to define the principles of his language and
prosody have failed to determine any one system as dominant, and indicate that the individual Wyatt poem must be
dealt with "in those terms which seem best suited to it."
His courtly love lyrics, those obviously on love as well
as those which reflect personal experience in the language
of love or are ambiguous in their intent, present a dramatic portrayal of an individual personality. His realistic
anti-Petrarchan poems portray a "manliness" and a wider
range of "out-of-love attitudes" than can be characterized
as simply heterodox or bitter. His Satires demonstrate
"narrative skill, forceful statement, individual adaptation of rhetorical patterns and native idiom, and, above
all, a fine sense of the dramatic." The Psalms, though
generally unsuccessful, do achieve unity through their
dramatic framework, the combination of narrative and lyric
voice, and imagery. And his miscellaneous, mainly political and occasional, lyrics demonstrate further his "diversity in method" and his "individual response to...
convention." Finally, with the recent accumulation of "a
body of decent critical materials on Wyatt," it is possible
to summarize the elements in his poetry that justify his
improved reputation: a "wide range of mood" within given
conventions, "emotional sincerity," "sheer energy" in
rhythm, idiom, imagery, and ideas; a "masculine strain,"
a "keen sense of the drama of self," and, particularly in
the English lyrics, "an unstrained purity of expression
and melodic simplicity." [Includes appendix of biographical and bibliographical data on the poems discussed.]

1   FRIEDMAN, DONALD M. "Wyatt and the Ambiguities of Fancy."
   JEGP, 67, no. 1 (January), 32-48.
      Sixteenth-century ideas about the "image-making faculty
   of the mind" ("'fancy,' 'fantasy,' or 'imagination'"),
   involved as they were with equivocal notions about

melancholy, produced two completely different attitudes
toward that faculty: psychological theorists and poets
alike considered it alternately as an anti-rational force
or as a positive creative power. These conflicting defi-
nitions are reflected in the courtly poetry of the period,
particularly in that of Wyatt, "because the mind is both
the scene of his erotic psychomachias and the major re-
source in his struggle to achieve integrity and permanence."
Even in his slightest courtly lyrics ("If fansy would
favor," for example), Wyatt penetrates beneath the superficial conflicts associated with the standard love situation to examine the effects of the ambivalent workings of
the fancy on the mind itself. More significantly, his
examination informs the "larger concerns" of Wyatt's work,
specifically the attainment of "quiet of mind" in the face
of the temptations of power and passionate love, and leads
him to conclude that the contradictory powers of the fancy
itself are more inimical to mental stability than the
vagaries of the external world.

2   HASHIGUCHI, MINORU. "Sir Thomas Wyatt--Kyuteifu Renai to
    Humanism" [Sir Thomas Wyatt: Courtly Love and Humanism],
    Oberon, 11, no. 1, 13-26.
        The execution of Anne Boleyn in 1536 marks the division
    in Wyatt's life between his "rosy" earlier period and the
    "grey" later one. This division is reflected in the con-
    trast between the Petrarchan/courtly love poems, which
    express one kind of humanism, and the Satires to Poins,
    in which the humanism takes on Stoic bitterness. [In
    Japanese.]

3   _____. "Wyatt Kenkyu no Mondaiten." Eigo S., 119: 222-231,
    306-307.
        Cited in MLA bibliography. [In Japanese.]

4   LOVEJOY, ROBERT BARTON. "Wyatt and the Tradition of the
    Middle English Lyric." Ph.D. dissertation, Case Western
    Reserve, 156 pp.
        "Wyatt's best poetry...is written largely in the tradi-
    tion of the medieval lyric." Of the various types of
    poems representative of that tradition--didactic and moral
    lyrics, narrative songs and carols, and courtly and popu-
    lar lyrics--he chose to write in the manner of those
    associated with the plain, rather than the ornate, style,
    and with the popular, rather than courtly, tradition.
    His choice was dictated by his "desire for justice, honesty,
    and loyalty in the face of the inconstancy of fortune, the
    fluctuations of political favor, and the capricousness of

1968

a woman's love." In his best poems (for example "It was
my choyce" and "Ys yt possyble"), he demonstrates his
originality by imposing on the tradition "the single innovation of an unwavering concentration of intelligence
and the emphatic force of plain and direct speech."

5   McCANLES, MICHAEL. "Love and Power in the Poetry of Sir
Thomas Wyatt." MLQ, 29, no. 2 (June), 145-160.
Wyatt's love lyrics, if read "as if they meant exactly
what they say," reveal "a coherent psychological situation"
in which the connection and interdependence of various
conventional situations serve to clarify the psychological
reality underlying them. The "typical Wyatt 'love situation'" involves a speaker who is a complex mixture of
idealism and cynicism, and whose attitude toward the lady
is marked by "paradoxical psychological movements," particularly by "the will to fail" and "a self-justifying
masochism" that, combined with his idealization of her,
leads inevitably to hostility and frustration. The lady,
in turn, is the "perfect correlative" to the speaker's
paradoxical attitude: "completely desirable and proportionately hateful," a projection of his fantasies whose
predominant role, as assigned her by the speaker's own
preconceptions, desires, and "fansy" (dreams), is that of
conqueror. Thus the tension of the situation is a product
of the fulfillment of the speaker's own desires: a love-
object that is superior and unattainable. This psychological approach informs not only those poems which mirror
the situation described (such as "They fle from me" and
"Suffryng in sorow in hope to attayn"), but also those few
that attain an unexpectedly peaceful synthesis of the
familiar paradoxes (such as "After great stormes the
cawme retornes").

6   ORMEROD, DAVID. "Wyatt and the Execution of Mark Smeaton."
PLL, 4, no. 1 (Winter), 101-103.
The execution of five men found guilty of being Anne
Boleyn's lovers is described in a poem ascribed to Wyatt
by Muir [W 1961.6]. The imagery of the stanza devoted to
Smeaton, one of the five, suggests that he was hanged
rather than beheaded, a reading supported by the evidence
of later chronicles of the episode.

7   WIATT, WILLIAM H. "Sir Thomas Wyatt and Anne Boleyn." ELN,
6, no. 2 (December), 94-102.
The available contemporary evidence suggests that
Wyatt's affair with Anne began in 1525 or 1526, and ended
in 1526, and that after his return from Rome in 1527

Wyatt, upon learning of her relationship with Henry VIII,
revealed to the King the earlier intimacy, and was banished
to Calais. After Wyatt's return to England in the Winter
of 1529-1530, then, the Duke of Suffolk, in an attempt to
ruin Anne, repeated the story of the old affair to the
King, who, after satisfying himself that it had not re-
vived, banished Suffolk.

1969

*DAALDER, JOOST. "Rhetoric and Revision in Wyatt's Poems."
AUMLA, 31: 63-75.
Cited in MLA bibliography, 1969.

1   INGLIS, FRED. "The Native Tradition, Italy, and Sir Thomas
Wyatt," in his The Elizabethan Poets: The Making of
English Poetry from Wyatt to Ben Jonson. Literature in
Perspective, edited by Kenneth H. Grose. London: Evans
Brothers, pp. 29-45.
Wyatt's best poetry brought together the form and substance of the Italian and native traditions by subordinating those traditions to a poetic voice characterized by
"the easy, unselfconscious utterance of a strong, honorable
man" and by subordinating the specific situations of individual poems to more universal moral considerations.
"His best love lyrics," for example, "are about something
more than love affairs, and...it is this something more
[the larger moral implication] which...is the real reward
Wyatt yields." And in the Psalm translations he portrays
an attitude that transcends the specifically religious
context to deal with its "essential experience" in a
"wholly non-sectarian way."

2   MAXWELL, J. C. Review of Kenneth Muir and Patricia Thomson,
eds., Collected Poems of Sir Thomas Wyatt [W 1969.3].
N&Q, 214, n.s. 16, no. 12 (December), 465-467.
"Here, at last, is a reliable and well-annotated edition of Wyatt's poems, together with his translation of
The Quyete of Mynde." However, its scope is "strictly
limited," with little criticism or biography, and with
only a brief treatment of the canon. Decisions about
emendations and choice of text are sometimes too liberal,
sometimes too conservative; punctuation and glossary are
sometimes "defective," and annotations are sometimes
questionable. The edition's "great strength," on the
other hand, is "its wealth of material on sources."

1969

3   MUIR, KENNETH and PATRICIA THOMSON. "Introduction," in their
    edition of <u>Collected Poems of Sir Thomas Wyatt</u>. Liverpool
    English Texts and Studies, edited by Kenneth Muir. Liver-
    pool: Liverpool University Press, pp. xi-xxvi.
        Provides brief account of the contents of the major
    manuscripts and printed sources, brief discussion of the
    Wyatt canon and the relationship of the Egerton, Devon-
    shire, and Blage MSS. to one another. The text provides
    "poems which are certainly by Wyatt, poems which have been
    ascribed to him either by one of the MSS., Tottel, or
    modern editors, and poems which are by Wyatt or one of his
    contemporaries." ["Commentary" provides notes to individ-
    ual poems; appendices include a "rejected poem" and the
    text of <u>The Quyete of Mynde</u>.]

4   TWOMBLY, ROBERT G. "Beauty and the (Subverted) Beast:
    Wyatt's 'They fle from me.'" <u>TSLL</u>, 10, no. 4 (Winter),
    489-503.
        The poem is an exception to the general run of Tudor
    love poetry because it portrays the love situation neither
    as a conventional and static spiritual ideal nor as a per-
    verse and equally static sexual counter to that ideal.
    Wyatt accomplishes this balance between extremes by creat-
    ing an "internal drama" in which the lady herself is a
    silent participant rather than a static object, and in
    which the speaker himself undergoes emotional change as
    he, along with the reader, gradually comes to recognize
    the ironic implications of the similarity between his
    role and hers and to finally understand the "emotional
    futility of desire," which is the poem's central theme.

<u>1970</u>

BERNARD, JOHN DANA. 'Love's Covenant: the Love Poems of
    Sir Thomas Wyatt,' in his "Studies in the Love Poetry of
    Wyatt, Sidney and Shakespeare." Ph.D. dissertation,
    University of Minnesota, pp. 35-108.
        By testing older love conventions with his own empiri-
    cal skepticism, Wyatt initiated a new "'dramatic'" treat-
    ment of love in lyric poems that explore "the <u>experience</u>
    of erotic life." In his Petrarchan poems he subjects the
    conventional attitudes to his own "austere" moral sensi-
    bility and critical intelligence. In his original sonnets
    he "recasts the form as a sort of microcosm of the world
    of the Tudor court," creating a dialogue between a courtly
    audience and a persona who both shares and challenges
    court values. And in his courtly lyrics he subjects his

persona-lover to a variety of attitudes that gradually
move away from that of Stoic renunciation toward a more
open-minded acceptance of the inevitable risk of a genuine
commitment to love as well as a sense of its value.

1   HARRIER, RICHARD [C.].   Review of Kenneth Muir and Patricia
    Thomson, eds., Collected Poems of Sir Thomas Wyatt
    [W 1969.3].   RQ, 23, no. 4 (Winter), 471-474.
         The edition is misnamed: it is "a miscellany of vari-
    ous lyrics that have clustered around Wyatt's name in
    early Tudor manuscripts." Also, it does not relate the
    other manuscripts to the Egerton (a problem in Muir's
    other editions of Wyatt as well [W 1949.1, 1961.6]). It
    overemphasizes the importance of the Blage MS., which "was
    not a collection of Wyatt poems," and it does not deal
    adequately with the Devonshire. "It is unfortunately true
    that most of the bibliographical work on the Wyatt MSS has
    still to be presented. In the meantime critics should
    base arguments concerning Wyatt's style upon the poems in
    the Egerton MS, which is the only solid foundation for the
    canon."

2   LaBRANCHE, ANTHONY.   "Imitation: Getting in Touch." MLQ,
    31, no. 3 (September), 308-329.
         Examines Wyatt's "Perdy I sayd hytt nott" and sonnets
    from Samuel Daniel's Delia in order to distinguish between
    imitation as "the imposition of a pre-established mental
    set upon whatnot material" and imitation as "the process
    of mental-setting." Sees Wyatt's transformation of the
    "self-protesting gestures" in his Petrarchan model into
    the "more argumentative" and moral stance of his own
    speaker as illustrative of the second type, which involves
    imitation in the "inspirational" rather than "regulatory"
    sense, i.e., imitation that involves "reaction, extension,
    reaffirmation, reincarnation, and definition of one's own
    self."

3   MERRILL, RODNEY HARPSTER.   "Formal Elements in the Late
    Medieval Courtly Love Lyric." Ph.D. dissertation, Stan-
    ford, pp. 113-141, 354-375, passim.
         Wyatt's "Goo burnying sighes" and Chaucer's "Canticus
    Troili" modify the "ideal postures" toward love of their
    Petrarchan originals in order to deal realistically with
    more earthly affairs, reversals which demonstrate the in-
    fluence of the French courtly lyric on their handling of
    love. French influence is also apparent in Wyatt's re-
    frains, which alternate between independent psychological
    statement and close dependence on the contexts of the
    poems in which they appear.

1970

4   O'NEEL, MICHAEL C. "A Wyatt Bibliography." BB, 27, no. 3
    (January-March), 76-79, 93-94.
        Includes "most Wyatt sources, principal editions, and
    critical studies through 1968," together with reviews.
    "The inclusion of most longer studies in which Wyatt is
    scantily treated...is highly selective."

5   SETAMANIT, SUDHA SASTRI. "The Place of Sir Thomas Wyatt's
    Lyrics in the Provençal-Italian Tradition of Amorous Poems."
    Ph.D. dissertation, University of Michigan, 1970.
        The principal source for the theme of Wyatt's courtly
    love lyrics was not the Italian, but the Provençal, lyric,
    as handed down by his medieval English predecessors. From
    the Italians he learned techniques and mannerisms that
    "enabled him to invest the familiar [Provençal] themes with
    more variations and a greater range of sentiments" that
    eventually produced his own individual style and attitude.
    Examination of nineteen of his translations and adaptations
    of Petrarch demonstrates his rejection of Petrarch's "un-
    English" "angelicization" of the lady, and while considera-
    tion of certain "'block'" references, or image groups,
    indicates Italian influence on his imagery, they are modi-
    fied to suit his own themes and expressions. Further
    comparisons show Wyatt to be more ideologically, psycho-
    logically, and technically inclined to, and influenced by,
    Serafino than Petrarch. Finally, an examination of seven
    main themes in Wyatt's poetry (the lady's faults, her
    power, the lover's sufferings, his qualities, solicitation
    for reward, abandonment of unsuccessful service, and fu-
    tility and death) against their English and Provençal
    origins bears witness to their return to England "for the
    first time after Chaucer," and also shows how Wyatt recap-
    tured "the wit, audacity, virility, and naturalness of the
    Provençal courtly lyric" that had been lost in Gower,
    Lydgate, and James I.

6   TWOMBLY, ROBERT G. "Thomas Wyatt's Paraphrase of the Peniten-
    tial Psalms of David." TSLL, 12, no. 3 (Fall), 345-380.
        Although Wyatt makes heavy use of others (John Fisher,
    Alamanni, Aretino, and Johannes Campensis) for the develop-
    ment of his paraphrases, he is almost completely original
    in his exploitation of the complex psychological drama
    implicit in the original source: his portrayal of David
    as "a Renaissance Christian penitent, solitary, morally
    hyperaware, theologically cocky, flamboyantly self-
    disgusted, more genuinely self-doubting, ironic," frees
    the poems from "theological case-making" and results in
    "some most subjective, contradictory, outrageous, and

shrewd intuitions about a man's hope for spiritual integra-
tion." Wyatt's approach, exemplified best in his treatment
of Psalm 51, concentrates on the subjective response of
the persona to the experience of moral/spiritual crisis,
and his persona's tone does not lose its sense of "metaphysical desperation" until the last two poems in the
sequence, when he begins to awaken to a historical sense
of his kinship with all men.

1971

BLEETH, KENNETH. "Wyatt and Chaucer's 'Lusty Leese.'" N&Q,
216, n.s. 18, no. 6 (June), 214.
The phrase "'lusty leese'" (from "Myne owne John
Poyntz") represents the "pastoral liberty" Wyatt experi-
enced after his release from the Tower in 1536. It also
appears in Troilus and Criseyde (II, 752), where it serves
as a metaphor for Criseyde's freedom.

1   BOYD, JOHN DOUGLAS. "Literary Interpretation and the Subjective Correlative: An Illustration from Wyatt." EIC, 21,
no. 4 (October), 327-346.
The presentation and examination of seven imaginary
explications of Wyatt's ambiguous lyric "There was never
nothing more me payned" illustrates the impossibility of
avoiding subjectivity in interpreting a poem in which
"the very data within the text...are themselves intrinsic-
ally subjective." The very different decisions made by
the seven mythical commentators about the roles of the
male and female personas, the tone of their comments, and
the relevance of the poem's literary milieu reveal that
while each informs his interpretation with preconceptions
based on his own experience, none of them violates the
principles of the New Criticism by committing Arnold's
personal fallacy. The experiment further demonstrates not
only that "there is simply no such thing as a 'pure'
reader, free from the subjective coloration of his own
unique sensibility and unique experience," but that such
an approach is a necessary complement to objective interpretation.

2   BRILLIANT, A. N. "The Style of Wyatt's 'The Quyete of
Mynde.'" E&S, 24: 1-21.
Wyatt's decision to translate Budé's Latin version of
Plutarch's De Tranquillitate rather than Petrarch's De
Remediis indicates not only his preference for practical
good sense over "total contemptuous rejection of worldly

things," but also his preference for the plain (Attic/
Senecan) over the eloquent (Asiatic/Ciceronian) style.
While his choice produces prose that is loosely structured,
inelegant, and often unclear, it also results in more
positive effects: "simple dignity," "forthrightness," and
the "sudden vivid phrase" that compare favorably with the
later English versions of Blundeville and Holland. But
while both the faults and the virtues of the prose are
partly attributable to his source, they also come from the
English plain-style tradition and from Wyatt's own stylistic proclivities, as evidenced in his correspondence, his
Defence, and, in more mature form, his Satires, where "the
concrete, colloquial English and the lucid, unaffected
Latin styles" produce "a synthesis of earthiness and
urbanity."

3   DAALDER, JOOST. "Some Problems of Punctuation and Syntax in
Egerton MS. 2711 of Wyatt's Verse." N&Q, 216, n.s. 18,
no. 6 (June), 214–216.
Silent changes in punctuation made in Collected Poems
of Sir Thomas Wyatt [Muir-Thomson, W 1969.3] alter the
syntax, and therefore the sense, of some of Wyatt's poems
from the Egerton MS. The examples cited suggest that "a
future edition of Wyatt ought to be more careful in its
handling of punctuation." [See also W 1971.4, 1975.]

4   _____. "The Sense of Some Passages in Wyatt." Parergon,
no. 1 (December), pp. 24–27.
Exemplifies how the editorial punctuation in the Muir-
Thomson edition of Collected Poems of Sir Thomas Wyatt
[W 1969.3] alters the sense of some passages. Suggests
that a new edition should either avoid tampering with MS.
punctuation altogether, or "come down on the side of what
makes straightforward sense" and explain fully any emendations. [See also W 1971.3, 1975.]

5   _____. "Wyatt's 'There was never nothing more me payned':
A Reply to John Douglas Boyd." EIC, 21, no. 4 (October),
418–424.
The critical problems brought up by Boyd [W 1971.1] are
"largely of his own making": subjective interpretation is
legitimate "only if it is supported by textual evidence";
furthermore, without that evidence, the interpretation is
incomplete. Finally, the study of "'moral, psychological
and ontological judgments derived from our experience
outside the poem' lies outside our province." Much of
what Boyd's imaginary critics say about the poem itself is
unconvincing because of the lack of objective evidence in
their arguments.

6   DEMBO, PAMELA. "Wyatt's Multi-Faceted Presentation of Love."
    <u>UES</u>, 9, no. 4, 5-10.
        Wyatt's love poetry portrays a variety of attitudes,
    situations, and moods, but it differs from many other
    examples of the genre in its concentration "on the experi-
    ence of love itself" rather than on the beloved, in its
    independence from conventional attitudes and imagery, and
    in its consistent portrayal of the manly integrity of the
    lover-persona.

7   FOX, DENTON. "A Scoto-Danish Stanza, Wyatt, Henryson, and
    the Two Mice." <u>N&Q</u>, 216, n.s. 18, no. 6 (June), 203-207.
        A Danish transcription of a stanza from a Scots song
    about the town mouse and country mouse might be a source
    for Henryson's fable and for Wyatt's "My mothers maydes."

8   FRANCON, MARCEL. "Wyatt et le Rondeau." <u>RQ</u>, 24, no. 3
    (Autumn), 340-343.
        Berdan [W 1920] is wrong in saying that the rondeau
    before Clement Marot was a loosely defined term that in-
    cluded a number of forms having nothing but the refrain
    in common; on the contrary, the rondeau had been a well-
    defined lyric genre since its origin in the thirteenth
    century. Wyatt wrote nine rondeaux, two of which are
    irregular and one of which has for its source an anonymous
    French poem; his versions should be printed in three
    stanzas. [In French.]

9   KAY, DONALD. "Wyatt's 'Dyvers Dothe Use': A Bibliographical
    Puzzle." <u>AN&Q</u>, 9, no. 5 (January), 73.
        It is generally thought that the poem was first pub-
    lished in Nott's edition [WS 1816.1] and that it is only
    to be found in the Devonshire MS. Yet Nott's introduction
    casts doubt on both of these conclusions.

10 LURIA, MAXWELL S. "Wyatt's 'The Lover Compareth His State'
    and the Petrarchan Commentators." <u>TSLL</u>, 12, no. 4 (Win-
    ter), 531-535.
        Unlike Wyatt's modern editors and critics, who usually
    read "My galy charged with forgetfulness" as a love com-
    plaint, Renaissance commentators on Petrarch "tended to
    read the poem as an allegory of the soul beset by unreas-
    on," an interpretation that is consistent with Petrarch's
    conception of the relationship between poetry and allegory
    and his moralistic view of the poet's task. Given Wyatt's
    career and his moral/ethical predilections, it is likely
    that his version should be read from the same point of
    view.

1971

11   MASON, H. A. "Editing Wyatt: Further Reflections on the Possibility of Literary Study." CQ, 5, no. 4 (Summer/ Autumn), 355-371.

        Describes the process of discovery that led to Editing Wyatt [W 1972.5] and relates the problems he finds in the Muir-Thomson edition [W 1969.3] to general principles of editing and studying poetry from 1450 to 1550.

1972

BONHEIM, HELMUT. "Notes on a Sonnet by Sir Thomas Wyatt." LWU, Band 5, Heft 1, 1-5.

        Although Wyatt is "an aristocratic formalist, not a social realist," his sonnet "Who so list to hunt" reveals a sociological portrait of his world. The image of the hunt implies an aristocratic, rather than working-class, milieu, and it also portrays two contrasting views of women: as socially inferior objects/pets, and as the superior beings who are part of the aristocratic game of courtly love.

1   BOYD, JOHN DOUGLAS. "The Subjective Correlative." EIC, 22, no. 3 (July), 329-331.

        Replies to W 1971.5 Daalder not only errs in assuming that "I endorse what one or another of my seven readers says," but he also "misconstrues my central thesis": the point is that true objectivity is impossible because we can only truly apprehend even "'the facts'" through our own minds; furthermore, identifying with the speaker is "precisely what one continually does, and must do, in reading a literary text"; finally, "I never claimed that we should study," but only "investigate" subjective judgments outside the poem."

2   DAALDER, JOOST. "Wyatt and Tottel: A Textual Comparison." SoRA, 5: 3-12.

        Evidence indicating that Tottel's modifications of Wyatt in the Songes and Sonettes were not prompted solely by metrical considerations suggests a more profound difference in sensibility between the two. The editor's titles often suggest that poems of "much more general significance" are about love; furthermore, this "falsification" often extends also to nonmetrical internal changes in the poems, changes aimed not only at ridding poems of repetition or at changing word order, but at changing meaning as well. Examples indicate that Tottel aimed at narrowing the perspective of individual poems "from general

to specific, from abstract to concrete," at sentimentaliz-
ing and personalizing the manly detachment of Wyatt's
persona, at censoring politically dangerous or morally
reprehensible language, and, finally, at clarifying "in-
congruity, paradox or irony" by means of "the obvious,
the commonplace, the powerless." These changes suggest
two possible motives: Tottel's desire to appeal to "a
large commercial market," and his inclination to model the
poems after other poets whose taste more closely resembled
his own--for example, Surrey. [A synopsis of this essay
appeared in the following monograph: Australian Universities Language and Literature Association, Proceedings
and Papers of the Thirteenth Congress Held at Monash University, 12-18 August, 1970, ed. J. R. Ellis (1971).]

3   LOW, ANTHONY. "Wyatt's 'What Word is That.'" ELN, 10, no. 2
    (December), 89-90.
        The poem was entitled "Anna" by a later hand in the
    Egerton MS., and the third line, "It is myn aunswer, god
    it wot," was changed in Tottel's Miscellany to "It is
    mine Anna god it wot," thus providing further evidence of
    Wyatt's relationship with Anne Boleyn. Although there is
    no authority for the change in the line, it does provide
    an appropriate solution to the riddle in the poem: "an na"
    forms a negative, suggesting not only Anne's name but the
    traditional negative response of the Petrarchan mistress.

4   MAHALANOBIS, SHANTA. "The Essential Wyatt: A Study of His
    Poetry." Essays Presented to Prof. Amalendu Bose, edited
    by Dipendu Chakrabarti. Bulletin of the Department of
    English, 8, no. 2, 9-21.
        Although "Wyatt was essentially of the court," evidence
    suggests that "in his writings he had dragged himself
    clear" of it. [Discusses biography, sociology, critical
    opinions, manuscripts.]

5   MASON, H. A. Editing Wyatt: An Examination of "Collected
    Poems of Sir Thomas Wyatt" Together with Suggestions for
    an Improved Edition. Cambridge: Cambridge Quarterly
    (Publications), 218 pp.
        First section corrects "the many hundreds of errors" in
    the Muir-Thomson edition of Collected Poems [W 1969.3] and
    points out similar errors in the other major printed
    sources of Wyatt's poetry; errors include misreadings as
    well as unrecorded and neglected variants discovered
    through comparison with transcripts, microfilms and photo-
    copies of the major manuscripts. Second section discusses
    the various procedures and considerations necessary for

1972

establishing a reliable Wyatt edition, and concludes that
the project--for Wyatt or any poet of the years 1450-1550--
requires a community of scholars divided into "sensible
working parties" controlled by a body of reputable author-
ities and a rigid system of thorough reviews as well as a
more thorough understanding of the period and "a new dic-
tionary of Early Tudor English."

6   O'NEEL, MICHAEL CHARLES. "Wyatt's MS Revisions." Ph.D.
    dissertation, University of Washington, 252 pp.
        Examination of the twenty-five poems in the Egerton MS.
    that contain "substantial" changes in Wyatt's own hand
    reveals relationships between his subject matter and style.
    Despite textural and procedural limitations (the condition
    of the MS., the problem of dating entries, the absence of
    an authorized version of the poems, our ignorance of
    Wyatt's prosody, the problem of context, and the danger of
    the intentional fallacy), it is possible to recognize that
    the changes represent apparently purposeful improvements
    in strategy and, more significantly, a developing pattern
    of relationship between the poet's search for "reciprocity
    in a mutable world" and his rhetoric, metrics, rhythm and
    diction. Specifically, the ironic rhetoric, the disruptive
    (if powerful) rhythms, and the indeterminate metrics of
    the decasyllabic love poems reflect Wyatt's failure to
    find that reciprocity in either the love relationship or
    the court. On the other hand, the dramatic and metrical
    "blend" in the Psalm translations reflects the stability
    he eventually found in the Protestant emphasis on the
    reciprocal relationship between the individual and God.

7   TILLEY, JR., EDMOND ALLEN. "Phonemic Differentiation Analyses
    of Poems by Sir Thomas Wyatt and Others." Ph.D. disserta-
    tion, University of Iowa, 158 pp.
        Uses fourteen Wyatt sonnets, ten of his <u>strambotti</u>
    and the first 140 syllables of <u>Quyete of Mynde</u>, together
    with examples of "non-poetry" and five sonnets by other
    poets, as material for a method of differentiating between
    vowel and consonant sounds in contiguous poetic lines,
    initial and terminal lines, and between different poems.
    Finds the method useful for distinguishing poems from one
    another, poetry from prose, language from nonlanguage, and
    poets from poets, as well as Wyatt's sonnets from his
    <u>strambotti</u>. Also finds that Surrey has a narrower "range
    of differentiation" and more "mirror symmetry" in "Love
    that doth reign" than Wyatt does in "The long love."

76

[Includes tables and graphs, an appendix defining and de-
scribing the method used, and a final chapter on projected
future uses of the method.]

1973

ANON. "Wyatt as he was?" [Review of H. A. Mason, Editing
Wyatt (W 1972.5)]. TLS, no. 3,722 (July 6), p. 768.
    Summarizes Mason's criticism of the Muir-Thomson edi-
tion of Collected Poems [W 1969.3], and finds his proposal
of a group effort aimed at producing a new Wyatt edition
"curious" but "attractive."

1   ASHTON, SUSAN EICHENFELD. "Sir Thomas Wyatt and the Struggle
of the 'Weried Mynde.'" Ph.D. dissertation, Loyala University, 197 pp.
    The theme of the unquiet mind, so important in Wyatt's
letters to his son, his Satires, and The Quyete of Mynde,
is a significant part of his Petrarchan poems as well.
From the Velutello edition of Petrarch he learned not only
structure, imagery and language, but also the proper tone
for dramatizing through "the speaking voice" the quest for
stability in the unstable world of the lover, and he employed that tone in his original love poems as well as in
his Petrarchan translations and adaptations. The quest is
made even more complex by Wyatt's plain style, which
qualifies--through devices like repetition and direct
address--the conventional Petrarchan devices, and comments
ironically on their inadequacy in dealing with the lover's
situation. Thus while The Quyete of Mynde, the Satires
and the letters represent the ideal (Stoic) answer to
life's instability, the love poetry records and dramatizes
"the continuing struggle."

2   BATH, MICHAEL. "Wyatt and 'Liberty.'" EIC, 23, no. 3
(July), 322-328.
    "Ons as me thought fortune me kyst" can be interpreted
in two ways, depending on one's reading of Wyatt's use of
"will" in line eighteen: "My will is alwaye at my hand."
If it means "the object of my will," the speaker is demand-
ing sexual satisfaction, but if it means "that part of his
mind that wills," then he is expressing the desire to ex-
tricate himself from the love that binds him and to
achieve Stoic quiet of mind. Each reading exemplifies one
of the "two ways to liberty" that Daalder [W 1973.4]
observes in Wyatt's poetry in general. However, a third
possibility, that "will" might mean "sexual organ" (not

found in the O. E. D.), provides further evidence of
"Empsonian ambiguity" in the poem by suggesting that the
line refers to masturbation. Finally the double (or
triple) meaning of the poem adds further to the possibility of multiple interpretation of Wyatt's poetry suggested
by Boyd [W 1971.1]. It also illustrates the essential
relationship between ambiguity and irony in Wyatt's
poetry.

3   BRODIE, PHILIP T. "So Kindly Served: Wyatt's Egerton MS. As
     Narrative Sequence." Ph.D. dissertation, University of
     Pittsburgh, 177 pp.
         The Egerton MS., perhaps because Wyatt was influenced
     by Vellutello's annotated edition of Petrarch, "presents
     a consistently developed persona, a coherent theme, and
     a plot with a definite sense of chronology" similar to
     Astrophil and Stella, the Amoretti, and Shakespeare's
     sonnets. The "story" of the sequence presents "a history
     of a man's private, inner responses to his failure to win
     a lady's favor, and...those personal, emotional and in-
     tellectual 'events' which mark the course of his gradual
     movement toward self-awareness." It falls into seven
     "dramatic units": (1) the introduction of persona, lady,
     and problem; (2) the persona's exploration of his options
     after being betrayed by the lady; (3) his recognition of
     the causes of his dilemma and his resolution to abandon
     reason for passion; (4) the depiction of his changing
     attitudes and his pursuit of a variety of unidentifiable
     females; (5) his disillusioned recognition of the vanity
     of his pursuit and the excessive nature of his passions
     and her cruelty; (6) his deeper understanding (in the
     Satires) of "the greed, excess, lust, and dishonesty of
     others"; and (7) his turning away from his own problems
     to a description of how David (in the Psalm translations)
     and Aeneas (in "Jopas' Song") overcame theirs. The key
     to understanding the theme of the sequence lies in the
     complementary discussions of Plato and Plutarch on "the
     wise and unwise man," wherein both find the principle of
     happiness to lie in the rejection of disordering passion
     for the order of the rational mind.

4   DAALDER, JOOST. "Wyatt and 'Liberty.'" EIC, 23, no. 1
     (January), 63-67.
         To Wyatt, "liberty" implied not only freedom from the
     bondage imposed on the male by the code of courtly love,
     but also, more significantly, the "psychological freedom
     from nervous tension" characteristic of quiet of mind, a
     "mental state" that could be attained through mature love

itself, or through the rejection of any mental prison
created by the passions. It is typical of Wyatt, however,
that the attainment of such freedom is regularly successful only through the aid of "external circumstances."

5   MICKEY, DAVID H.   "The Moral Vision in the Poetry of Sir
      Thomas Wyatt."   Ph.D. dissertation, Kansas State Univer-
      sity, 216 pp.
         The unity of the Wyatt canon resides in the "moral and
      ethical element" that underlies both his love poems and
      his "non-love" poems. The discovery of that element comes
      from one's recognition of the relationship in both kinds
      of poem between the persona's response to the specific
      situation and the poet's more general response to "experi-
      ence that is human and moral"; in the love poems between
      the literal man-woman conflict and its metaphorical ana-
      logue, the conflict between "right and erroneous behavior."
      Wyatt criticism, in dividing itself between the study of
      his place in the development of Italianate humanism on the
      one hand and his role as "romantic" psychotherapist on the
      other, has heretofore failed to recognize that in the
      union between his various personae and the "ethical voice"
      of his moral poetry and prose, he belongs to a tradition
      of ethical poetry that includes Chaucer, Gascoigne, Ral-
      egh, Jonson, and Donne.

6   OKUMA, SAKAE.   "Sir Thomas Wyatt no Kozai" [Sir Thomas Wyatt's
      Merits and Demerits].   Oberon, 14, no. 2, 60-86.
         General discussion of Wyatt's ideas, literary tech-
      niques and life. Finds one of his chief merits to be his
      ability to change "static theme" into "dynamic poetry,"
      as pointed out by Tillyard [W 1929.2], but finds him in-
      ferior to Surrey in "rhythm," "lucidity," and "fluency."
      [In Japanese.]

1974

BOKROSS, AGNES H.   "Unidentified Sources of Sir Thomas Wyatt:
    Their Scope and Implications."   Ph.D. dissertation, McGill
    University, 164 pp.
       Because of its overemphasis on his Italian sources,
    Wyatt scholarship has generally ignored the "international
    and polyglot" environment of sixteenth-century poetry in
    general and the classical influence on his poetry in par-
    ticular. Examination of two European Petrarchan poets
    contemporary with Wyatt, Maurice Scève and Garcilaso de
    la Vega, illustrates by analogy how the Italian influence

was modified by a synthesis of other sources, contemporary and classical. More specific comparison shows that the influence of the thematic, structural, and stylistic characteristics of Horace on Wyatt's poetry goes beyond the similarities of common topoi and philosophies, and establishes Wyatt as the most thoroughly Horatian and classical of English poets up to his time.

1 CURLEY, STEPHEN J. "Of Man and the Wheel: Poetic Attitudes Towards Fortune in the Verse of Sir Thomas Wyatt." Ph.D. dissertation, Rice University, 178 pp.
    Wyatt's poems fall into four thematic categories, based on "the implied relationship" between speaker and fortune in each: (1) those in which he depends completely on a fortune that is favorable to him; (2) those in which his dependency is not matched by fortune's favor; (3) those which "illustrate that man and fortune are equal in power"; and (4) those which "reject or ignore" her influence. This classification demonstrates the universality of the individual dramatic experiences in Wyatt's poetry in general.

2 GOLDEN, WILLIAM. "I. Johnson on Colonization. II. A Study of Transcendent Moments in the Poetry of Eliot and Yeats. III. Wyatt and the Court of Henry VIII." Ph.D. dissertation, Rutgers, pp. 83-103.
    The "twenty or so" poems in which Wyatt portrays his attitude toward life at and away from court can be divided into three groups, each related to one of his imprisonments and dependent for its tone on the gravity of the charges involved in each case. The poetry written in response to the 1534 imprisonment is light, highly conceited, and composed mainly of epigrams on the capriciousness of Fortune. The Satires, written after the 1536 imprisonment, express the smugness of one who has left the court for the life removed. In the final group, written during the dispute with Bonner and after the 1541 imprisonment, Wyatt eschews detachment to express personal bitterness at the charges against him and the desertion of friends in poems that resemble his Penitential Psalms in tone and content. [Foxwell's dating of the poems (W 1911, 1913) is used as the basis for the divisions.]

3 GREENE, RICHARD LEIGHTON. "A Carol of Anne Boleyn by Wyatt." RES, n.s. 25, no. 100 (November), 437-439.
    A first-person carol with a young woman as speaker and "plausibly attributed to" Wyatt has as the first line of its burden a translation of "the motto or device used by

Anne Boleyn on her servants' liveries...in 1530." This
not only dates the poem, but it identifies Anne as its
speaker. Furthermore, evidence in the text indicates that
the subject of the poem is Anne's love for Henry VIII.

4 GUSS, DONALD. "Wyatt's Petrarchism: An Instance of Creative
   Imitation in the Renaissance," in Übersetzung and Nachah-
   mung im europäischen Petrarkismus: Studien und Texte.
   Edited by Luzius Keller. Stuttgart: J. B. Metzler,
   pp. 218-232.
      Reprint of W 1965.4.

5 HANNEN, THOMAS A. "The Humanism of Sir Thomas Wyatt," in
   The Rhetoric of Renaissance Poetry From Wyatt to Milton.
   Edited by Thomas O. Sloan and Raymond B. Waddington.
   Berkeley and Los Angeles: University of California Press;
   London: University of California Press, pp. 37-57.
      Wyatt's humanism is most clearly indicated in his con-
   cern with the Isocratean, Ciceronian ideal that coupled
   rhetorical ability and the requirements of moral wisdom
   and political involvement--more specifically, with the
   problem of applying to public life "the wisdom and stability usually found only in philosophy." Close examination
   of the relationship of his diction and his rhetorical and
   rhythmic structures to the mental states of his various
   dramatic personae in "What vaileth trouth," "Ys yt possyble," and "It may be good" demonstrate not only that he
   possessed a sophisticated understanding of textual rhetoric, but, more importantly, that he was seriously searching
   in his poems for "a theory of poetic structure" that would
   reconcile "the rhetoric of oratory" with "the rhetoric of
   allegory" and would analyze the mind not in isolation but
   in the active world. The indecisiveness of his various
   dramatic stances and the variety of forms in which he presented them indicate that "every poem was a new search"
   for "an eloquence that would reconcile thought and action
   so as to create a human society in which a man could par-
   ticipate without losing his self-respect."

6 MAXWELL, J. C. "Wyatt and 'Liberty.'" EIC, 24, no. 1 (January), 104.
      The O. E. D. does not, as asserted by Bath [W 1973.2],
   maintain silence on all the sexual implications of its
   entries.

1974

7   OGLE, ROBERT B. "Wyatt and Petrarch: A Puzzle in Prosody."
    JEGP, 73, no. 2 (April), 189-208.
        Confusion about the "roughness" of Wyatt's translations
    from Petrarch can be resolved by the recognition that both
    poets were imitating "logaoedic" rhythmic patterns from
    classical prosody. Originally perfected by Horace and
    Catullus, these patterns were later applied to the con-
    struction of medieval Latin verse and the Italian hende-
    casyllabic line. They are "essentially trochaic, with
    irrational feet in regularly prescribed positions," and
    when they consist of five feet, they provide a line com-
    posed of two parts. Similarities between Petrarch's lines
    and Wyatt's indicate the possibility that Wyatt was imi-
    tating his Italian source with the full knowledge of
    logaoedic prosodic principles in mind.

8   SOUTHALL, RAYMOND. "Wyatt and Kytson." N&Q, 219, n.s. 21,
    no. 11 (November), 403-404.
        Wyatt's advice to Bryan in the third Satire that he
    should not lend "Onles it be as to a dogge a chese" repre-
    sents cheese as an emetic; the revolting nature of the
    image is perhaps the reason "dogge" is changed to "calfe"
    in Tottel's Miscellany and the Arundel MS. The "Kittson"
    referred to in the same poem was probably Sir Thomas
    Kytson, a notably successful businessman who became
    Sheriff of London in 1533 and was knighted in the same
    year.

9   THOMSON, PATRICIA. "Introduction," in Wyatt: The Critical
    Heritage. Edited by Patricia Thomson. The Critical
    Heritage Series, edited by B. C. Southam. London and
    Boston: Routledge & Kegan Paul, pp. 1-20.
        Surveys selected commentary, criticism, and scholar-
    ship on Wyatt from the sixteenth century through C. S.
    Lewis [WS 1954], concentrating on major turns in the dev-
    elopment of Wyatt's reputation up to recent decades, when
    Wyatt studies become "too numerous to be named separately."
    [Main text contains extracts from major critical docu-
    ments.]

                          1975

    DAALDER, JOOST. "Introduction," in his edition of Sir Thomas
    Wyatt: Collected Poems. London: Oxford University
    Press, pp. xi-xx.
        Evidence from his revisions suggests that, while Wyatt
    displays "no consistent desire to make his lines iambic,"

he was interested in syllabic regularity and was probably
"working towards iambic pentameter...." Examination of his
poetry alongside his life and letters suggests that they
should all be read as part of "an integrated whole."
[Includes discussion of textual sources, appendix, and
"selected textual notes."]

1   HARRIER, RICHARD [C.]. "Part One. Textual Studies," in The
      Canon of Sir Thomas Wyatt's Poetry. Cambridge, Massachu-
      setts: Harvard University Press, pp. 1-92.
          Provides histories of all major contemporary MSS. and
      printed sources of Wyatt's verse (Egerton, Arundel Haring-
      ton, Devonshire, Blage, Park-Hall, and minor MSS.; The
      Court of Venus and Tottel's Miscellany), and provides
      physical descriptions of Egerton, Arundel Harington, Dev-
      onshire, and Blage. Concludes that the Egerton is the
      "cornerstone of the Wyatt canon." ["Part Two" includes a
      transcript of the Egerton, with variants from the other
      contemporary sources.]

2   HOUGH, GORDON. 'Sir Thomas Wyatt,' in "A Quiet Image of Dis-
      quiet: The Persona in the Lyrics of Wyatt, Sidney and
      Donne." Ph.D. dissertation, University of New York at
      Buffalo, pp. 9-56.
          Applies D. W. Winnicott's distinction between the "true"
      and "false" selves to Wyatt's second letter to his son,
      "My mothers maydes," "I am as I am," "Synce loue wyll
      nedes," "My lute awake!" "They fle from me," and "Blame not
      my lute" in order to demonstrate that Wyatt's persona
      serves as an "operational center" between the poet's feel-
      ings (the "true self") and poetic convention ("false self").
      The method also reveals that the sense of frustration and
      futility in his poems comes from the persona's awareness
      of his "tenuous" position between the two, and his recog-
      nition of its threat to the "whole self." The dilemma is
      not pathological, however, because it results in the dev-
      elopment of "a relationship between the feelings and the
      conventions."

3   WINSER, LEIGH. "The Question of Love Tradition in Wyatt's
      'They Flee From Me.'" Essays in Literature (Western Illi-
      nois University), 2, no. 1 (Spring), 3-9.
          The poem belongs to the tradition of the dubbi, or
      questioni--which introduce "a question of love for judgment
      by court lovers"--popular in Renaissance Europe and prac-
      ticed by Boccaccio, Bembo and Castiglione, among others.
      The structure of the dubbio is threefold, involving first
      a covert approach to the subject, then a more direct

1975

statement, and finally "an invitation for judgment" on the
part of the listeners. Wyatt uses the form more clearly in
"Like as the bryde," but the many "answers" to the problems
of "They flee from me" by modern critics suggests that it
is "one of the most successful" examples of the dubbio ever
invented.

1976

BARON, HELEN V. "Wyatt's 'What rage.'" The Library, 5th
ser., 31, no. 3 (September), 188–204.
Ultra-violet examination of the Egerton MS. version of
the poem reveals that Wyatt used two different colors of
ink while composing and revising it. This discovery makes
possible a comparison of three stages of its composition
and leads to conclusions about the poem's meaning and
about Wyatt's principles and methods of composition, as
well as suggesting the possibility that the poem is a
translation.

1   GRAZIANI, RENÉ. "Sir Thomas Wyatt at a Cockfight, 1539."
RES, n.s. 27, no. 107 (August), 299–303.
The record of an incident in which Wyatt offered a defense of the art of cockfighting confirms that the poet
was in England between April and November of 1539.

2   MASON, H. A. "Editing Wyatt" [Reviews of Joost Daalder, ed.,
Sir Thomas Wyatt: Collected Poems (W 1975), Richard C.
Harrier, The Canon of Sir Thomas Wyatt's Poetry (W 1975.1),
and Patricia Thomson, ed., Wyatt: The Critical Heritage
(W 1974.9)]. SR, no. 4 (Fall), 675–683.
Finds fault with Daalder's "meaningless" groupings of
the poems, his lack of criteria for determining ascrip-
tions, and his gratuitous explanations; criticizes Harrier's proofreading and his evidence for attributions to
Wyatt; questions Thomson's selections and points out her
erroneous transcriptions. Prefers the editions of Nott
[WS 1816.1] and Swallow [W 1949.2], and calls attention to
the continuing need for an edition of Wyatt that will determine his true canon and, in so doing, clear up the
continuing confusion over his prosody.

3   MISKIMIN, ALICE S. "Counterfeiting Chaucer: The Case of
'Dido,' Wyatt, and the 'Retraction.'" SMC, 19: 133–145.
Wyatt's "Lyke as the swan" is based on the spurious
"Letter of Dido" from Pynson's corrupt 1526 edition of

Chaucer. Other Wyatt poems are based on Chaucer's "Truth," and his "Farewell Love" is "an original tour de force reply to the Merchant's Tale."

4   RAY, DONALD LOUIS. "I. Howard's End: The Novel 'Opening Out.' II. Sir Thomas Wyatt's Protestant Petrarchanism. III. Flannery O'Connor's Satires on American Liberalism." Ph.D. dissertation, Rutgers, pp. 68-167.
Wyatt's courtly love poems show "the emergence of a moral-reflective strain" that differs from the conventional courtly stance in its honesty, from the aesthetic abstraction of the meditative Petrarch in its moralistic realism, and from contemplative Stoicism in its dramatic specificity. The attitude is best characterized as a "'Protestant' independence--or isolation" that at once condemns the standard duplicity and obeisance required of the conventional courtly persona and looks toward Wyatt's criticism of the Tudor court itself, an institution which demands the same behavior.

1977

CHIAPELLI, CAROLYN. "A Late Gothic Vein in Wyatt's 'They Fle From Me.'" Ren&R, n.s. 1, no. 2, 95-102.
The abstract imagery that results from the projection of the poem's narrative and images over the full three stanzas, the similarity between its metaphors and the image of Fortune's Wheel in medieval iconography and between its structure and that of the "tragedy of fortune," as well as the poem's resemblance to other Wyatt poems about Fortune, all suggest that "Fortune in its manifold aspects is the one who flees" in the poem. Whatever the circumstances of the poem's composition, it "marks the moment in English literature when the tragedy of fortune...enters to become what it would be for the Elizabethans: the vehicle for an arrogant cry of heroic acceptance.

1   DAALDER, JOOST. "Wyatt's Prosody Revisited." Lang&S, 10, no. 1 (Winter), 3-15.
Scansion of passages and lines from Wyatt's Psalms, taking into account his verb endings, pronunciation, orthography, Romance accents, elisions, and the long argument about iambic and accentual verse, leads to the inevitable conclusion that "he saw the decasyllabic line as a norm, but one which he was at liberty to depart from." Specifically, his method involves "'balanced pentameters,'" which are characterized by the interplay of classic iambic

1977

            pentameter with the alliterative tradition. This investi-
gation thus shows that Wyatt was "a transitional poet
prosodically as he was in other matters."

2   SIEK, WAYNE H. "A Note on Some Handwriting in Wyatt's
Holograph Poetic Manuscript." N&Q, 222, n.s. 24, no. 6
(December), 496-497.
        Disputes Harrier's claim that the Egerton MS. version
of "Vulcane bygat me Mynerva me taught" is in Wyatt's hand
[W 1975.1] by pointing out differences between its paleo-
graphy and orthography and Wyatt's usual poetic practice.

3   TILLEMANS, TH[OMAS]. King and Courtier: A Cultural Reconnaissance into an Age of Transition With Illustrations
Drawn from the Poetry of Sir Thomas Wyatt and other
Sources. Folcroft, Pennsylvania: Folcroft Library Editions, 62 pp.
        Reprint of W 1951.2.

<u>1978</u>

KOZISKOWSKI, STANLEY J. "Wyatt's 'They Flee From Me' and
Churchyard's Complaint of Jane Shore." N&Q, 223, n.s. 25,
no. 5 (October), 416-417.
        Churchyard's analogy between Shore and Dame Fortune in
the Mirror for Magistrates "probably reflects a Tudor understanding of Wyatt's lyric, which likewise views the
wayward mistress in the guise of Fortune." Wyatt's
imagery, like Churchyard's, clearly reflects the relationship.

1   MERMEL, JERRY. "Sir Thomas Wyatt's Satires and the Humanist
Debate over Court Service." SLitI, 11, no. 1 (Spring),
69-79.
        Interpretations that see all three Satires as exclu-
sively anti-court in attitude (Southall and Thomson, for
example [W 1964.10, 1964.13]), fail to recognize the complex assessment of court life and service presented in the
poems. Even "Myne owne John Poynz," which is the most
hostile in its attitude toward court, qualifies its criticism by indicating that "country life is a [reluctant]
second choice" compelled only by court corruption. "My
mother's maids" is much more ambivalent, suggesting "that
the source of inner peace is a disciplined mind" rather
than one's environment. And "A spending hand" is as
sympathetic to Bryan's idealistic determination to be an

"honest courtier" as it is to Wyatt's satiric anti-court persona. Thus Wyatt's Satires, like the Utopia and Colin Clouts Come Home Againe, "explore the arguments...on both sides of the humanist debate over court service."

2   REBHOLZ, RONALD A. "Love's Newfangleness: A Comparison of Greville and Wyatt." SLitI, 11, no. 1 (Spring), 17-30.
    The theme of "'newfangleness'" (infidelity, promiscuity) in love is common to both Wyatt and Greville, but they deal with it differently. Wyatt's poems are more dramatic because his speakers are less aware than the poet of their situations; thus they often express surprise at discovering unfaithfulness and fear of the risk of loving again, betraying feelings of disillusion, exhaustion, devastation, bitterness, contempt for women in general, and/or the desire for vengeance. Greville's speakers, on the other hand, share his ironic detachment, his cynicism, and the "Christian contempt" that sees infidelity as the inevitable result of the Fall--a response that Wyatt only approaches in his Satires and Psalms. [Mentions having recently completed a "re-edited and modernized version" of Wyatt's poems; in notes on the contributors the editors of SLitI announce that the edition will be published by Penquin in Summer, 1978.]

3   SIEK, WAYNE H. "Uncertain Geographic References in Wyatt's Diplomatic Correspondence." N&Q, 223, n.s. 25, no. 5 (October), 414-416.
    Provides historical information on "Napoly in Romania," "Syo," "Vincentia," "Bishop of Lynden/Lyndon/London," and "Suyzer" from Wyatt's letters and asks for more information on them.

4   TILLEMANS, TH[OMAS]. King and Courtier: A Cultural Reconnaissance into an Age of Transition With Illustrations from the Poetry of Sir Thomas Wyatt and Other Sources. Norwood, Pennsylvania: Norwood Editions, 62 pp. Reprint of W 1951.2.

5   TILLYARD, E. M. W. "Introduction," in his The Poetry of Sir Thomas Wyatt: A Selection and a Study. St. Clair Shores, Michigan: Scholarly Press. Reprint of W 1929.2.

Writings about Surrey

1554[?]

OWEN, WYLLYAM. "To the most puissant prince Thomas Duke of
Norfolke, Wyllyam Awen hys most humble Oratour wysheth
perpetual health and felicitie," in his edition of The
fourth boke of Virgill, intreating of the loue betwene
Aeneas & Dido, translated into English, and drawne into
a strauge metre by Henrye late Earle of Surrey, worthy
to be embraced. London: printed by John Day for William
Awen.
Owen's dedication of the Fourth Boke to Surrey's son;
says that his copy, the basis for the printed text, was
"wrytten wyth the authors owne hande," but informs Norfolk that he "conferred with" two other copies of the
text before printing it because Surrey "had not tyme
sufficiet to the due examinacion therof" and also because
the author's copy was "somewhat doutful" "by reason of
speedye wrytyng thereof." [From Hartman, S 1933.]

1586

WEBBE, WILLIAM. A Discourse of English Poetrie. Together
with the Authors iudgement, touching the reformation of
our English Verse. London: printed by John Charlewood
for Robert Walley [STC 25172].
Notes, in a discussion of "Hexametrum Epicum," that
Surrey was "the first that attempted to practise thys
verse in English" in his translation of Virgil, but also
points out that the translation was "without regard of
true quantity of sillables." [From ECE, I, 283.]

1594

NASHE, THOMAS. The Vnfortvnate Traveller. Or, The life of
Iacke Wilton. London: printed by T. Scarlet for C. Burdy.

89

1594

    Includes the fictional narrative of Surrey's courtship
of "Geraldine" and the travels and knightly contests and
poetry he engaged in for the sake of her love. [From <u>The
Works of Thomas Nashe</u>, ed. Ronald B. McKerrow. Vol. 2.
Oxford: Basil Blackwell, 1958; rpt. 1966, pp. 199-328.]

1595

SIDNEY, SIR PHILIP. <u>An apologie for poetrie</u>.... London:
    printed for H[enry] Olney [STC 22534].
       Finds in "the Earle of Surries <u>Liricks</u> many things
tasting of a noble birth, and worthy of a noble minde."

1605

[CAMDEN, WILLIAM]. <u>Remaines of a Greater Worke, Concerning
    Britaine, the inhabitants thereof, their Languages, Names,
    Surnames, Empreses, Wise Speeches, Poesies, and Epitaphs</u>.
    London: printed by G. E. for Simon Waterson, p. 50.
       Contains Surrey's epitaph on Thomas Clere, "Norfolk
sprang thee." Surrey is referred to as "Thomas, Earle of
Surrey."

1619

DRAYTON, MICHAEL. <u>Englands Heroical Epistles</u>. London:
    printed for John Smethwicke.
       Includes an epistle from Surrey to "the Lady Geraldine,"
with excerpts from his poems, and a reply from the Lady;
based on Nashe's romance in <u>The Vnfortvnate Traveller</u>
[S 1594]. [From <u>The Works of Michael Drayton</u>, ed. J.
William Hebel. Vol. 2. Oxford: published for the Shakespeare Head Press by Basil Blackwell, 1961, pp. 277-294.]

1831

ANON. "Memoir of Henry Howard, Earl of Surrey," in <u>The Poems
    of Henry Howard Earl of Surrey</u>. The Aldine Edition of the
    British Poets. London: Bell and Daldy, pp. xiii-lxxiv.
       Biography of Surrey, with texts of letters, documents,
conversations relating to his life. [Reprinted: S 1866,
1871.]

1854

BELL, ROBERT. "Henry Howard, Earl of Surrey, 1517-1547," in his edition of <u>Poetical Works of Henry Howard, Earl of Surrey, Minor Contemporaneous Poets and Thomas Sackville, Lord Buckhurst</u>. The Annotated Edition of the English Poets, edited by Robert Bell. London: John W. Parker and Son, pp. 7-36.
    Biography, with an account of Surrey's influence on English poetry and his literary reputation from the sixteenth to the nineteenth centuries.

1866

ANON. "Memoir of Henry Howard, Earl of Surrey," in <u>The Poems of Henry Howard Earl of Surrey</u>. The Aldine Edition of the British Poets. London: Bell and Daldy, pp. xiii-lxxiv.
    Reprint of S 1831, with minor changes.

1871

ANON. "Memoir of Henry Howard, Earl of Surrey," in <u>The Poems of Henry Howard Earl of Surrey</u>. The Aldine Edition of the British Poets. London: Bell and Daldy, pp. xiii-lxxiv.
    Reprint of S 1831.

1881

SCHROEER, ARNOLD. "Ueber Die Anfaenge Des Blankverses in England." <u>Anglia</u>, 4: 1-72.
    A study of the beginnings of blank verse in England, starting with Surrey. Discusses his prosody, accentuation, rhythms, and related matters (trochaics, enjambment, caesuras), comparing Surrey with later sixteenth-century writers and examples of blank verse (Grimald, <u>Gorbuduc</u>, Turberville, van der Noodt, Spenser, <u>Tancred and Gismond</u>, Gascoigne, Barnabe Rich, Lyly, Peele, Greene, Marlowe, and <u>The Famous Victories of Henry V</u>). Incorporates comments on blank verse by Gascoigne, Webbe, Puttenham, Sidney. [In German.]

1883

*FEHSE, HERMAN. <u>Henry Howard, Earl of Surrey, ein Beitrag zur Geschichte der Petrarchismus in England</u>. Chemnitz.
    Cited in S 1920.1. [In German.]

1886

MAYOR, JOSEPH B. "Blank Verse in Surrey and Marlowe," in his Chapters on English Metre. Second Edition [1901]. Cambridge: Cambridge University Press, pp. 157-167.
Points out that Surrey uses the initial trochee as often as Milton, that his rhythm is often harsh, and that when he provides a middle pause, it is usually after the fourth syllable.

1889

EMERSON, OLIVER FARRAR. "The Development of Blank Verse-- A Study of Surrey." MLN, 4, no. 8 (December), 233-236.
The differences in the frequency of run-on lines, couplets, weak endings, feminine endings, "mid-stopt lines," and pauses, together with the difference in average sentence length, between Book II and Book IV of Surrey's Aeneid show "a gradual development toward freedom" in his use of blank verse.

1891

BAPST, EDMOND. "Henry Howard, Compte de Surrey," in his Deux Gentilshommes-Poetès de la Cour de Henry VIII. Paris: Librairie Plon, pp. 145-376.
Biography aimed at distinguishing between the true facts about Surrey's life and poetry and the fictional nature of earlier accounts. Refutes specifically (1) the belief that Surrey traveled to Italy, (2) the possibility of an intimate friendship between Surrey and Wyatt, and (3) the likelihood of a real relationship between Surrey and "Geraldine" (Lady Elizabeth Fitzgerald). Suggests that Surrey wrote about love because of the imported inspiration of Petrarch, because it was a traditional and diverting pastime, and because it was a safe subject in a politically dangerous court. Assesses Surrey's character as unusually straightforward, generous, and chivalric, but pridefully disdainful of inferiors and potentially violent. Sees the Aeneid translations as hastily done and derivative of Gavin Douglas, and notes the increasingly religious nature of the later verse. [In French.]

1902

*DITTES, R[UDOLF]. Zu Surrey's Aeneisübertragung, Beiträge zur
    Neueren Philologie. Vienna.
        Cited in S 1920.1. [In German.]

1903

FEST, OTTO. Über Surrey's Virgilübersetzung, nebst Neuausgabe
    Des Vierten Buches nach Tottel's Originaldruck und der
    bisher ungedruckten Hs. Hargrave 205 (Brit. Mus.).
    Palaestra[:] Unterschingen und Texte aus der deutschen und
    englischen Philologie, 34, edited by Alois Brandl, Gustav
    Roethe and Erich Schmidt, 146 pp.
        Detailed comparison/examination of matters of form and
    content related to Surrey's Aeneid IV in Tottel's Certain
    Bokes and the newly discovered BM Hargrave MS. 205. The
    last chapter provides a reprinting of Tottel's Book IV
    with variants from the Hargrave in notes. Fest finds that
    the differences between them suggest that the Hargrave
    compiler was concerned with removing irregularities, metri-
    cal and otherwise, from Tottel's version. [In German.]

1905

IMELMANN, RUDOLF. "Zu den Anfängen des Blankverses: Sur-
    rey's Aenis IV in ursprunglicher Gestalt." Jahrbuch der
    Deutschen Shakespeare-Gesellschaft, 41: 81-123.
        Examines the variants between the versions of Surrey's
    Aeneid IV in Tottel's Certain Bokes and Hargrave MS. 205
    and their relation to Gavin Douglas's Eneados, the Italian
    versions, and the translation by Thomas Phaer. Suggests,
    on the basis of verbal correspondences, that Phaer used
    the Day-Owen version of Surrey's translation. Also ques-
    tions Fest's belief [S 1903] that the Hargrave version is
    a result of the editing of Tottel's. [Willcock (S 1919)
    finds Imelmann "far more valuable" than Fest. In German.]

1906

PADELFORD, FREDERICK MORGAN. "The Manuscript Poems of Henry
    Howard, Earl of Surrey." Anglia, 29: 273-338.
        Describes the contents of seven British Museum MSS.
    containing poems by Surrey: Egerton 2711, Harleian 78,
    Hargrave 205, Devonshire 17492, Add. MS. 28635, Add. MS.

1906

28636, and Add. MS. 36529. Also discusses the missing
"Hill" MS. and "Harrington MS. No. ii." Points out differences in readings among the MSS. and Tottel's Miscellany. Prints poems from Add. MS. 36529 and 28635, with
textual notes.

1919

WILLCOCK, GLADYS D. "A Hitherto Uncollated Version of Surrey's Translation of the Fourth Book of the 'Aeneid' (I)."
MLR, 14, no. 2 (April), 163-172.
  While Surrey's translation of Book II of the Aeneid is
extant in only one version, Tottel's Certain Bokes of Virgil's AEneis (T), Book IV is preserved not only in that
text but in two others: "an undated and hitherto uncollated quarto edition printed by John Day [D], and the MS.
Hargrave 205 [H] in the British Museum." Internal and
external evidence point to D as the earliest, with "the
end of 1554" its likely date; T was published in 1557; H,
erroneously described as a "'Poetical Commonplace Book by
Henry, Earl of Surrey,'" and written in two different
hands, has "independent authority...even though it was
copied out when both D. and T. were in circulation."
Imelmann's contention [S 1905] that Thomas Phaer used D
for his 1555-1558 translation is not convincing, but his
inadvertent establishment of the authenticity of D and H
is significant. [See also S 1920.2, 1922.1.]

1920

BERDAN, JOHN M. "Henry Howard, Earl of Surrey," in his Early
Tudor Poetry. New York: Macmillan Co., pp. 504-545.
  Surrey's poetry represents the maturity in both literary technique and literary substance achieved during the
last stage of the early Tudor period, and is the product
of both his individual poetic sensibility and the merging
in his work of the Italian, native, classical (humanistic)
and medieval Latin traditions. His "London" satire shows
a "lightness of touch" not seen since Chaucer; his translation of Petrarch's "Amor, che nel penser mio vive e
regna" illustrates an advance in technique and language
over Wyatt's more literal and archaic version; his translations from Martial and Horace, compared with other
English versions, exemplify his modern phraseology and
his concise, if awkward, syntax. But it is in poems like
"The soote season," and, more specifically, in his free

use of accent in his Aeneid translations, that we observe
that merging of individuality and tradition that marks his
poetry as the culmination of the "'prentice work" that
characterizes early Tudor poetry. [Includes some biography, and questions evidence of Surrey's relationship
with Wyatt and Elizabeth Fitzgerald. See also W 1920.]

1   PADELFORD, FREDERICK MORGAN. "Introduction," in his edition
    of The Poems of Henry Howard Earl of Surrey. University
    of Washington Publications in Language and Literature,
    Vol. 1. Seattle: University of Washington Press, 7-42.
        Wyatt deserves credit for his major reforms in prosody
    and diction, particularly for his "reformation of the
    iambic pentameter line," and Surrey's verse shows his in-
    fluence. Surrey's own contributions to English prosody
    lay in his development of the English sonnet and blank
    verse: although settling on the quatrain-couplet rhyme-
    scheme for the sonnet, he followed a variety of sense-
    divisions; his blank-verse translation of the Aeneid is
    "succinct, forceful and spirited, and the movement fairly
    rapid"; it is further distinguished by its "severe dig-
    nity" and marked by the use of run-on lines, caesuras, and
    alliteration. He also experimented with other forms:
    poulter's measure (an "unfortunate" choice), terza rima
    (in both pentameter and tetrameter), and "various stanzas
    of three and four-foot lines" (following Wyatt). His
    diction, influenced by foreign words and Chaucer, is
    "direct, firm, and muscular, but flexible and euphonious."
    But finally, that which most influenced the Elizabethans
    was the "dramatic quality" of his verse--the "interpreta-
    tion of experience through pictorial and vivid action."
    [Includes biography that views Surrey's life as an "impres-
    sive tragedy" and the poems as its "lyrical accompaniment."
    Revised edition: S 1928; reprint: S 1966.1.]

2   WILLCOCK, GLADYS D. "A Hitherto Uncollated Version of Sur-
    rey's Translation of the Fourth Book of the 'Aeneid' (II)."
    MLR, 15, no. 2 (April), 113-123.
        Provides collation of the three extant versions of the
    translation--the printed versions of Day and Tottel and
    MS. Hargrave 205--, using Tottel's as "the standard" and
    noting deviations in the other two. [Continuation of
    S 1919; see also S 1922.1.]

1921

ANON. Review of Frederick Morgan Padelford, ed., The Poems
of Henry Howard Earl of Surrey [S 1920.1]. SP, 18, no. 3
(July), 370-371.
Padelford's "scholarly volume" is particularly valuable
because it classifies the poems by subject matter, which
complements the biographical introduction by providing
more "human interest" in Surrey.

1   BASKERVILL, C[HARLES] R[EAD]. "Recent Works on Phases of the
English Renaissance" [Review of Frederick Morgan Padelford,
ed., The Poems of Henry Howard Earl of Surrey (S 1920.1)].
MP, 18, no. 9 (January), 507.
"Unusually important" edition.

2   BRIGHT, J. W. Review of Frederick Morgan Padelford, ed., The
Poems of Henry Howard Earl of Surrey [S 1920.1]. MLN, 36,
no. 3 (March), 188-191.
This is a book "'published to the common profit and
delectation of the many,' rather than a monograph for the
use of specialists." It is not arranged well, it devotes too much attention to "grammatical forms" and it
misinterprets "metrical details." Furthermore, it does
not record the textual work done on Surrey by German
scholars. While valuable for its inclusion of passages
from the three sixteenth-century versions Book IV of his
Aeneid, it adds nothing to our knowledge of Surrey's uses
of earlier translations or the order in which he translated
Books II and IV. The biography is good, but the critical
introduction is too general and superficial.

3   WILLCOCK, G[LADYS] D. Review of Frederick Morgan Padelford,
ed., The Poems of Henry Howard Earl of Surrey [S 1920.1].
MLR, 16, nos. 3-4 (July-October), 336-339.
The edition is useful for "both general and specialist
students": it supersedes the "modernized text" of the
Aldine edition [S 1831] and profits from the work on Surrey's sources and meters done by modern English and German
scholars. It is accurate in seeing Surrey's prosodic
forms (particularly blank verse) as peculiar to him rather
than as "a stage" in literary history. However, its account of Wyatt's metrics and of sixteenth-century prosodic
theory are questionable.

1922

C[RAIG], H[ARDIN]. Review of Frederick Morgan Padelford, ed.,
The Poems of Henry Howard Earl of Surrey [S 1920.1]. PQ,
1, no. 1 (January), 74-76.
   The edition provides "the first satisfactory text of
Surrey's poems," embodying previous work done on Surrey
by German scholars, and printing "correct punctuation, and
many restorations of true readings," as well as important
critical notes. However, it does not account adequately
for French influence on Surrey, it makes the contrast between Wyatt and Surrey "more violent than it is," and, in
its emphasis on the influence of Italian versions on Surrey's Aeneid translations, it does not take into account
the possibility that annotated editions of Virgil were
used in common by Surrey and the Italian translators, as
suggested by Berdan [S 1920].

1   WILLCOCK, GLADYS D. "A Hitherto Uncollated Version of Sur-
rey's Translation of the Fourth Book of the 'Aeneid'
(III)." MLR, 17, no. 2 (April), 131-149.
   Examines variations among the three early versions of
the translation--Tottel's Certain Bokes of Virgils AEneis
(T), the Day-Owen undated quarto (D), and MS. Hargrave 205
(H), concluding that while all three have undergone some
editing, T has been more carefully and completely revised
by someone "thoroughly in tune with Surrey's manner," that
T represents the later version despite the fact that H is
"the actually latest text," and that comparison with Gavin
Douglas's Eneados provides proof of the authenticity of D
and H. Also points to evidence indicating "a certain pre-
ponderance of probability in favour of author's [Surrey's]
revision in T," and discounts the probability of Nicholas
Grimald's participation in the translation. [Continuation
of S 1919, 1920.2.]

1923

HUDSON, HOYT HOPEWELL. "Surrey and Martial." MLN, 38, no. 8
(December), 481-483.
   A version very close to "Martiall, the thinges that do
attayn" was printed in William Baldwin's Treatise of Morall
Phylosophie in 1547/48, almost ten years before the poem,
ascribed to Surrey, was printed in Tottel's Miscellany. In
"at least one early edition of the Treatise," the poem is
ascribed to Surrey, indicating that Baldwin may have taken
the poem from the Surrey manuscript also used by the Miscellany's editor. If that is the case, the translation represents "the earliest publication of any of Surrey's poems.

1924

ROBERTSON, J. M. "The Evolution of English Blank Verse."
The Criterion, 2: 171-187.
Surrey's contact with verso sciolto probably came
through the Italian translations of the Aeneid by Liburnio, Piccolomini, and Molza rather than Trissino's
Sofonisba. Piccolomini and Molza were particularly important in influencing his "lining," which is more concise
than that of Gavin Douglas. But the Italian influence on
Surrey was negligible "when the start was once made":
that which distinguished his blank verse, "the free play
of fluid rhythm" (sentence endings at various points in
the line, variation in sequences of feet, run-on lines,
trochaic substitution at the beginnings of, and within,
lines), is apparent in Virgil and Surrey, but less so in
other writers of blank verse, Italian or English; Sackville, Norton, Gascoigne, and Kinwelmershe are "thralled
metrists" who apparently "learn[ed] nothing from Surrey."

1925

LEACH, H. S. "Earle Surrey's Songs and Sonnets." N&Q, 148,
no. 20 (May 16), 349.
A copy of the first volume of Bishop Percy's edition of
the Songes and Sonettes (1767-1807), together with 48
pages of Surrey's Aeneid, II and IV, resides in the Lehigh
University Library. Is this one of the four copies of
Percy's edition that survived the 1808 fire, or is it a
fifth?

1   MERRILL, L. R. "Preface" to "The Shorter Poems of Nicholas
Grimald," in his The Life and Poems of Nicholas Grimald.
Yale Studies in English, Vol. 69, edited by Albert S.
Cook. New Haven: Yale University Press; London: Hum-
phrey Milford, Oxford University Press, pp. 361-374.
Tottel's Miscellany ranks as equal in historical
importance to the Lyrical Ballads: it marks the advent of
modern verse. Surrey is given first (titled) position in
the anthology because of his rank, but credit is also due
Wyatt and Grimald for introducing the sonnet to England
through its publication. Also, evidence suggests that,
contrary to the belief of Willcock [S 1919, 1920.2,
1921.3], Grimald's blank verse in the Miscellany, rather
than Surrey's Aeneid, IV, was the first published example
of the form; it was also the most influential, because of
the many reprintings of the Miscellany in the sixteenth
century.

1928

PADELFORD, FREDERICK MORGAN. "Introduction," in his edition
of The Poems of Henry Howard Earl of Surrey. Revised
edition. University of Washington Publications[:] Language and Literature, Vol. 5. Seattle: University of
Washington Press, pp. 3-55.
Revised edition of S 1920.1.

1929

_____. "A Sixteenth Century Courtier: Henry Howard, Earl of
Surrey." The Johns Hopkins Alumni Magazine, 17 (November,
1928-June, 1929), 332-372.
Biography of Surrey that portrays him as the incarna-
tion of Castiglione's ideal Courtier, meeting death as
"a high minded gentleman" in the "coarse, craven, and
often stupid society" of the court of Henry VIII.

1933

HARTMAN, HERBERT. "Introduction," in his edition of Surrey's
"Fourth Boke of Virgill." Privately printed [by John
Johnson at the Oxford University Press] for Carl H.
Pforzheimer, Purchase, New York, pp. ix-xxvii.
The text of the John Day-William Owen undated edition
of the Fourth Boke [D] was for two centuries confused
with Tottel's Certain Bokes [T], and later with the Hargrave MS. version [H]. The terminus a quo for the publication of D is August 25, 1554, the terminus ad quem
October 16, 1554, despite evidence suggesting later dates;
thus D represents the first published blank verse in
English, despite arguments that Grimald's verses in Tottel's Miscellany are. Collation of D, T, and H reveals
D to be the most authentic as well as "the very earliest
and least corrupt," and to represent "the older tradition
of accentual pentameter as practiced by Surrey and his
friend and master Wyatt, rather than the 'old Iambicke
stroake' of strict decasyllables"; T and H betray the
desire for "a tight iambic decasyllable," and therefore
represent a later tradition than the more medieval D.
Comparison of the D text with Italian writers of verso
sciolto (Liburnio, de Medici, Piccolomini) and Gavin
Douglas' Scots Eneados indicates Surrey's independence,
and suggests the possibility that Servius' commentary on
the Aeneid was the common source, and thus explanation,

1933

for the parallels between Surrey's text and the others.
[Mentions all references to Surrey's translations from 1557
through its purchase by Pforzheimer.]

1934

*BROOKS, CLEANTH, JR. "The History of Percy's Edition of
Surrey's Poems." ESt, 68 (1933-1934), 424-430.
Cited in MLA bibliography.

1935

LATHROP, H[ENRY] B[URROWES]. Review of Herbert Hartman, ed.,
Surrey's "Fourth Boke of Virgill" [S 1933]. MLN, 50,
no. 3 (March), 198-200.
The evidence that Surrey owed little to Gavin Douglas'
Eneados or to Italian translators of Virgil is "cogent but
not conclusive"; the task of comparing Surrey's translations line-by-line with the other versions still remains
to be done.

1   WILLCOCK, G[LADYS] D. Review of Herbert Hartman, ed. Surrey's "Fourth Boke of Virgill" [S 1933]. MLR, 30, no. 1
(January), 73-75.
Hartman reaffirms that the Day-Owen version is earlier
and closer to Surrey's autograph than either Tottel's
Certain Bokes or MS. Hargrave 205. However, he overempha-
sizes the early popularity of the translation, he is wrong
in separating English from European humanism, and he errs
in dismissing the influence of Gavin Douglas' Eneados on
Surrey's translations.

1936

BANNISTER, EDITH. "Surrey's Vocabulary." TLS, no. 1812
(October 24), p. 863.
Replies to Gray [S 1936.4], offering more examples of
Surrey's debt to Douglas' Eneados, focusing on words Sur-
rey misinterpreted and "northern and rare words" he bor-
rowed.

1   BYROM, H. J. Review of Herbert Hartmen, ed., Surrey's "Fourth
Boke of Virgill"[S 1933]. RES, 12, no. 45 (January), 81-
83.

Hartman's contention that the parallels between the translation and those of others was caused by all having used Servius' Commentary is "valuable" but "contentious"; furthermore, the related argument--that English humanism was independent of Italy--is wrong. However, the book is valuable for providing evidence that Surrey wrote blank verse before Grimald, and for providing "material for a fuller examination" of the regularization of Surrey's metrics in both Tottel's Certain Bokes and Tottel's Miscellany.

2   CASADY, EDWIN R. "A Reinterpretation of Surrey's Character and Actions." PMLA, 51, no. 3 (September), 626-635.
        The traditional view of Surrey as "'the most folish prowde boye that ys in Englande'" is belied by the facts of his life and death. He was born to "the leadership of the conservative nobility" and "trained to accept and fulfill the responsibilities of his inheritance." He was an astute military leader and a wise and able public and private citizen. Incidents interpreted as examples of his "rashness" rely upon "unwarranted assumptions." His execution, finally, resulted not from flaws in his character, but from "the tragic conflict which has inevitably accompanied the shifting of power from one group to another." [See also S 1938.]

3   CASSON, LESLIE F. "Surrey's Vocabulary." TLS, no. 1814 (November 7), p. 908.
        Replies to Gray [S 1936.4]. Explores the English poetic history of the word "feddrame" from Surrey's Aeneid.

4   GRAY, M. M. "Surrey's Vocabulary." TLS, no. 1809 (October 3), p. 791.
        Comparison between selected words, lines, and passages in Surrey's Aeneid and Gavin Douglas' version indicates that Surrey "continually consulted" a manuscript of Douglas' translation while doing his own. However, the examination also reveals that he introduced in his translation "a number of words from Latin, and also some new English forms." [See also S 1936, 1936.3.]

5   _____. "Surrey's Vocabulary." TLS, no. 1813 (October 24), p. 887.
        Replies to Bannister [S 1936], suggesting that Surrey's use of "tallowit" and "feddrame" was independent of Douglas' Aeneid translation.

1937

CAMP, TRUMAN W. "Another Version of 'The Thinges That Cause A Quiet Lyfe.'" MLN, 52, no. 3 (March), 186-188.
    The text of Surrey's translation of Martial, x. 47, that appears in William Baldwin's A treatise of Morall Phylosophie (1547/48) differs from the version in Tottel's Miscellany. That the Baldwin version begins with "'My frende'" indicates "that Baldwin knew Surrey well enough to receive a manuscript of the poems from the author."

1938

CASADY, EDWIN [R.]. Henry Howard, Earl of Surrey. The Modern Language Association Revolving Fund Series, 8. New York: The Modern Language Association of America, 269 pp.
    Biographical study that reinterprets Surrey's character in light of contemporary evidence and errors of fact and interpretation in earlier accounts; aims specifically at disproving the traditional view of Surrey as a "'folish prowde boye,'" arguing that his conduct consistently re-flected "sound Judgment" given the fundamental conflict between his hereditary ties to the old nobility and the economic, political, and religious changes involved in the development of a strong Tudor monarchy and a unified national order. [See also S 1936.2.]
    Appendix I, "Surrey's Contribution to English Litera-ture," details the characteristics and accomplishments of his poetry: he refined English diction by discarding archaisms and borrowings from Latin and French; he re-formed English metrics by using "a fixed rhythmical stan-dard for a word," by placing tonic accent "only on the even syllables" (exception: initial trochees), by experi-menting with a large variety of iambic verse forms and patterns, by making free use of pauses and run-on lines, and by demonstrating for the first time the "possibilities" of poulter's measure; he translated Petrarch accurately but not slavishly, avoiding his more "preposterous" con-ceits, and his Italian rhyme scheme, and emphasizing nature more than individual emotion. His blank verse, the most important contribution, was probably more direct-ly influenced by Alamanni's Opere Toscane than to any other specific source, but its main connection is the humanistic one to the Aeneid itself. Finally, it is cor-rect to view Surrey's poetry as "'polite verse'": both his love poetry [see Appendix II, on "Geraldine"] and his

"autobiographical" pieces are less personal than literary; it is only in his Biblical paraphrases that the personal element dominates.

1939

ANON. "Pioneer Tudor Poet" [Review of Edwin Casady, Henry Howard, Earl of Surrey (S 1938)]. TLS, no. 1929 (January 21), p. 44.

Agrees for the most part with Casady's fatalistic interpretation of Surrey's life and sees the study of the poetry as "independent and thorough."

1   BYROM, H. J. Review of Edwin Casady, Henry Howard, Earl of Surrey [S 1938]. RES, 15, no. 59 (July), 342-344.

Casady's is "the most complete and accurate narrative" of Surrey's life that we have, although it is overly deterministic--and thus oversimplified--in its historical point of view. His discussion of the poetry "breaks no new ground."

2   GILBERT, ALLAN H. Review of Edwin Casady, Henry Howard, Earl of Surrey [S 1938]. MLN, 54, no. 8 (December), 611-612.

Relegating the discussion of Surrey's poetry to an appendix is consistent with "the current tendency of literary scholars to have little to do with poetry." Casady does not investigate Surrey's attitude toward Italian art, and he presents the poet as a writer of "'polite'" verse except in the Biblical translations. Some of the biographical evidence subverts the attempt to portray Surrey in a positive light.

3   MATTINGLY, GARRETT. Review of Edwin Casady, Henry Howard, Earl of Surrey [S 1938]. Journal of Modern History, 11, no. 1 (March), 113-114.

Casady provides valuable (if sometimes misleading) information about Surrey's career as a soldier and diplomat, but nothing new about his poetry, sustaining the "now usual" rejections of the Geraldine legend and the possibility of a personal friendship between Surrey and Wyatt.

4   PADELFORD, FREDERICK MORGAN. Review of Edwin Casady, Henry Howard, Earl of Surrey [S 1938]. JEGP, 38, no. 3 (July), 457-461.

Because he is too much Surrey's advocate, Casady fails to prove his case in the biography, operating from conjectures "that are more fanciful and farfetched than

1939

than those of Nott and Bapst [WS 1816.1, S 1891] that he seeks to discredit." While the evidence suggests that Surrey was indeed brave, loyal, and devoted to his family, it also shows him to be hot-tempered, impulsive, "scornful of men of meaner birth," and "greedy for family aggrandizement and power." Casady's is "a sentimental and modernistic interpretation." The appendices on the poetry and the Geraldine myth add "nothing new."

5 PUTT, S. GORLEY. "A Suppressed Henidadys in a Poem by Surrey." MLR, 34, no. 1 (January), 66-67.
   The absence of the comma between the second and third lines of the 1542 printing of An excellent Epitaffe [W 1542.2] suggests that Surrey was there employing the figure hendiadys, "'in which a single idea is expressed by two words connected by a conjunction'"; thus the lines would read "disdainful virtue," implying Wyatt's Coriolanus-like character.

6 _____. Review of Edwin Casady, Henry Howard, Earl of Surrey [S 1938]. MLR, 34, no. 2 (April), 258-259.
   The appendix on Surrey's contribution to English literature is "for the most part a summary of other opinions," and is inferior to Berdan's [S 1920].

1940

ZANDVOORT, R. W. Review of Edwin Casady, Henry Howard, Earl of Surrey [S 1938]. ES, 22: 178-179.
   Casady's "grimly determinist" reading of Surrey's life will "probably remain the standard biography...for many years to come."

1946

BENNETT, J. A. W. "The Early Fame of Gavin Douglas's Eneados." MLN, 61, no. 2 (February), 83-88.
   Surrey's use of Scots words and phrases in his Aeneid translations prove that he had read Douglas' translation carefully, "even though he did not always understand its Scots idioms."

1947

ANON. "Surrey's Triumphs." TLS, no. 2,346 (January 18), p. 37.

Extols Surrey's many literary "triumphs"--in diction, translation, in adapting the English sonnet from the Italian, in adapting poetry to music--and focuses particularly on the "one triumph all his own": blank verse, which has yet to be superseded by any other "metrical idea." In observance of the 400th anniversary of the poet's execution.

1949

TOWNE, FRANK. "Surrey's Certain Books of Virgil's Aeneis, II, 272." Explicator, 8, no. 3 (December), item 25.

"'Raught'" is a form of the word "'reach,'" as used by both Surrey and Virgil.

1951

ORAS, ANTS. "Surrey's Technique of Phonetic Echoes: A Method and its Background." JEGP, 50, no. 3 (July), 289-308.

The "grave stateliness" of Surrey's Aeneid results partly from "clear, intelligible, and effectively graded" arrangements of assonantal echoes, reinforced somewhat by consonance and even rhyme. These patterns, which are most apparent in passages of high emotional intensity, occur in all three sixteenth-century versions of the translation in varying degrees, as well as in the blank verse written by Surrey's immediate followers, although "between Surrey and Marlowe...[the use of them] tends to degenerate into a mechanical habit." While Virgil and Wyatt may have provided Surrey with precedent for the technique, his main sources were probably Italian: Petrarch and, especially, Italian writers of verso sciolti and Italian translators of Virgil.

1952

CHAPMAN, RAYMOND. "The Earl of Surrey in France." TLS, no. 2,614 (March 7), p. 173.

It was Surrey's father, not Surrey, who was part of the English contingent at the Field of the Cloth of Gold

1952

in 1520, contrary to the information reported in the
Cambridge History of English Literature [WS 1909] and
other works.

1953

MAXWELL, J. C. "Surrey's Lines on Wyatt." N&Q, 198 (March),
    100.
    The source for the first line of "Wyat resteth here" is
    the epitaph on the tomb of Trivulzio: Hic quiescit qui
    numquam quievit.

1955

_____. "Surrey's Lines on Wyatt." N&Q, 200, n.s. 2, no. 1
    (January), 41.
    Apologizes for an oversight in a previous note on "Wyat
    resteth here" [S 1953].

1956

JUEL-JENSEN, BRENT. "The Poet Earl of Surrey's Library."
    BC, 5, no. 2 (Summer), 172.
    Reports the existence of a copy of Castiglione's Libro
    del Cortegiano with Surrey's name on the title page and
    annotations in the text "in his autograph."

1   MUMFORD, IVY LILIAN. "Musical Settings to the Poems of Henry
    Howard, Earl of Surrey," EM, 7: 9-20.
    Five of Surrey's poems "are known to have existed as
    songs," and appear with or without accompanying tablatures
    in various MSS. and printed sources: "If care do cause
    me(n) cry," "In winter's just return," "O happy dames,"
    "My friends" ["Martial"], and "When youth had led me half
    the race." In fact, we know more about musical settings
    for Surrey's poems than we do about those for Wyatt's.
    [Includes discussions of the sources and the relationship
    of the music to the poems, and prints photocopies of
    pages from several of the sources: the Mulliner Book,
    Royal App. 58, BM MS. Stowe 389, and BM Add. 33933 (The
    Scottish Metrical Psalter).]

1960

ANON. "Booked for Tragedy" [Review of Hester W. Chapman, Two Tudor Portraits (S 1960.1)]. TLS, no. 3,044 (July 1), p. 412.

    Questions Chapman's assumptions about Tudor attitudes toward human life and finds her treatment of Surrey's poetry "somewhat perfunctory."

1   CHAPMAN, HESTER W. Two Tudor Portraits: Henry Howard, Earl of Surrey and Lady Katherine Grey. London: Jonathan Cape, pp. 13-147.

    Biography that sees Surrey's rash temperament and premature downfall as the result of his isolated, privileged (yet tempestuous) early upbringing and his long-held status as King Henry's court favorite, conditions that produced in him an inflated sense of the significance of his noble heritage and an oversimplified and archaic attitude toward the changing realities of Tudor court life and politics. Considers his poetry mainly from the biographical point of view, emphasizing its often arrogant tone and its ties to medieval courtly sensibility.

2   DAVIES, M. BRYN. "Surrey at Boulogne." HLQ, 23, no. 4 (August), 339-348.

    Reports the existence of an eye-witness account of the battle between Surrey's English troops and the French on January 7, 1545: a chronicle written in Welsh by Elis Gruffydd that is preserved in the National Library of Wales. The account may be relevant to Surrey's allusions to his Boulogne experience in several poems.

3   ECKERT, CHARLES WILLISON. 'Critical Introduction' [Chapter I], in his edition of "The Poetry of Henry Howard, Earl of Surrey." Ph.D dissertation, Washington University of St. Louis, pp. 1-65.

    (Divided into Surrey's "Character and Tastes," the relationship of Surrey and Wyatt to "'Poesia per Musica,'" Petrarchan and Chaucerian influences, prosody, and "Surrey's Personality and His Poetry.") Surrey was possessed of "an extreme sensitivity" in his dealings with others, one that eventually turned him away from court intrigue to poetry. His break with medieval song was caused by the new Italianate forms--strambotto, frottolo (the form for "almost half of his secular poems"), capitolo, canzone, sonnet--and the advent of poulter's measure, which both Wyatt and Surrey wrote in imitation of Petrarch's canzoni, and which was probably often set to music. His

1960

Petrarchan poems are more directly influenced by contemporary <u>Petrarchismo</u> than Petrarch, and his debt to Chaucer is clear not only in his "diction, conceits and rhetorical habits" but in his adaptation of "a number of Chaucer's poems." His prosody is characterized by a deemphasis on "rhyme as a major poetic element," and the regularization of metrics, which was also affected by "'poesie per musica.'" The distinguishing mark of the verse of both Wyatt and Surrey is that it "consistently reveals personality within quite conventional forms and is often deeply saturated with the character of the poet"; this is less true of Surrey's Petrarchan poems than those poems that accomplish "the impression of immediacy" through "more concrete, visual imagery...and by his use of definite settings." [Also includes chapters on texts, canon, chronology; text does not include the <u>Aeneid</u> translations.]

4   ELTON, G. R. Review of Hester W. Chapman, <u>Two Tudor Portraits</u> [S 1960.1]. <u>The Listener</u>, 63, no. 1628 (June 9), 1025.
    Chapman's is a "far from necessary book." Surrey is a "not very good poet."

5   MUIR, KENNETH. "Surrey Poems in the Blage Manuscript." <u>N&Q</u>, 205, n.s. 7, no. 10 (October), 368-370.
    Evidence indicates that three poems in the MS.--"Such wayward wayes hath loue," "Yf Ryght be rakt and ouer Ron," and a six-line fragment--are Surrey's. [Includes the texts of the poems, with variants from other sources.]

1961

RIDLEY, FLORENCE H. "Surrey's Debt to Gawin Douglas." <u>PMLA</u>, 76, no. 1 (March), 25-33.
    Reviews scholarship on the relationship between Surrey's <u>Aeneid</u> and Douglas' <u>Eneados</u>, and provides selective collation to demonstrate that "although Douglas contributed little or nothing to the technical form of Surrey's work...he contributed greatly to its content," influencing over forty percent of Surrey's lines. Also includes external evidence supporting the likelihood that Surrey had seen Douglas' translation. [<u>See also</u> S 1963.2.]

<u>1963</u>

LITTLEFIELD, THOMAS HASTINGS. "Of Ancient Liberty: A Study
of Surrey's Translation of Books II and IV of the <u>Aeneid</u>."
Ph.D. dissertation, Columbia, 188 pp.
    The uneven quality of the translation--a third of it
good, a third bad, a third adequate--demonstrates that it
should properly be considered "essays in translation"
that illustrate the Renaissance passion for imitation and
serve merely as "a source of information about Surrey's
attitudes and mode of thought." The best passages are
those dealing with "martial exploits," "princely splen-
dors," "manly duty," and love--concerns consistent with
Surrey's biographical and literary character. Of possible
sources, Douglas' <u>Eneados</u> was the only one Surrey "con-
sulted frequently." The variants among the three extant
versions of Book IV (Day-Owen, Tottel's and MS. Hargrave
205) do little to clear up the textual difficulties;
Hargrave, the latest, "appears most remote from the influence of any Surrey autograph"; and the other two, when
they concur against it, "are to be preferred" despite
their corruptions. The translation was "not recognized
for at least a century and a half after its appearance,"
and it exercised only a remote influence on later writers
of blank verse; it does not merit "a revival of interest."

1   PHILBIN, JOAN HONOR. "A Metrical Analysis of the Blank Verse
of Henry Howard, Earl of Surrey." Ph.D. dissertation,
Yale, 244 pp.
    Analysis of Surrey's <u>Aeneid</u> translations (based on the
texts of Padelford and Hartman [S 1920.1, 1933]) indicates
that, despite the lack of an authorized text and uncer-
tainties about Tudor accentuation of Romance words, the
"decasyllabic and iambic nature" of his lines is definite-
ly apparent. Over 94 percent of the lines in the Day-
Owen version, the most irregular of the texts, "contain
exactly ten syllables" when one takes into account metrical doublets and contractions. Furthermore, over 98
percent of the lines are in "perfectly regular iambic
meter," and Surrey's intention to achieve that regularity
is made clear by his frequently inverted word order.
Other characteristics of his lines include occasional accidental rhymes, alliteration, some instances of trunca-
tion, anacrusis, and feminine endings, and some alexan-
drines and Virgilian short lines. Rhythmical variation in
the otherwise regular translation is provided through
trochaic inversions and caesuras.

1963

2 RIDLEY, FLORENCE H. "Introduction," in her edition of The
    "Aeneid" of Henry Howard Earl of Surrey. Berkeley and Los
    Angeles: University of California Press, pp. 1-48.
        Although insufficient evidence prevents determining
    conclusively either the definite date of Surrey's Aeneid
    translations or the relative authenticity of the three
    extant versions of Book IV, it is possible to establish
    through both external and internal evidence the extent of
    his borrowings from Gawin Douglas' Eneados. Although not
    printed until 1553, the Scottish translation circulated in
    manuscript before 1539-1540, and it was probably well-
    known in Surrey's circle. Furthermore, as the only Aeneid
    translation in English, it was precisely the kind of work
    that would have interested Surrey the humanist. Other
    explanations for the similarities between the two transla-
    tions--the possibility that Surrey and Douglas used the
    same Latin version as copy-text or relied on the same com-
    mentaries on Virgil, or that they result from the tamper-
    ing of a later Surrey editor--can be dismissed. Of the
    available Continental translations, that of Saint Gelais
    influenced him only indirectly through the Eneados, and
    those of de Molza, Liburnio, and Piccolomini only provided
    him with the example of verso sciolto, which helped him
    attain the metrical versatility, the precision, concise-
    ness, and epic cadence, of unrhymed Latin hexameter; while
    Douglas' couplets could not achieve such qualities, his
    version is more expansive and less literal than Surrey's,
    and it conveys more successfully Virgil's suggestiveness
    and significance--"and therefore his full, true meaning."
        In spite of these differences, however, the comparison
    shows that Surrey relied on Douglas for phraseology "in
    more than 40 percent of his lines," apparently to convey
    the latter's "color, vividness and life." This edition,
    taken from Tottel's 1557 version, "is designed to make as
    clear as possible the evidence of his [Surrey's] borrowing
    from Douglas; thus apparent borrowings from Douglas are
    italicized [in the text] and their source is given at the
    bottom of each page," along with relevant Latin passages
    and commentaries.

1964

JONES, EMRYS. "Introduction," in his edition of Henry Howard,
    Earl of Surrey: Poems. Clarendon Medieval and Tudor
    Series, edited by J. A. W. Bennett. London: Oxford Uni-
    versity Press, pp. xi-xxv.

The quality and significance of Surrey's poetry is best
understood through its relationship to the new approach to
the formal qualities of Latin diction, syntax, quantity,
number, and rhythmical balance fostered by the early humanists. And because it is likely that Latin, rather than
Italian, poetry represented the "main formative influence
in his literary development," his connection with the
humanists is best illustrated through his Aeneid translations, where, faithful to Virgil's example, he bases his
structural unit not on the poetic line, but on "phrasal
shapes and patterns." While his fidelity to the Latin
sometimes produces awkward and overly-compressed English
idiom, "pure verbality," or "loss of ordinary vitality,"
it accomplishes humanist elegance in the more oratorical
passages and, particularly, in single lines.

His other poetry shows the influence of the neoclassical
bias of the Aeneid translations: the Petrarchan poems are
of interest "not as love poems but (to use the term in no
very disparaging sense) as performances in elocution"; and
his best original poems "are those of a man who has
studied Latin poetry in the neoclassical way." His poetry
is thus of more historical than intrinsic worth.

1   TUCKER, MELVIN. "California MS. AC 523, Formerly Phillipps
    MS. 3841." N&Q, 209, n.s. 11, no. 10 (October), 374-376.
        The MS., long considered lost, contains information
    about the young Surrey's daily life. It was used by Nott
    [WS 1816.1], the editors of the Aldine edition [S 1831],
    and Bapst [S 1891]. It also provides insight into John
    Skelton's relationship with the Howard family.

2   WILLIAMS, NEVILLE. "Kenninghall Palace (1538-1547)," in his
    Thomas Howard Fourth Duke of Norfolk. London: Barrie and
    Rockliff, 1-22.
        Brief discussion of Surrey's life, character and death
    in a biography of his son.

1965

ELLIOT, A. H. Review of F[lorence] H. Ridley, ed., The
    "Aeneid of Henry Howard Earl of Surrey [S 1963.2]. RES,
    n.s. 16, no. 61, 106.
        The italicizing of words and phrases indicating Sur-
    rey's dependence on Douglas is "nonsensical" and "mis-
    leading." In fact, Douglas' influence on Surrey is not
    nearly as pervasive as the large number of verbal paral-
    lels indicates. The English poet "remained almost immune

1965

from Douglas's style," regularly borrowing his words, but
just as regularly restoring the line "to Virgil's cadence."
Perhaps Surrey's major achievement in the translations
lies in his having recaptured Virgil's "quietness."

1 HUTTAR, CHARLES A. "Poems by Surrey and Others in a Printed
Miscellany Circa 1550." EM, 16: 9-18.
    The miscellany, entitled Certayne Chapters of the
prouerbes of Sālomon drawen into metre by Thomas sterneholde... and existing in a single copy in the British
Museum (STC 2760), contains three chapters of Surrey's
Ecclesiastes paraphrases and his paraphrase of Psalm 88.
In addition, it contains versions of Psalms 31 and 51 that
resemble Surrey's other Biblical paraphrases in style,
theme, and spirit. Thus the book provides not only "the
earliest substantial body of Surrey's verse in print and,
apart from Book IV of his Aeneid, the largest publication
of Surrey's verse before Tottel," but two additions to his
canon as well.

2 MUIR, KENNETH. Review of Emrys Jones, ed., Henry Howard,
Earl of Surrey: Poems [S 1964]. MLR, 60, no. 2 (April),
244-245.
    The introduction is "more illuminating" than the criti-
cism of Surrey by Warton [WS 1781], Nott [WS 1816.1],
C. S. Lewis [WS 1954], and Maurice Evans [WS 1967.1], and
it is "particularly good" in its comparison between the
Aeneid translations of Surrey and Gavin Douglas. The
edition is "disappointing," however, because it omits
seven poems and provides silent emendations, and because
its source for poems from BM Add. MS. 28635 "seems to be
derived from the Arundel MS. itself or from Miss Hughey's
careful transcript" [WS 1960.2].

3 MUMFORD, IVY L. "Italian Aspects of Surrey's Lyrics." EM,
16: 19-36.
    Scholars have overemphasized Surrey's contributions to
the English lyric and his relation to Italian poetic
sources because of his traditional association with
Tottel's Miscellany, the popularity of which obscured
from the beginning his one certain "metrical innovation,"
the blank verse of his Aeneid translations. In fact,
compared to Wyatt, Surrey wrote proportionately few genuine lyrics, and of those, only seven (five of which are
sonnets) show the direct influence of Italian sources.
Even in the sonnets one finds sufficient departures in
imagery, emphasis, and form to suggest that "it is the
Petrarchan spirit, rather than Petrarch in translation,
which characterizes Surrey's verse."

4   THOMSON, PATRICIA. "Firenzuola, Surrey, and Watson." RN,
    18, no. 4 (Winter), 295-298.
        Surrey's "Geve place ye louers" shows "several distinct
    likenesses" to Agnolo Firenzuola's "Deh le mie belle donne
    amorose," suggesting that he had read the Italian poem in
    manuscript. However, he does not incorporate Firenzuola's
    images from nature, choosing instead the familiar topic
    which pictures the subject as Nature's masterpiece, and
    his persona's stance is more aggressive. Thomas Watson's
    Passion xxxiv, from the Hekatompathia, was probably influ-
    enced by both poems, although Watson acknowledges only
    Firenzuola's.

                          1966

    CHALKER, JOHN. Review of Emrys Jones, ed., Henry Howard,
        Earl of Surrey: Poems [S 1964]. SN, 38: 154-155.
            Jones' Introduction "vindicates Thomas Warton's pro-
        nouncement that he [Surrey] was 'the first English classi-
        cal poet' [WS 1781], and convincingly demonstrates the
        poet's interest in syntactic patterning and his verbal
        sensitivity." The edition "fills a distinct need" because
        of the inaccessibility of Padelford's [S 1920.1, 1928,
        1966.1].

1   PADELFORD, FREDERICK MORGAN. "Introduction," in his edition
        of The Poems of Henry Howard Earl of Surrey. Revised
        edition. University of Washington Publications[:] Lan-
        guage and Literature, Vol. 5. New York: Haskell House,
        3-55.
            Reprint of S 1928.

2   THOMSON, PATRICIA. Review of Emrys Jones, ed., Henry Howard,
        Earl of Surrey: Poems [S 1964]. N&Q, 211, n.s. 13,
        no. 1 (January), 33-34.
            "This is an almost complete edition of Surrey's poems,"
        more accurate than Padelford's [S 1920.1, 1928, 1966.1],
        but with some misprints. Its main contribution lies in
        Jones' "valuable re-emphasis on the neoclassical and
        humanistic elements in the poetry," particularly in the
        Aeneid translations, which he shows to be "more Virgilian
        than Douglas's" as well as more compressed and varied.
        Because he dates the translations earlier than Ridley
        [S 1963.2], Jones sees them as a more significant part of
        Surrey's development and uninfluenced by the Italian
        translations of Ippolito de' Medici and Molza. This,

1966

together with the question of the influence of the Vir-
gillian commentaries on Surrey, is still open to debate.

3   VERHOEFF, A.   Review of Emrys Jones, ed., Henry Howard, Earl
of Surrey: Poems [S 1964].   Neophilologus, 50: 203-204.
The critical notes to the edition are often irrelevant
and the introduction, a "random anthology of critical
comments" that are often misleading, would have been more
valuable if it had discussed "the development of critical
opinion about Surrey's work."

1968

MATHEW, T. C.   "Surrey's 'Prisoned in Windsor, He Recounteth
His Pleasure There Passed,' 7."   Explicator, 27, no. 2
(October), item 11.
"'The Maiden's tower'" referred to in "So cruel prison"
was probably a place from which the ladies of Windsor
Castle watched the games played by the young men. [Uses
Nott's edition (WS 1816.1).]

1969

HARRIS, WILLIAM O.   "'Love That Doth Raine': Surrey's Creative Imitation."   MP, 66, no. 4 (May), 298-305.
Modern comparisons between Wyatt's translation of Petarch's "Amor, che nel pensier mio vive e regna" and Surrey's have often applied "inconsistent criteria" in order
to demonstrate the superiority of the former, failing to
consider the possibility that the different effects in
Surrey's poem "may result...from quite different, but
equally valid, purposes."   Explication of Surrey's version
shows that he provides the original with a "historical
dimension" that forms the basis for a dramatic conflict
between the real action of the lady and the metaphorical
response of personified Love, a conflict that, in focusing
specifically and exclusively on the dilemma of the persona, "recreates that [larger] conflict between the inner
and outer existences of the passion-driven man."   That
focus is then echoed in a syntactical division into two
tercets that subordinates Surrey's standard quatraincouplet
rhyme scheme and concludes the sonnet not with the quiet
surrender of the persona, as in Petrarch and Wyatt, but
with the objectification of "that moment of psychological
reality when a lover chooses...the senses over the reason,

          although clearly aware of the implications of such a
choice, the ceaseless betrayals and tyrannies of the
flesh."

1   JENTOFT, CLYDE WILLIARD. "Rhetoric and Structure in the
Poetry of Henry Howard, Earl of Surrey." Ph.D. dissertation, Ohio State, 235 pp.
        Examines the influence of traditional rhetorical patterns on selected Surrey poems: finds that four poems
("O happy dames," "Good ladies," "Geue place ye louers,"
and "London") reflect the structure of the classifical
oration; sees in the elegies on Wyatt, Norfolk, and Richmond a reflection of the praise-lament-consolation pattern
recommended for such poems by sixteenth-century and classical theorists; and suggests that Surrey's use of larger
rhetorical patterns helps to explain the differences
between his Petrarchan poems and their originals. Finally, the examination notes four characteristic qualities in
Surrey's verse: (1) a tendency toward "generalized opening statement"; (2) a "sense of dramatic situation"; (3)
economy of expression; and (4) associative but logically
connected imagery. [Includes transcripts of poems discussed. See also S 1973, 1976.]

1970

PRATT, SAMUEL M. "Surrey and the Fair Geraldine: A Review
and a Discovery." CLJ, no. 10 (Winter), pp. 35-39.
        Surveys accounts of the dubious Surrey-Elizabeth Fitzgerald relationship and reports the existence of one
heretofore unknown: A Brief Memoir of the Lady Elizabeth
Fitzgerald Known as the Fair Geraldine (1874), by James
Graves, which rejects the reality of the relationship well
before it had been questioned by others.

1971

MASON, H. A. "The First Two Printed Texts of Surrey's
Poems." TLS, no. 3, 614 (June 4), p. 656.
        Huttar's discovery [S 1965.1] of an early printed version of Surrey's versification of Campensis' paraphrases
of Ecclesiastes and Psalm 88 failed to note "another,
possibly earlier," edition (STC 12634) which contains
versions of Surrey's Ecclesiastes purloined by John Hall
from a "corrected version" of the earlier one. The text
based on both printed versions provides "several readings

1971

which an editor might ponder and one or two which he would
certainly adopt," but on the whole it demonstrates that
the two main sources of the poems, Add. MSS. 36529 and
28635, were edited only slightly by the original owners,
the Haringtons. Collation of the versions of Psalm 88
and the texts discovered by Huttar leads to the same
conclusion.

1973

JENTOFT, C[LYDE] W[ILLARD]. "Surrey's Four 'Orations' and
the Influence of Rhetoric on Dramatic Effect." PLL, 9,
no. 3 (Summer), 250-262.
  Examination of Surrey's use of classical rhetorical
patterns in "O Happy dames," "Good Ladies," "Geue place
ye louers," and "London" reveals how his poetry "demonstrates more clearly than most the intimate relationship
between the theory and practice of composition in the
sixteenth century" and also counters the modern dismissal
of his verse as lacking in drama and "'feeling.'" Specifically, all four poems follow in different ways the
structure of the classical oration; but Surrey mitigates
that traditional influence with alterations that provide
the poems with imaginary contexts, recognizable personas
and audiences, and irony, indicating that they might
properly be termed "'dramatic orations.'"

1   TROMLEY, FREDERICK B. "Two Tudor Epitaphs: Surrey on Wyatt;
Baldwin on Edward VI." AN&Q, 12, no. 2 (October), 24-25.
  Verbal echoes in Baldwin's poem indicate that he was
heavily indebted to Surrey's. However, he fails to reproduce Surrey's "concision, poise, and complexity," his
"balanced and antithetical structure," his "solemn movement," and his "tone of considered assessment." Thus
Surrey's "is one of the best poems of the mid-16th century, while Baldwin's is a good example of what is wrong
with the poetry of the time."

1974

BAWCUTT, PRISCILLA. "Douglas and Surrey: Translators of
Virgil." E&S, 27: 52-67.
  The differences between Douglas' Eneados and Surrey's
Aeneid epitomizes the "contrast between the translator as
teacher and expositor...and the translator as courtly poet."
Comparison indicates the truth of the standard view of their

differences--"'Douglas is diffuse, Surrey terse'"--but the
differences go deeper: Surrey was attempting to "'imitate'
some of the more striking formal qualities of Virgil's poetry" in his blank verse, his unfinished lines and his Virgilian verse paragraphs, whereas "Douglas was rarely a stylistic innovator," as indicated by his traditional couplets
and narrative style. But Douglas was also aiming at scholarly completeness, and thus often provided what amounts to
"translation and running commentary, all in one," in an effort at conveying Virgil's true meaning. Surrey's best
lines thus bring out Virgil's "polished surface, while those
of Douglas go beneath that surface to articulate "something
of Virgil's mysterious latencies of feeling." On the whole,
Douglas' is the "more successful" translation.

1   DAVIS, WALTER R. "Contexts in Surrey's Poetry." _ELR_, 4,
     no. 1 (Winter), 40-55.
         Surrey's classicism--his "concern for wholeness, for
     singleness of effect"--is exemplified by the organic re-
     lationship he often establishes between personal experi-
     ence and its larger contexts, spatial, temporal, social,
     political and literary. In the poems of natural descrip-
     tion he is "less interested in metaphor, in projecting the
     self onto nature, than in seeing the self in _relation_ to
     nature." This neoclassical tendency toward simile rather
     than metaphor is also apparent in poems alluding to clas-
     sical personages and events, which both redefine the pres-
     ent in terms of the past and the past in terms of the
     present. In poems like "Wrapt in my carelesse cloke" and
     "Gyrtt in my giltlesse gowne" his context is social; in
     "O happy dames" he combines the natural and the social.
     But it is in his elegies that he most clearly fuses "broad
     objectivity with intense personal feeling," merging larger
     temporal, social, and political contexts with the form and
     sentiments of the literary love tradition in "Norfolk
     sprang thee," "So crewell prison," and "Dyvers thy death."

1975

RUDICK, MICHAEL. "Two Notes on Surrey's Psalms." _N&Q_, 220,
     n.s. 22, no. 7 (July), 291-294.
         STC 22134, _Certayne Psalmes select out of the Psalter
     of Dauid_...(1553), by Francis Seager, contains paraphrases
     of Psalms 88, 31, and 51 that first appeared in Stern-
     hold's _Certayn Chapters of the prouerbes of Saloman_ (STC
     2760). All three paraphrases have been ascribed to Sur-
     rey; thus Seager's appropriation of them "presents us with

1975

a plain case of literary plagiarism," and his revisions
of them show his well-known ineptness.

Seven corrections made over erasures in the Arundel
Harington Manuscript version of Surrey's paraphrase of
Psalm 88 suggest the likelihood of "a substantive copy of
Psalm 88 no longer extant." None of the corrections ap-
pear in Add. MS. 36529; three of them are consistent with
readings in Sternhold's <u>Certayn Chapters</u>.

1976

JENTOFT, C[LYDE] W[ILLARD]. "Surrey's Five Elegies: Rhetoric, Structure, and the Poetry of Praise." <u>PMLA</u>, 91, no. 1
(January), 23-32.

Surrey's five "personal elegies" demonstrate his
sophisticated use of traditional rhetorical patterns,
specifically his manipulation of the two types of structure for epideictic praise, that focusing on the subject's
life, and that emphasizing his virtues. His sonnet on
Thomas Clere follows the first type, and the <u>excellent
Epitaffe</u> on Wyatt adheres closely to the second, but even
in these pieces Surrey departs from convention when it
suits his larger rhetorical and poetic purposes. Individual modifications are even more apparent in his three less
public tributes: the two sonnets on Wyatt, "Dyvers thy
death" and "In the rude age," serve as sequels to the
satiric ending of the <u>Epitaffe</u>, and "So crewell prison"
extends personal grief over the death of the Earl of Richmond to the level of an <u>ubi sunt</u> lament for the passing
of an age. The elegies illustrate, finally, that the
successful manipulation of convention by a good Tudor
poet is itself a kind of originality.

1   RICHARDSON, DAVID A[NTHONY]. "Humanistic Intent in Surrey's
<u>Aeneid</u>." <u>ELR</u>, 6, no. 2 (Spring), 204-219.

Surrey's <u>Aeneid</u> translations, despite their defects,
represent a "humanistic milestone" because they render
more faithfully than heretofore realized the form and
style of the original. By capturing the rhythmic sweep
and freedom of Virgil's verse paragraphs, the compressed,
abstract, non-colloquial dignity of his diction, and the
connotative power of his metaphors, Surrey successfully
reproduces his quintessential spirit, and, in contrast to
Douglas' <u>Eneados</u>, effects a "radical break with the forms
and language of medieval tradition." This leads to the

conclusion that Surrey's humanism is Erasmian rather than
didactic or mechanical, and justifies his traditional
reputation as "the first English classical poet."

1977

NATHAN, LEONARD. "The Course of the Particular: Surrey's
Epitaph on Thomas Clere and the Fifteenth-Century Lyric
Tradition." SEL, 17, no. 1 (Winter), 3-12.
   "Norfolk sprang thee" illustrates that Surrey as well
as Wyatt was responsible for a "revolutionary" departure
from the courtly subjects, the pathetic and hierarchical
attitudes, the accumulative, linear, and static structure,
and the aureate style of the simplistic fifteenth-century
lyric. Rather than presenting a formulaic catalogue ac-
cumulating around an abstract ideal, Surrey presents in
the poem an "experiential" approach to his subject that
communicates the "human and humane particularity" of
Clere's life through "complex syntax," "tonal variety and
depth," "a good range of pitch and volume"--in short,
through "a distinctive voice, one which it is possible to
imagine speaking." He thus departs from the sense of
social hierarchy apparent in his tributes to Wyatt as well
as from the accumulative formula of "The soote season,"
and succeeds in writing "one of the few poems before the
Elizabethan era that offers a sense of an authentic personal life."

Writings about Wyatt and Surrey

1557

TOTTEL, RICHARD (?). "The Printer to the Reader," in his
edition of SONGES AND SONETTES, written by the ryght
honorable Lorde Henry Haward late Earle of Surrey, and
other. London: Richard Tottel, sig. Alv.
That the English language is equal in eloquence to
Latin and Italian is demonstrated by "the honorable stile
of the noble earle of Surrey, and the weightinesse of the
depewitted sir Thomas Wyat the elders verse." [From
WS 1929.]

1570

ASCHAM, ROGER. "Of Imitation," in his The Scholemaster.
London: John Daye [STC 832].
Gives credit to Wyatt and Surrey, among others, for
their imitation of the ancients, but chastises them for
following "rather the Gothes in Ryming than the Greekes in
true [quantitative] versifying." Praises Surrey for having "auoyded the fault of Ryming" in Book IV of his Aeneid,
but finds his lines also lacking in "trew quantity of
sillables." [From ECE, I, 30, 32.]

1576(?)

A book of songs and sonetts, with longe discoorses sett with
them, of the chylds lyfe, togyther with A yoong mans lyfe,
and entring into the old mans lyfe. devysed and written
with A new Orthografye by Thomas Whythorne, gent.
Whythorne mentions copying out poems by Wyatt, Surrey,
and William More for his master, John Heywood. Some of
Whythorne's early verses were influenced by Surrey, Thomas
Sternhold and, especially, Wyatt. [From The Autobiography
of Thomas Whythorne, ed. James M. Osborn. Oxford: Clarendon Press, 1961, pp. liv, 14, 44.]

121

1589

PUTTENHAM, GEORGE. The Arte of English Poesie. Contriued
into three Bookes: The first of Poets and Poesie, the
second of Proportion, the third of Ornament. London:
printed by Richard Field.
    Early commentary on Wyatt and Surrey that hails them
as "the first reformers of our English meetre and stile"
for having "pollished our rude & homely maner" after
traveling to Italy and discovering Petrarch. Sees "very
little differēce" between the two English poets: "their
conceits were loftie, their stiles stately, their conuey-
ance cleanely, their termes proper, their meetre sweete
and well proportioned, in all imitating very naturally
and studiously their Maister Francis Petrarcha." Illustrates various rhetorical/poetic principles and practices
with extracts from their poetry. [From The Arte of
English Poesie by George Puttenham, ed. Gladys Doidge
Willcock and Alice Walker. Cambridge: Cambridge University Press, 1936, passim.]

1591

HARINGTON, SIR JOHN. "A Preface, or rather a Briefe Apologie
of Poetrie, and of the Author and Translator," in his
translation of Orlando Furioso in English heroical verse.
London: printed by R[ichard?] Field [STC 746].
    Observes that Wyatt and Surrey, as translators of
Italian, "are yet called the first refiners of the English
tong" in a discussion of the virtues of translation.
[From ECE, I, 219.]

1598

MERES, FRANCIS. Palladis tamia, Wits treasury being the
second part of Wits Commonwealth. London: printed by
P. Short for C. Burbie [STC 17834].
    Includes Wyatt and Surrey in a list of those who "are
the most passionate among vs to bewaile and bemoane the
perplexities of loue," and praises Surrey's Aeneid, Book
IV. [From ECE, II, 320-321.]

1606

FLETCHER, ROBERT. The Nine English Worthies: Or, Famous and Worthy Princes of England, being All of one name....
London: printed by H.L. for John Harrison the yonger, p. 51.
Laments not having the "learned pen" of "Princely Surrey" or Wyatt to pay proper tribute to Prince Henry.

1618(?)

BOLTON, EDMUND. Hypercritica: or A Rule of Judgement, for writing or reading our History's.
The "Songs and Sonnets" of Wyatt and Surrey, despite their "Noble, Courtly, and Lustrous English," are but "Foils and Sportives" to Surrey's Aeneid. [From CESC, I, 111.]

1622

PEACHAM, HENRY. "Of Poetrie," in his The Compleat Gentleman.
London: printed by W. Stansby (?) for F. Constable [STC 19502].
Praises the "excellent facultie in Poesie" in the "Songs and Sonnets" of Wyatt and Surrey. [From CESC, I, 133.]

1641

JONSON, BEN. Timber: or, Discoveries; Made Vpon Men and Matter: As They have flow'd out of his daily Reading; or had their refluxe to his peculiar Notion of the Times.
Mentions Wyatt and Surrey, among others, as writers who "were for their times admirable." [From Ben Jonson, eds. C. H. Herford Percy and Evelyn Simpson. Vol. 8. Oxford: Clarendon Press, 1947, 591.]

1679

[LLOYD, DAVID]. State-Worthies. Or, the Statesmen and Favourites of England Since the Reformation. Second edition. London: printed for Peter Parker, pp. 76-81, 134.

1679

Includes a brief account of Wyatt's life and character.
Mentions Surrey's execution in an account of his father,
the Duke of Norfolk.

1687

WINSTANLEY, WILLIAM. The Lives of the Most Famous English
   Poets. London: printed by H. Clark for Samuel Manship.
   Brief biographies of both poets. Follows Nashe's
"Geraldine" myth [S 1594] for Surrey. [From facsimile,
Gainesville, Florida: Scholars Facsimiles & Reprints,
1963, pp. 49-58.]

1691

À WOOD, ANTHONY. Athenae Oxonienses: An Exact History of All
   The Writers And Bishops Who Have Had Their Education In The
   University of Oxford To Which Are Added The Fasti or Annals
   of the Said University. London: printed for Tho. Bennet
   [STC 3382].
   Brief biographies of Wyatt and Surrey. Retains the view
that both went to Italy, and repeats the Nashe account
[S 1594] of Surrey and "Geraldine." [From a facsimile of
the London edition of 1813. Vol. 1. New York and London:
Johnson Reprint Corp., 1967, cols. 124-129, 153-161.]

1723

[GILES, JACOB]. The Poetical Register: or, the Lives and
   Characters of All the English Poets. With an Account of
   their Writings. Vol. 1. London: printed by A. Bettes-
worth, W. Taylor, and J. Batley for J. Wyatt, C. Rivington,
E. Bell, W. Meadows, J. Pemberton, and J. Hooke, pp. 76-
78, 229-230.
   Includes brief accounts of the lives and literary
accomplishments of Wyatt and Surrey.

1781

WARTON, THOMAS. The History of English Poetry, From the Close
   of the Eleventh to the Commencement of the Eighteenth
   Century. Vol. 3. London: printed for J. Dodsley, J.
Walter, J. Robson, G. Robinson, J. Bew, and Messrs.
Fletcher, pp. 1-40.

Surrey's sonnets have "nothing of that metaphysical cast which marks the Italian poets"; his "sentiments are for the most part natural and unaffected...[and] unembarrassed by learned allusions or elaborate conceits." "Give place, ye Lovers" exemplifies the correctness, the polish, and the musical nature of his versification, which almost matches "the ease and gallantry of Waller." The Wyatt epitaph contains "nervous and manly quatraines" and "The great Macedon" exemplifies the "great dignity and propriety" of his verse. He also wrote successfully of nature in "The soote season," and produced the first English blank verse in his <u>Aeneid</u>, "a noble attempt to break the bondage of rhyme." His Biblical translations "shew that he was a friend to the reformation." He was "the first English classical poet." [Includes biographical sketch, with a lengthy account of Surrey's relationship with "Geraldine."]

Although Wyatt cooperated with Surrey in correcting "the roughness of our poetic style," he is inferior to Surrey "in harmony of numbers, perspicuity of expression, and facility of phraseology" as well as in "elegance of sentiment,...nature and sensibility." His style is "not intelligible," his versification "negligent." His imitation of Italian poets resulted in "prolix and intricate comparisons, and unnatural allusions." While "My Lute awake" possesses "lyric sweetness," Wyat's main strength "was of the moral and didactic species," as exemplified by the excellence of his Satires. [Includes short account of Wyatt's death, placing it in 1541.]

1810

CHALMERS, ALEXANDER. "The Life of Henry Howard, Earl of Surrey" and "The Life of Sir Thomas Wyatt," in his edition of <u>The Works of the English Poets from Chaucer to Cowper</u>. Vol. 2. London: printed for J. Johnson, et al.; Cambridge: printed for Deighton & Son; New York: printed for Wilson & Son, pp. 311-322, 361-367.

Surveys earlier biographies of Surrey, finding the "Geraldine" myth improbable. Sees Surrey's "<u>songs and sonnets</u>" as "of the elegiac strain," his scriptural paraphrases as consolatory exercises of his latter years. Quotes liberally from Warton [WS 1781], agreeing with his assessment that the paraphrases indicate Surrey's Protestant leanings.

1810

      Reports that Wyatt and Surrey were friends. Agrees
with Warton's view of Wyatt, finding him inferior to Surrey "in all respects," but noting his importance as
England's "first moral satirist," one who follows "the
true spirit of the didactic muse."

<u>1816</u>

ANON. Review of George Frederick Nott, ed., <u>The Works of</u>
    <u>Henry Howard Earl of Surrey and of Sir Thomas Wyatt the</u>
    <u>Elder</u> [WS 1816.1]. <u>Edinburgh Review</u>, 27, no. 54 (Decem-
    ber), 390-422.
      Finds the volume on Surrey to be at least worthwhile,
but dismisses the usefulness of the volume on Wyatt because, while Wyatt "was a man of wit, a shrewd observer, a
subtle politician..., in no true sense of the word, was he
a <u>poet</u>." Goes on to discuss Nott's biography, criticism
and notes on Surrey exclusively, with no further mention
of Wyatt. Sees Surrey as "a light in a dark age" between
Chaucer and the Elizabethans.

1 NOTT, GEO[RGE] FRED[ERICK]. "A Dissertation on the State of
    English Poetry Before the Sixteenth Century" and "An Essay
    on Wyatt's Poems," in his edition of <u>The Works of Henry</u>
    <u>Howard Earl of Surrey and of Sir Thomas Wyatt the Elder</u>.
    2 vols. London: printed by T. Bensley for Longman, Hurst,
    Rees, Orme, and Brown, 1, cxxxvii-clxxxvi, 2, cxv-clxviii.
      English versification before Surrey's time was deca-
syllabic but not iambic, and rhythmical rather than metrical; as such, it "admitted of redundant and defective
lines," and it became unsatisfactory when poetry ceased to
be sung and began to be read. Surrey, the first to per-
ceive this problem, invented a new system of versification
marked by metrical rather than rhythmical principles, and
composed of ten syllables divided into "five equal Iambic
feet" with varied pauses--thus establishing the system
adopted and employed "by our standard writers, with hardly
any variation, ever since." Wyatt's versification, on the
other hand, is principally rhythmical.
      "Wyatt, as a poet, can lay little claim to originality":
his works are virtually all imitations or translations.
His sonnets fail because they imitate Petrarch's worst
examples and because they are "uniformly harsh and unmelo-
dious." His rondeaux are ill-fitted to "solemn complaint."
His epigrams are influenced by the extravagant conceits
of Serafino, but two of them, "Tagus farewell!" and "A
face that should content me wondrous well," are excellent.

His Psalms are plagued by "crabbed and inharmonious" versification and "unequal" language based on French pronunciation, although they display learning and Christian
feeling. His Satires, on the other hand, are "unquestion-
ably his happiest and most finished productions," unappre-
ciated by his contemporaries because they are so far
advanced. And his prose letters and his Defence show him
to be "the first English writer...to have aimed at anything
like legitimate style in prose." Also praiseworthy are his
"amatory odes," which resemble more closely the Spanish
style than either the French or Italian, and which owe
their excellence to their naturalness: "they were composed
probably on the impulse of the moment." In general,
Wyatt's early poems resemble the versification of Hawes
and Barclay, but his later ones show that he eventually
learned the "Iambic form" from Surrey. Throughout his
career, however, his verse is "disfigured by...the old
rhythmical system" and by "a far greater number of antiquated words, and obsolete forms of speech" than Surrey's.
   Finally, general comparisons between the two reveal that
Wyatt had "a deeper and a more accurate penetration into
the characters of men," that Surrey was a better observer
of nature, more universal in his observation, and generally
superior in taste and propriety.
   [Volume 1 (1815) is devoted to Surrey, Volume 2 (1816)
to Wyatt; includes biographies, letters, notes, indices,
appendices, glossaries, collation of Surrey's Aeneid with
Douglas' Eneados, "Memoirs of the Earl of Northhampton,"
contents of the "Harington" and Devonshire MSS.]

1820

COLLIER, J[OHN] PAYNE. "The Second Conversation," in his The
   Poetical Decameron, or Ten Conversations on English Poets
   and Poetry, Particularly of the Reigns of Elizabeth and
   James I. Edinburgh: Archibald Constable & Co.; London:
   Hurst, Robinson, and Co., pp. 77-145.
      Surrey and Wyatt are discussed in a conversation about
   blank verse. Also, errors in Nott's edition [W 1816.1]
   are pointed out.

1887

SAINTSBURY, GEORGE. "From Tottel's 'Miscellany' to Spenser,"
   in his A History of Elizabethan Literature. Vol. 2.
   London: Macmillan, pp. 1-8.

1887

Although Surrey was Wyatt's disciple, he "is a far superior artist." Wyatt is generally awkward.

1889

BROOKS, SARAH W. "Some Predecessors of Spenser." Poet-Lore, 1, no. 5, 214-223.
    The poetry of Surrey ["Thomas Howard"] is "remarkable for its flowing melody, correctness of style, and purity of expression," but that of Wyatt has "more depth of sentiment as well as more force."

*1 NAGEL, HEINRICH. Sir Thomas Wyatt und Henry Howard, Earl of Surrey.
    Cited in S 1920.1. [In German.]

1890

KOEPPEL, EMIL. "Studien zur Geschichte des englischen Petrarchismus im sechzehnten Jahrhundert." Romanische Forschungen, 5: 65-86.
    Lists poems in Tottel's Miscellany by Wyatt and Surrey that are translations or adaptations of Petrarch, and lists with them the Petrarchan originals; also includes Wyatt's poems from Serafino with their originals. Annotates the individual poems, citing liberally from Nott's comments [WS 1816.1]. Goes on (pp. 87-97) to discuss "Uncertain Authors" and Sidney. [In German.]

1897

COURTHOPE, W. J. "Sir Thomas Wyatt: Originality of Thought: Imitation of Foreign Models of Expression" and "The Earl of Surrey: Decay of Chivalry: Reform of Poetical Diction and Versification," in his A History of English Poetry. Vol 2: The Renaissance and the Reformation: Influence of the Court and the Universities. London and New York: Macmillan, pp. 44-67, 68-101.
    Wyatt's poetry is best when untrammeled by foreign influences. His best sonnets and epigrams are those least influenced by their models, when his individual attitude, his "manliness," is most distinct. His best poems in general are those influenced by music and written in simple, native forms. His Satires and Psalms, though also influenced by foreign models, are also best when his

individuality comes through, particularly in those that
show his Protestant sympathies. In his poetry, "matter
prevails over form"; unfortunately, "his art was not equal
to his imagination."

Surrey, without Wyatt's "vehement individuality," expresses in his poetry the lament for a decaying chivalric
aristocracy. He is more successful than Wyatt at natural-
izing foreign ideas because of his style, which is his
"predominant poetical virtue," and is thus of more historical significance. His love poems follow closely the
matter and form of Courtly Love and Petrarch, eschewing
originality in favor of the eloquent expression of their
commonplaces. His reform of the sonnet demonstrates his
understanding not only of Petrarch but of the principles
of English prosody that go back to Chaucer. His improvements include the development of iambic decasyllables, the
harmonious use of the rhythmical pause, the "rejection of
weak syllables for the purposes of rhyme," blank verse,
and the refinement of "poetical diction." [Includes
biographies.]

1899

ALDEN, RAYMOND MACDONALD. The Rise of Formal Satire in
England Under Classical Influence. University of Pennsylvania Series in Philology, Literature and Archaeology,
Vol. 7, No. 2. Philadelphia: Published for the University of Pennsylvania, pp. 52-60.

Wyatt's reputation as "'the first polished English
satirist'" represents the prevailing opinion: his style
is "compact but smooth, and noticeably urbane," epistolary, and Horatian in its "ease and naturalness." His
three Satires betray his familiarity with Horace and
Persius, but his main source was Alamanni, from whom he
learned terza rima, the epistolary form, and the idea of
"adapting the classical method to the conditions of his
own time and place." Surrey's "London has thow accused
me" is a satire in name only.

1901

HANSCOM, ELIZABETH DEERING. "The Sonnet Forms of Wyatt and
Surrey." MLN, 16, no. 5 (May), 137-140.

While both poets divide their sonnets into three
quatrains and a couplet and use run-on lines between
metrical divisions, they differ in ways that demonstrate

1901

Surrey's formal superiority: Wyatt normally uses Petrarch's enclosed rhyme, Surrey the alternating rhyme that
resembles the strambotti and anticipates Elizabethan practice; furthermore, Wyatt is guilty of several "errors"--
--rhyming by grammatical/inflectional endings, rhyming
final vowels "without regard to preceding consonants,"
rhyming "words with different accents," and using feminine
rhyme--not normally commited by Surrey. Also, while both
alter the iambic pattern, particularly with initial tro-
chees, Surrey does so more logically and consistently.

1 SEGRE, CARLO. "Due Petrarchisti del Secolo XVI." Nuova
   Antologia di Scienze ed Arti, 4th ser., 96 (Novembre-
   Dicembre), 45-67, 256-277.
      Wyatt found that Italian poetry answered his needs
   better than its English counterpart. Unfortunately he
   chose to imitate contemporary Petrarchism, which was ornament without passion, or the worst, most affectatious and
   conceited, examples of Petrarch. However, he was essentially a serious and practically minded English Petrarchan,
   one who could reconcile the laws of honor and duty with
   the poetic muse. He was the first English poet to use
   terza rima, ottava rima and (unfortunately) the strambotto.
   Surrey, who learned Italian culture from John Clerke and
   the French court, continued Wyatt's developmentof Petarchan culture in England. However, he was an Italian,
   not an English, Petrarchan: his love poetry is conventional, and he rivaled the Italians in artificiality.
   His importance lay in his understanding of iambic rhythm,
   pauses and rhyme, and in bringing verso sciolto (Italian
   blank verse) to England. Both he and Wyatt demonstrate
   that poetry, like all artistic expression, is principally
   a matter of form. [Includes biographical matters, particularly the Wyatt-Anne Boleyn relationship (possible but
   not probable) and Surrey's education. In Italian.]

1902

EINSTEIN, LEWIS. "The Italian Influence in English Poetry,"
   in his The Italian Renaissance in England: Studies.
   Burt Franklin Research and Source Works Series, No. 26.
   New York: Burt. Franklin, pp. 321-330, 351-353.
      Wyatt and Surrey were "the first to make use in English
   of the new Italian poetic forms." However, their individual contributions were quite different. Wyatt was the
   innovator ("the father of modern English poetry"), but the
   deficiencies in the English language, together with his

rebellion against Petrarch's conceits and his inability to
reproduce Petrarchan sonnet structure, rhythm, and imagery,
caused his individual shortcomings. Surrey, who learned
his technique from Wyatt and others, was a better techni-
cian, and thus imported "the Italian artistic conscience,
the love of polish and style," and introduced innovative
forms: the English sonnet, blank verse, and terza rima.
Wyatt's introduction of classical satire to England was
also influenced by the Italians, as were the Biblical
paraphrases of both poets.

1903

ERSKINE, JOHN. The Elizabethan Lyric. New York: Columbia
University Press, pp. 71-78, passim.
Although Surrey is perhaps a better poet, Wyatt, as
"the earliest singer of the Elizabethan subjective lyric"
and as a writer of "art lyrics" ("songs meant to be en-
joyed without music"), is more important in the development of the lyric itself. Wyatt's love lyrics, unlike
his lighter poems, are too analytical and intellectual to
succeed as songs. Surrey "was a lyrist only in the sense
of being a poet of subjective expression, and he lacked
almost entirely the song-quality of words." He is dramatic, not personal, and the lyric quality of his sonnets
is the product of his quatrain organization rather than
intrinsic lyric capability.

1   WINTERMANTEL, EGON. Biographisches in den Gedichten von Sir
Thomas Wyatt und Henry Howard, Earl of Surrey. Furtwangen:
Wilhelm Kirchberg's Buchdruckerei, 81 pp.
A study of biographical elements in the poetry of Wyatt
and Surrey, specifically, Wyatt's relationship with Anne
Boleyn and Surrey's with "Geraldine." Discusses the historical relationships; theories about the significance of
the ladies to the poetry; their appearance in translations,
imitations, and revisions; poems that relate to the
ladies' lives; and provides the contents of all relevant
poems. Dates the Wyatt poems according to their postures
toward the lady, using Simonds' categories [W 1889]. Discusses the Surrey-Geraldine relationship in Nashe [S 1594],
Drayton [S 1619] and others. Concludes that the evidence
from the poems does not prove the authenticity of a real
love affair in either case. [In German.]

1905

LATHROP, H[ENRY] B[URROWES]. "The Sonnet Forms of Wyatt and
     Surrey." MP, 2, no. 4 (April), 463-470.
          Wyatt's sonnets in the Egerton and Devonshire MSS. all
     contain octave rhymes of abba/abba, and all but two con-
     tain sestets rhyming cdd/cee, evidence which suggests that
     he intended the sestet to be divided into two "terzets"
     rather than into a quatrain and couplet. Surrey's sonnets
     are, with one exception, in alternate rhymes with coup-
     lets. It is probable that Wyatt's departures from his
     normal practice are the result of mistakes or inferior
     Italian models, and that Surrey's rhyme-pattern derives
     from the strambotto.

1906

JUSSERAND, J. J. A Literary History of the English People.
     Vol 2, Part 2. New York and London: G. P. Putnam's Sons,
     The Knickerbocker Press, pp. 134-149.
          Wyatt is the most important contributor to Tottel's
     Miscellany; although his love poems are probably all
     imitations, he demonstrates his "gift of poetry" in those
     poems containing "a personal note"--the Satires, "Tagus,
     farewell," and some passages in the Psalm paraphrases.
     Surrey possesses the "same merits" as Wyatt, but "in a
     somewhat higher degree"--particularly in "So crewell
     prison" and his Aeneid translations, although the latter
     lack the "refined tact" of later blank verse.

1   PADELFORD, FREDERICK MORGAN. "The Relation of the 1812 and
       1815-16 Editions of Surrey and Wyatt." Anglia, 29: 256-
       270.
            Internal evidence reaffirms the traditional view that
       the 1812 edition, which exists in four copies without
       cover, title-page or preface in the British Museum, was
       originally prepared by John Nott, and that his work was
       incorporated without acknowledgment by his nephew, George
       Frederick Nott, for his edition [WS 1816.1]. The evidence
       documents "one of the most surprising cases of 'literary
       borrowing' in the history of our literature."

2   SAINTSBURY, GEORGE. "The Turn of the Tide--Italian Influ-
       ence," in his A History of English Prosody From the
       Twelfth Century to the Present Day. Vol. 1. London and
       New York: Macmillan, 303-317.

Though neither of them was a poet of "the first class,"
Wyatt and Surrey "heralded the Renaissance of English in
poetry." Wyatt, though "capricious" in accentuaton and
uncertain in rhyme because of the uncertain state of
English pronunciation, contributed to the development of
the English sonnet by adapting rhyme-royal stanzas to
sonnet structure; by adapting various Continental short
forms (madrigals, epigrams, octaves, rondeaux, and
"refrain-pieces"); by writing poulter's measure, which,
despite its "jog-trot" rhythm, linked literary and popular
verse; and by writing the "intertwined decasyllables" of
his Satires, which contributed to Surrey's blank verse.
Surrey, the pupil to Wyatt the "pioneer and master," was
better: his sonnets are "better phrased, more concen-
trated in general ordonnance, and, consequently, more
musical"; his poulter's measure and other line combina-
tions are smoother and more effective; and he produced
blank verse, which in his hands was rhythmically stiff
despite "metrical and grammatical overlapping," but which
lost its stiffness with Shakespeare.

1907

PADELFORD, FREDERICK MORGAN. "Introduction," in his edition
of Early Sixteenth Century Lyrics. Boston and London:
D. C. Heath & Co., pp. ix-lviii.
Wyatt's translations and imitations of Petrarch generally fail not only because he often selected Petrarch's
lesser poems for models, but also because his versions of
the better ones are marked by a failure to appreciate
their real virtues: in general, he ignores their "gra-
cious sweetness," "feeling for color," idealization of
the heroine, and feeling for nature in favor of subtle
conceits, "artificial antitheses," "factitious pictorial
allegory," "feeble personification" and "trite metaphor."
The same can be said of his poems inspired by the French.
In his best love poems, however, he penetrates beneath
the rhetorical and emotional artificiality and succeeds
in realizing experience in "simple, fervent, and sincere
language"; these poems read "like monologues snatched
from intense situations" and surpass Petrarch and the
other Italians. And his Satires excel in their combination of classical purity, "Christian feeling," and honest
realism.
Surrey, in contrast, "was in all respects a successful
pupil of Petrarch" without being slavishly imitative.
His Italianate verse is distinguished by "technique, care

1907

for form, clearness and compression, felicity of diction, and rhythmical ease"; it is also well organized and concise, and better than the Italians' in its treatment of nature, which was influenced by Chaucer. His best poems are occasional, and his translations of the Psalms are superior to Wyatt's.

1909

CHILD, HAROLD H. "The New English Poetry," in Renascence and Reformation. The Cambridge History of English Literature, Vol. 3, edited by A. W. Ward and A. R. Waller. New York: G. P. Putnam's Sons; Cambridge: University Press, 187-196, passim.

English prosody, confused and irregular after Chaucer, regained order with Wyatt's Italian sonnets, which provided the necessary corrective to the "vague thought, loose expression and irregular metre" of the Chaucerians. However, Wyatt's inclusion of the couplet (influenced, perhaps, by rhyme-royal) altered the Petrarchan form, and his metrical practice shows uncertainty in accent and rhythm--shortcomings due, probably, to the instability of English pronunciation and the faulty text of Tottel's Miscellany. Italian influence also led him to introduce the "personal note" into the conventional sentiments of Courtly Love, giving them a "genuineness and originality" that often "flies in the face of the slavery to the mistress prescribed in the code." His other lyrics, some of which represent his best work, express the same attitudes, but with a "sweetness, a dignity, a sincerity" that comes from the refrains and short stanzas of poems meant to be sung. His epigrams, consisting usually of "a single conceit or paradox," reflect Serafino's strambotti in form and classical authors in content. His Satires, in Alamanni's terza rima, express more fully his strong personal feelings, and their "ruggedness of form" looks forward to Donne and Marston. His Psalms, in the same form, are very free translations which he uses as "pretexts" for the communication of his own sentiments.

Surrey's poetry conforms consistently to the code of Courtly Love rather than expressing the manly independence of Wyatt, while his sonnets are more technically advanced, without Wyatt's roughness and archaisms. In thus improving on Wyatt, "he makes of the sonnet--what had never existed before in English poetry--a single symphonic effect." Even his poems in poulter's measure reveal that he was "a born poet, with a good ear and a knowledge of

134

the necessity of relating line to line and cadence to cadence." His Aeneid translations, probably influenced by Italian poetry, represent "his clearest title to fame" because of their later influence, and his own blank verse, "if a little stiff and too much inclined to make a break at the end of each line," nevertheless proves his ability. In "So cruell prison," perhaps his "best and sincerest" poem, he describes the world of decaying chivalry, which was the chief inspiration for both his life and his poetry.

1910

LEE, SIDNEY. "French Influence on English Literature," in his The French Renaissance in England. Oxford: Clarendon Press, pp. 109-126.
   Emphasis upon the Italian heritage of the verse of Wyatt and Surrey ignores the fact that both acquired much of that heritage in France, particularly through the work of the Florentine exile Luigi Alamanni, who influenced Surrey's blank verse and Wyatt's Satires and Penitential Psalms, as well as their sonnets. Furthermore, native French influence, particularly the work of Clement Marot, is observable in Wyatt's diverse stanzaic forms and rondeaux. Indeed, it can be observed that the link between early Tudor and early Elizabethan poetry is "largely of French texture."

1914

THOMPSON, GUY ANDREW. Elizabethan Criticism of Poetry. Menasha, Wisconsin: George Banta Publishing Co., passim.
   Cites numerous references to Wyatt and Surrey in the sixteenth century.

1917

CROSLAND, T. W. The English Sonnet. London: Martin Secker, pp. 125-128, passim.
   Wyatt and Surrey, along with Chaucer, "may be considered to have laid the technical foundations of modern English poetry," although their departures from Petrarch's rhyme-pattern make difficult the classification of their sonnets.

1918

1918

SHAFER, ROBERT. The English Ode to 1660: An Essay in Literary History.
Wyatt and Surrey did not write true "odes"; the term
was not used in English until forty years after Wyatt's
death. [From rpt., New York: Gordian Press, 1966, pp. 6,
36-42.]

1923

BULLOCK, WALTER L. "The Genesis of the English Sonnet Form."
PMLA, 38, no. 4 (December), 729-744.
Wyatt was the originator of three-quatrain-plus-couplet
form, and Surrey "gave it its final permanent shape by
relaxing and simplifying the type which Wyatt had adopted."
Wyatt found his model for the rhyme-pattern of the octave
in Petrarch, but for the quatrain-couplet form of the
sestet he very likely found his models in the Raccolta dei
Giunti, a collection of Italian lyrics published in 1527
that contains five sonnets with that division by Cino da
Pistoia and one with a variation on it by Guido Cavalcanti, and in the unpublished sonnets of Benedetto Varchi,
eight of which contain the same division with slight variations. [See also WS 1905.]

1925

WHIPPLE, T. K. 'The New Poetry and the Epigram,' in his
"Martial and the English Epigram from Sir Thomas Wyatt to
Ben Jonson." University of California Publications in
Modern Philology, 10, no. 4, 311-319.
Wyatt was the first and only English poet to cast
"Italian lyrics in the form of English epigrams." In
this he was influenced by Serafino's strambotti, the
source for his ottava rima, and by his subject matter (love)
and style ("far-fetched similitudes"). Surrey's "Martial,
the thinges that do attayne" is "the first English rendering of Martial," an "almost literal" translation that is
admirable for its "concision."

1926

SCHIRMER, WALTER F. "Das Sonett in Der Englischen Literatur." Anglia, 49: 1-31.
 General survey of the sonnet from Wyatt and Surrey
through the Rossettis and Robert Bridges. [In German.]

1928

SAINTSBURY, GEORGE. "The School of Elizabethan Literature,"
in his The Earlier Renaissance. Periods of European Literature, Vol. 5, edited by George Saintsbury. Edinburgh
and London: William Blackwood and Sons, pp. 263-277,
passim.
 Wyatt and Surrey represent the turn in English poetry
from French to Italian influence. Despite the inevitable
shortcomings inherent in English versification and pronunciation during their time, their development of the
English sonnet form, their transformation of the fourteener
into quatrains of alternating rhyme, and Surrey's pioneer
work with blank verse were important in English literary
history.

1929

ROLLINS, HYDER EDWARD. "Introduction," in his edition of
Tottel's Miscellany (1557-1587). Vol. 2. Cambridge,
Massachusetts: Harvard University Press, 3-124.
 Surrey's rank and the involvement of Wyatt's son in the
rebellion against Queen Mary in 1554 account for the ex-
clusion of Wyatt's name from the title-page despite the
fact that he was the pioneer and, from a historical point
of view, "by far the most important contributor." Despite
Wyatt's historical importance, however, "no one should be
tempted to put too high a value on his intrinsic merit";
his "genius was chiefly derivative," he was overly fond of
"elaborate conceits" and "grotesque imagery," and he reflected the practice of his contemporaries in "the uncertain accents, the strange pronunciations, [and] the rough
movement of his lines," faults corrected by Surrey. [In-
cludes discussion of the Miscellany's various editions,
other editions of the two poets' works, the major contri-
butors (Wyatt, Surrey, Grimald), its editor, style, and
influence; Vol. 2 also contains "Notes," "Appendix," and
"Glossarial Index," and photographic facsimiles of the
title pages of the first nine editions of the Miscellany.

1930

GIBBON, JOHN MURRAY. Melody and the Lyric from Chaucer to the Cavaliers.

Prints the words and music for Wyatt's "Hey Robin" (music by Cornysshe) and "I loathe that I did love," which has been ascribed to both Surrey and Lord Vaux. [From rpt., New York: Haskell House, 1964, pp. 35-36.]

1 HAMER, ENID. The Metres of English Poetry. London: Methuen & Co., pp. 61-63, 177-178, 186-190, 287.

Surrey's blank verse is characterized by regular pauses at the ends of lines, but few within the lines themselves; although he occasionally uses the trochee ("almost his only modulation"), he builds his lines mainly by counting syllables. Wyatt's sonnets are marred by unsteadiness in metre, double rhymes, rhyming of weak syllables and similar problems. Surrey benefited from Wyatt's experiments and his own practice with blank verse, and thus created. firmer metres and the simpler rhyme-schemes of the English forms. [Mentions Wyatt's stanza forms and rondeaux.]

1933

LATHROP, HENRY BURROWES. Translations from the Classics into English from Caxton to Chapman[,] 1477-1620. University of Wisconsin Studies in Language and Literature, No. 35. Madison: [University of Wisconsin Press], pp. 93-101, passim.

Wyatt and Surrey were the most important early Tudor translators of the classics. Wyatt is "most himself" in the Satires, where he combines Horace's "artistic form" with "reality of content." He shows the influence of Virgil, Boethius, Seneca, Ausonius, and Josephus. Surrey betrays no real evidence of classical reading aside from his Aeneid translations, which were probably influenced principally by Cardinal Hippolyto de Medici. Douglas' Eneados influenced his diction, but nothing else.

1 PEARSON, LU EMILY. "Petrarchism," in her Elizabethan Love Conventions. Berkeley: University of California Press, pp. 58-74.

Wyatt is "un-English" in his "predominant interest in form" and in his failure to grasp Petrarch's harmonious fusion of earthly and spiritual love. Nevertheless, he is to be credited with combining Petrarchan sonnet form with Chaucerian versification and with discovering, through

Petrarch and Chaucer, "a new convention of voicing personal emotion," and particularly for his independent and
original poetic attitude toward injustice in the courtly
love situation. Surrey's appeal is the opposite: unlike
Wyatt he is absorbed in natural settings, in the expression of conventional Petrarchan attitudes, and in the
spiritualization of love. In these two poets, then, are
to be seen the English beginnings of both anti-Petrarchan
and Petrarchan poetry.

1935

CECCHINI, ANTONIO. "Vita ed opera poetica del Cavaliere
Thomas Wyatt (Il Sonetto in Inghilterra)," "La vita e
l'opera poetica del Conte di Surrey," and "Serafino,
Wyatt, Surrey e il grande Shakespeare," in his Serafino
Aquilano e la Lirica inglese del '500. Aquila: Casa, ed.
Vecchio, pp. 77-155.
     Provides a biography of Wyatt through his visit to
Italy, followed by comparisons of his translations of
Serafino with their originals ("Venemous thorns," "He is
not dead," "My heart I gave thee," "Resound my voice,"
"Perdie I said it not," "Process of time"); emphasizes
that Wyatt was much more than a servile translator. Also
includes a discussion of the development of the sonnet
from Wyatt to Keats. Provides a biography of Surrey,
emphasizing the influence of the French court and John
Clerke on his Italian learning; finds Surrey a more scru-
pulous Petrarchan than Wyatt because he was a less subjective translator, more the artist while Wyatt was more
the man; compares "Alas! so all things now do hold their
peace!" with Serafino; also discusses Surrey's introduction of verso sciolto to England. Concludes that both
poets learned elegance of expression through Serafino more
than through Petrarch, and suggests that, while neither
Wyatt nor Surrey was a great poet, they were important
because they introduced to England "il culto della forma,"
which influenced Shakespeare and Elizabethan drama. [In
Italian.]

1   HUGHEY, RUTH. "The Harington Manuscript at Arundel Castle
and Related Documents." The Library, 4th ser., 15, no. 4
(March), 388-444.
     Reports the discovery of the Manuscript, describes its
contents, and relates it, along with the "Related Documents," to other sources for the poetry of Wyatt and
Surrey. Includes the following facts and observations:

(1) the MS. contains 18 poems by Surrey, 67 by Wyatt; (2) it was used for the 1769-1775, 1779, and 1792 editions of the Nugae Antiquae, but not for Park's 1804 edition; (3) it is the Harington MS. No. II used by George Frederick Nott [WS 1816.1]; (4) Nott's Harington MS. No. I is Egerton MS. 2711; (5) among the related Surrey documents in the collection are several editions of Tottel's Miscellany, three copies of "the 1717 Meares-Brown edition of the Poems of Henry Howard, Earl of Surrey," Nott's edition of Wyatt and Surrey, and his mysterious 1814 edition; (6) the "Hill Ms.," used by Chalmers [WS 1810] and Nott is B.M. Add. MS. 36529; (7) the Arundel MS. and Add. 36529 are "the two most important manuscript sources for Surrey's poems"; (8) the Arundel was "in many cases" the copy text for Add. 36529; (9) the Egerton and Arundel MSS. were once companion volumes, the Arundel a later version that "shows an attempt to smooth out Wyatt's uncouth lines"; (10) the Arundel version of Wyatt's Penitential Psalms was "quite clearly taken directly from that in the Egerton MS."; (11) other Wyatt poems in the Arundel incorporate changes in the Egerton made by Wyatt and others (including Nicholas Grimald); (12) emendations in the Arundel that are not in the Egerton sometimes agree with changes in Tottel's Miscellany; (13) Wyatt sonnets in the Arundel follow the Egerton more closely than his epigrams, while his Satires are closer to the Miscellany; (14) while there appears to have been "cooperative editing" in the compilation of the Arundel and the Miscellany, they do not always agree in ascribing Wyatt and Surrey poems. [Appendix II records changes made in Add. 36529 to conform to Surrey poems in the Arundel; Appendix III records variants among the Egerton, Arundel and 1549 printed version of Wyatt's Psalms.

1938

DE SOLA PINTO, V. The English Renaissance: 1510-1688. Introductions to English Literature, Vol. 2, edited by Bonamy Dobrée. London: The Cresset Press, pp. 148-154, and passim.

Includes brief bibliographic guides to Wyatt and Surrey and brief general remarks on both in the opening chapter.

1   JOHN, LISLE CECIL. "Introduction," in his <u>The Elizabethan</u>
     <u>Sonnet Sequences: Studies in Conventional Conceits</u>. New
     York: Columbia University Press, pp. 5-9, passim.
          Discusses the Italian influence on the sonnets of Wyatt
     and Surrey and summarizes their contributions to the
     development of sonnet form and rhyme.

                         <u>1939</u>

WINTERS, IVOR. "The 16th Century Lyric in England: A
     Critical and Historical Reinterpretation: Part II."
     <u>Poetry: A Magazine of Verse</u>, 53, no. 6 (March), 320-
     322.
          Names 28 poems by Wyatt that rank him with Gascoigne,
     the chief representative of the non-Petrarchan, "plain"
     school of sixteenth-century poetry--a poetry that is
     superior to that of the Petrarchans in its intellectual
     depth and complexity, its restrained, direct style, and
     its "sombre and disillusioned" tone. Finds Surrey's
     poetry to be closer to the Petrarchan school but, partly
     because of Wyatt's influence, sometimes suggestive of the
     plain school. ["Part I" (Vol. 53, no. 5, February, 258-
     272) contrasts the qualities of the two schools.]

                         <u>1940</u>

SWEETING, ELIZABETH J. <u>Early Tudor Criticism: Linguistic</u>
     <u>and Literary</u>. Oxford: Basil Blackwell, pp. 52-53, 164-
     166.
          Wyatt's prefatory remarks to his translation of the
     <u>Quyete of Mynde</u> indicate the difficulty of translating the
     classics into Tudor English. The significance of Wyatt
     and Surrey is due mainly to their "combination of serious
     purpose and conviction of the possibilities of the English
     language, with the taste for form and style which led them
     to supplement English resources with foreign models."
     English poetry "regains its prestige" with them and be-
     comes a vehicle for the expression of "personal emotion."

                         <u>1941</u>

RUBEL, VERÉ L. "The New Idiom of Sir Thomas Wyatt" and
     "Henry Howard, Earl of Surrey," in her <u>Poetic Diction in</u>
     <u>the English Renaissance From Skelton Through Spenser</u>.

                         141

1941

New York: Modern Language Association of America; London:
Oxford University Press, pp. 47-56, 57-82, and passim.

Wyatt, influenced by Pynson's edition of Chaucer and
the attitude toward vernacular language expressed in Il
Cortegiano, wrote in that kind of Chaucerian diction that
employed "native or naturalized archaisms," whereas Lydgate, Skelton, and Hawes were primarily influenced by
Chaucer's borrowings from the Romance languages. Chaucerian echoes are also apparent in Wyatt's "figures of ornament," which are of particular importance because of their
influence on later poets through Tottel's Miscellany,
which itself contributed to the "expanding concern with
rhetorical figures as the century progressed." Indeed,
Wyatt's poems provide "illustrations of most of Puttenham's classifications" of figures in The Arte of English
Poesie [WS 1589].

Surrey's poems contain verbal echoes of both Chaucer
and Wyatt, some of which are apparently from Wyatt alone.
But an examination of Surrey's influence on the diction
and rhetoric of later poets must take into account the
changes in his poems made by the editor of Tottel's Miscellany, changes that on occasion alter his sense, and
others that "result in smoothing...the line, in regularizing the meter, in increasing melody by alliteration, in
modifying Surrey's customarily rather rugged expression."
Despite these changes, however, Surrey's diction still
provided many "innovations and archaisms." In order to
study the influence of his Aeneid translations, it is
necessary to recognize his dependence on Gavin Douglas'
Eneados, which influenced his use of native archaisms;
nevertheless, he differs from Douglas in being more compressed, closer to Virgil's Latin, and "at times more
archaic," suggesting the influence of Chaucer. His Biblical paraphrases, which show the continued influence of his
work with the Aeneid, and of Wyatt, are still characterized
by "archaisms, interspersed by an occasional Latinism."

1   SWALLOW, ALAN. 'Sir Thomas Wyatt' and 'Henry Howard, Earl of
     Surrey,' in his "Principles of Poetic Composition from
     Skelton to Sidney." Ph.D. dissertation, Louisiana State,
     pp. 112-210, 211-248.

     Wyatt is the first poet to replace the medieval alle-
gorical poetic and Skelton's "repetitive and accumulative"
one with a method of dramatic structure and with various
devices (image, metaphor, pun, word-play) and metrical
variations within that structure that provide "a means of
dramatically objectifying the experience of the poem in

its empirical particularity" and "techniques adapted to
the needs of an inductive approach to experience." His
was the method adopted by the great Elizabethans. [Dis-
cusses, in chapter on Skelton, pp. 52-111, Wyatt's use
of iambic pentameter; see also W 1949.2.]

In contrast to Wyatt's, Surrey's method involved "surrounding a central idea or theme with many analogous
ideas," without Wyatt's dramatic structure or internal
devices. His method was adopted in the Elizabethan miscellanies.

1942

KREMER, CHARLES FREDERICK. 'Wyatt' and 'Surrey,' in his
"Studies in Verse Form in Non-Dramatic English Poetry from
Wyatt to Sidney." Ph.D. dissertation, Northwestern,
pp. 10-30, 31-38, and passim.

Lists and examines all the verse forms used by Wyatt,
Surrey, and others, clasifying the forms by meter, line
length, and rhyme and stanza patterns. Also traces foreign and native models. Includes lists of poems in particular forms and summary lists of the various forms used
by each poet.

1943

POLICARDI, S. Lyrical Poetry in Renaissance England. Bib-
lioteca Di Saggi e Lezioni Accademiche, No. 9. Milan:
Montuoro Editore, pp. 41-53.

Wyatt was more important than Surrey because he was
"without doubt the more powerful intellect of the two"
and thus influenced the "matter" and "spirit" of English
poetry while Surrey only influenced its "manner." Nevertheless, both are "epoch-making" because they express
"more imaginatively, more individualistically" and with
"greater psychological verisimilitude" the conventional
situations of the subjective lyric. Wyatt's specific importance lay in his introduction into England of the form
and subject matter of the Petrarchan sonnet. His most
typical poems are "art lyrics" ("song[s] not meant for
music"). Surrey's major importance was metrical and linguistic, and he is typically "dramatic rather than personal...inclined to depict an imaginary happening rather
than one which is within his own experience." His lyrics
are thoroughly English, and inspired by medieval chivalry.

1943

His moral poems are more personal than such poems were
before him, and his literary tributes are of particular
interest because they look toward "the intimate literary
life" of the Elizabethans. [No index.]

1946

SMITH, HALLETT. "English Metrical Psalms in the Sixteenth
Century and their Literary Significance." HLQ, 9, no. 3
(May), 249-271.
Wyatt, Surrey and Sir Thomas Smith differed from other
sixteenth-century writers of metrical Psalms in that
theirs came from private, rather than public, motives.
Wyatt's seven Penitential Psalms, deriving from David's
remorse at ridding himself of Uriah to have Bathsheba,
are "romantic," voicing "a kind of de remedia amoris," and
they demonstrate his ability to turn his sources into
"dramatic and rhetorical situations." Surrey's Psalms,
composed during his final imprisonment, voice the more
general theme of the courtier: the mutability, treachery,
and malice of life at court.

1947

BULLETT, GERALD. "Introduction," in his edition of Silver
Poets of the Sixteenth Century. London and New York:
Everyman's Library, pp. vii-xii.
The metrics of both Wyatt and Surrey can only be un-
derstood and appreciated if we recognize that "like all
true poets they wrote by ear, not by counting syllables."

1948

MILES, JOSEPHINE. "The Poetry of the 1540's and the 1640's,"
in her The Primary Language of Poetry in the 1640's.
Berkeley and Los Angeles: University of California Press,
pp. 1-45.
Provides tables collating the use of adjectives, nouns,
verbs, and specific words by various poets, including
Wyatt and Surrey. [Printed with Miles' The Continuity of
Poetic Language: Studies in English Poetry from the
1540's to the 1940's. Berkeley and Los Angeles: University of California Press, 1951.]

144

1949

MILLER, AUDREY BERRYMAN. "Themes and Techniques in Mid-Tudor
Lyric Poetry: An Analytical Study of the Short Poems from
Wyatt to Sidney." Ph.D. dissertation, Northwestern,
241 pp.
Discusses the themes of love, friendship, life, death
and immortality, beauty, fortune, the Golden Mean and
virtue (Part I), together with basic techniques drawn from
rhetorical, Petrarchan, classical traditions and the practice of figurative ornamentation (Part II) in English
lyric poetry from Wyatt to the year 1581. Includes observations on both thematic and technical trends (Part III)
and "addenda" listing additional stylistic devices, the
principles of Courtly Love, and illustrative quotations.

1951

MILES, JOSEPHINE. "The Language of the Donne Tradition."
KR, 8, no. 1 (Winter), 37-49.
Donne's "predicative poetry," which is "clausal, con-
ceptual, full of logical subordination" and characterized
by the "intensification of the human, the temporal, the
active and rational," belongs to the tradition of language
that goes back to Chaucer, Wyatt and Surrey. It is to be
distinguished from the "substantive" poetry of Spenser,
Sackville, Dryden and Milton.

1952

TILLYARD, E. M. W. The English Renaissance: Fact or Fiction? Baltimore: The Johns Hopkins Press, pp. 48-65,
and passim.
With Wyatt and Surrey, the "recreational" function and
the anonymous nature of the English lyric are replaced by
serious moral purpose and identifiable poets whose lives
and moral personalities are impressed upon their poems.
Wyatt's lyrics, which capture "the luminous and critical
spirit of contemporary Italian literature" more successfully than his workmanlike sonnets, are characterized by
their union of tradition and individuality, and by their
dramatic and introspective presentation of "independent
psychological experience" that extends beyond his age and
looks forward to Donne. Surrey, "with less originality,"
is "centrally of [his age]" in his desire for the classical qualities of "balance and harmony": his sonnets are

more ordered, his meter more flowing, his poetry in general
"a highly reasonable, civilized affair" similar to that of
the Augustans. "O happy dames," however, is uncharacter-
istically dramatic, and "Alas so all things now do hold
their peace" contains a "totally new" description of
nature.

1953

BALE, JOHN CHRISTIAN. "The Place of Chaucer in Sixteenth
Century English Literature." Ph.D. dissertation, University of Illinois, pp. 162-197.
   Questions several assumptions made by Foxwell [W 1911]:
that Wyatt modeled his versification on Pynson's Chaucer;
that the Egerton poems are in chronological order; that
Wyatt "was consciously trying to write regular decasyl-
labics"; and that his model for regularity was Chaucer.
Agrees with Foxwell's contention that Chaucer influenced
Wyatt's diction and content, but finds Chaucerian influence on his rhetoric "probably secondary rather than
primary." Sees Chaucerian influence on Surrey in "verbal
parallels and apparent echoes," but none on his versification.

1   MASON, H. A. "Wyatt and the Psalms--II." TLS, no. 2,666
(March 6), p. 160.
   Surrey was strongly influenced by Wyatt's Prologues to
the Seven Penitential Psalms in his versions of both the
Psalms and Ecclesiastes, and he shared Wyatt's debt to the
Psalm versions of Campensis and Zwingli as well. Yet
despite these debts, the two poets' treatments of the
Psalms differ significantly: while both applied their
versions to personal situations, Wyatt did so through
translation, Surrey through paraphrase; it is thus paradoxical that while Surrey "exhibits greater 'independence,'" he "gives a feebler impression of personal urgency"
than Wyatt. The comparison thus indicates that Wyatt "is
a far more isolated genius than is commonly supposed."
[See also WS 1959.]

2   McDOWELL, DIMMES. 'Tottel's Miscellany,' in his "Courtly
Love in the Early English Renaissance: 1485-1557."
Ph.D. dissertation, Cornell, pp. 230-263.
   While both Wyatt and Surrey were influenced by Petarch's style, and while Wyatt in particular is often new
in "poetical form" and unique in tone, both poets consistently express the traditional attitudes and content of
medieval courtly love.

146

<u>1954</u>

LEWIS, C. S. "Drab Age Verse," in his <u>English Literature in</u>
<u>the Sixteenth Century</u> Excluding Drama. The Oxford History
of English Literature, Vol. 3, edited by F. P. Wilson and
Bonamy Dobrée. London and New York: Oxford University
Press, pp. 223-235, passim.

Wyatt's place in literary history is "an unfortunate
one": he begat poulter's measure; he had little effect on
the development of the sonnet; and whatever his rhythmical
method was, it had no effect on the Elizabethans. His
real value lies in the intrinsic merits of his lyrics,
where he demonstrates both the weaknesses and the strengths
of plain, unadorned song; at their worst they are dreary
and unstructured; at their best they produce "an intonation
that would occur in real speech" and reach a dramatic intensity seldom attempted in the English lyric. "His fame
is in the ascendent."

Surrey, less medieval than Wyatt and unaffected by the
song tradition, is more historically "useful" because of
his experiments with sonnet structure, poulter's measure
and blank verse and "more accomplished" at providing a
"completeness" and "shape" and "a certain smooth and controlled dignity and propriety" often missing in Wyatt.
In his poetry, "the Drab age is fully established," and
its affinities with the Augustans demonstrated.

1 POTTER, JAMES LAIN. 'The Sonneteers of Tottel's <u>Miscellany</u>,'
in his "The Development of Sonnet-Patterns in the Sixteenth Century." Ph.D. dissertation, Harvard, pp. 11-45.

Although most of Wyatt's sonnets end with the rhymed
couplet, his sense divisions more often follow the octave-
sestet arrangement of the Italian form, even in those
poems with final "sense-couplets." He can be credited,
therefore, with inventing "not the Shakespearian sonnet...
but at least the English." And while Surrey invented the
Shakespearean rhyme scheme and obviously valued the "emphatic final sense-couplet," his sonnets on the whole
vary between Italian and English thought patterns.

<u>1955</u>

SELLS, A. LYTTON. "'Two Courtly Makers,'" in his <u>The Italian</u>
<u>Influence in English Poetry</u>. Bloomington, Indiana:
Indiana University Press, pp. 68-81, passim.

Wyatt's influence on later poetry originated in his
visit to France in 1526, where he probably encountered

1955

Petrarchan poetry in the work of Saint-Gelais and the
rondeaux and penitential Psalms of Marot, and on his mis-
sion to Italy in 1527, where he became acquainted with the
strambotti of Serafino, the terza rima of Alamanni, the
penitential Psalms of Aretino, and the sonnets and canzoni
of Petrarch. He used the strambotti for his epigrams, and
terza rima for his Satires and penitential Psalms. He
found it "easier to naturalize Petrarch's themes than to
imitate his verse," and thus adapted his forms into octo-
syllabic quatrains and decasyllabic six-verse stanzas with
refrains; and while he wrote only one regular Petrarchan
sonnet, his experiments with the form mark him as "the
real inventor" of the Shakespearean type.

Surrey, who became acquainted with Italy's "artistic
prestige" during his visit to France in 1532, had "a far
surer instinct for the English iambic," and thus succeeded
where Wyatt failed in anglicizing the Petrarchan sonnet
form. Through the influence of Trissino's versi sciolti,
as used by Alamanni in his eclogues and by Caro, Liburnio,
and Ippolito de' Medici in their Aeneid translations, he
also succeeded in capturing the dignity and rapidity of
Latin hexameter verse in his blank-verse Aeneid, correcting
Gavin Douglas' prolixity and replacing rhyme with internal
pauses and enjambment.

1956

CLINARD, TURNER NORMAN. 'The Sonnets of Sir Thomas Wyatt'
and 'The Sonnets of Henry Howard, Earl of Surrey,' in his
"A Critical History of the Pre-Elizabethan English Sonnet."
Ph.D. dissertation, Vanderbilt, pp. 39-179, 180-265.
The growing appreciation for Wyatt's poetry in the
twentieth century has not yet included his sonnets. This
analysis renders the following conclusions: (1) while his
experiments with the Italian hendadecasyllabic line and
English accentual verse and his mastery of conversational
rhythmic speech contributed to the development of iambic
pentameter, he did not intentionally aim toward it; (2)
his Petrarchan translations generally fall into the fourfold thought division of two quatrains and two tercets,
his original sonnets generally into three quatrains and a
couplet, but variations in both kinds indicate that he was
not a slavish imitator in either his thought-divisions or
rhyme scheme; (3) there are original qualities in the
translations and Petrarchan characteristics in the original sonnets, but on the whole he ignored Petrarch's

Platonizing attitudes and foreshadows Donne in his adaptation of Petrarchan conventions to subjects other than
love, in his attitude and tone, and in his dramatic and
forceful diction.

Analysis of Surrey's sonnets indicates that his rhythms
are smoother and more consistently in iambic pentameter
than Wyatt's; that he was principally influenced by Wyatt
in the development of the Shakesperean thought-and rhyme-
division; that he is more Petrarchan and Platonic in
spirit; that, unlike Wyatt, he departs from the love situation in order to use the sonnet for occasional purposes;
and that he was influenced more fundamentally by classical
precedent.

1   HUTTAR, CHARLES A.   "English Metrical Paraphrases of the
    Psalms, 1500-1640."   Ph.D dissertation, Northwestern,
    pp. 116-121.

    Wyatt and Surrey belong to that group of versifiers who
    translated the Psalms "as a pastime" rather than for pub-
    lic consumption or for serious literary or religious pur-
    poses. Wyatt was probably inspired to write his after
    observing in Paris the esteem accorded Marot and Alamanni
    for their versions, although his model was the prose ver-
    sion of Aretino. The exclusively literary nature of
    Wyatt's version is indicated by its highly dramatic nature.
    Surrey's literary purpose is revealed in the freedom he
    asserted in expanding the originals.

2   LEVER, J. W.   "Wyatt" and "Surrey," in his The Elizabethan
    Love Sonnet. London: Methuen and Co., pp. 14-36, 37-50,
    passim.

    Wyatt's development of a sonnet form proper to his own
    expression involved two "interdependent" processes:
    verbal changes that gradually affected Italian structure
    and prosody, and the development of the decasyllable and
    the final couplet, which affected content. These proces-
    ses, in turn, can be seen operating in three stages: (1)
    the earliest phase of experimentation with form, which
    produced three decasyllabic quatrains, the couplet, and
    iambic feet with Chaucerian accentual freedom, together
    with the imposition of his own "vigorous personality" on
    traditional love themes; (2) a middle stage of freer
    adaptation and improvisation, without preoccupation with
    technical matters and exemplified by "Dyvers dothe vse,"
    "a sonnet of entirely English stamp"; and (3) a final
    period in which he turned to subjects other than love for
    his themes (exemplified by "The flamyng sighes") and

1956

nearly completed the move toward the rhyme scheme Surrey
produced. Throughout this development there is observable
Wyatt's preoccupation with "personal dignity," which led
necessarily to his rejection of Petrarchan attitudes.
In his sonnets on love Surrey was either experimenting
with prosody or simply using Italian models for reflections unrelated to the sonnet's thought patterns. Because
he did not share Petrarch's "intuitive" poetic response to
the Mediterranean sense of "an inherent sympathy between
man and nature," his sonnets are characterized by objective observation and logical connection. His desire for
"logical exposition" is the basis for his development of
the English rhyme scheme as well as his compression and
precision; at the same time, it results in poems that work
as "descriptive or near-narrative verse," but not as sonnets. However, when he departs from the subject of love
in the sonnets on social and public life, his "true field,"
he achieves poetic effects that look forward to the
Augustans.

3   SEATON, ETHEL. "The Devonshire Manuscript and Its Medieval
    Fragments." RES, n.s. 7, 55-56.
        The manuscript contains fragments from the fourteenth
    and fifteenth centuries as well as the early sixteenth.

1957

THOMPSON, JOHN. 'Wyatt, Tottel, and Surrey,' in his "The
    Iambic Line from Wyatt to Sidney." Ph.D. dissertation,
    Columbia, pp. 20-51.
        The irregularity of metrical pattern in Wyatt's Satires
    ("ten syllables more or less, five relatively strong
    stresses, more or less") show that his interest lay not in
    attaining metrical regularity but in reproducing "the
    language of a man speaking." The regularization of his
    lines in Tottel's Miscellany indicates an entirely dif-
    ferent metrical principle. Surrey's practice, on the
    other hand, appears to have been consistent with the Mis-
    cellany's principles, particularly in the "fatal sing-
    song" of poulter's measure and even in his Aeneid transla-
    tions. [See also WS 1961.1]

1959

MASON, H. A. Humanism and Poetry in the Early Tudor Period.
    London: Routledge and Kegan Paul, pp. 143-178, 179-235,
    236-254.

The study of Wyatt's Devonshire lyrics "belongs to
sociology rather than literature." It is likely that, if
all the court songs written between Chaucer and Wyatt were
available, one would find Wyatt's to be all composed of
"conventional phrases" and "set forms" written for "social
occasions" and as anonymous as their medieval predecessors.
Furthermore, the convention of which they are a part is
"linguistically bad and bad in sentiment."
  Wyatt's best and most significant poetry is to be found
not in his lyrics but in his translations, where he consistently "takes over the general framework and order of
ideas from his original[s]," "recasts foreign idiom into
English idiom," and uses the originals "as a Mask or
Persona, as a means of finding and creating himself." He
uses Petrarch "to find an analogy to his own position, and
struggles to transmute the dead language and trite sentiments of Courtly Love into fresh idiom and specific re-
sponses to his own experience." His Psalms change the
Catholic emphasis on penance in the originals to a "drama
of repentance" that suggests the influence and spirit of
Luther. In the Satires he attempts to convert the classical abstractions of his models into a "convincing concrete
presentation of the moral facts" relevant, again, to his
own experience and suggestive of Chaucer (though without
Chaucer's connection to a Catholic universe). As "the
only poet of the first period of Humanism," then, Wyatt is
to be considered, with More and Erasmus, as representative
of the period "in which the first attempt to be modern
since Chaucer's comes to an end."
  Unlike Wyatt's, Surrey's poetry is marked by "commonplace sentiments, smooth metre, and the lack of any
commanding idiom." While influenced by Wyatt in translating Petrarch and in writing poulter's measure, he only
repeats Wyatt's shortcomings. In fact the only real bond
between the two is an historic one: Surrey's Psalm
translations and his "London" satire indicate that he
shared Wyatt's Protestant inclinations, but nowhere does
he demonstrate Wyatt's abilities as a poet and translator.
Even his Aeneid translations, his chief claim to literary
fame, are awkward, and at their best only when influenced
most clearly by Gavin Douglas' much superior version.
Surrey is better in his two translations on the golden
mean, but even these belong to the translations in Tottel's Miscellany, which, with the exception of some of
Wyatt's poems contained therein, represents "the grave
of Early Tudor poetry."

1959

1 THOMSON, PATRICIA. "The First English Petrarchans." HLQ,
   22, no. 2 (February), 85-105.
     "Both for historical and intrinsic value Wyatt's
   translations and imitations of Petrarch deserve a higher
   place than Surrey's." Comparison of their very different
   versions of Petrarch's "Amor, che nel pensier mio vive e
   regna," for example, shows that, while Surrey's is "rhythmically firmer," Wyatt's renders more faithfully the fundamental meaning and structure of the original, and relates
   conceit to structure in a manner that looks forward to
   Donne. Examination of Wyatt's alterations of Petrarch
   provide further evidence that he is "the key figure in
   this first phase of English Petrarchianism": in his direct translations he expresses a more self-centered, less
   transcendental attitude toward love than that in the Italian; and in his looser imitations/adaptations he departs
   further from the originals by simplifying them, consistently choosing to concentrate on a single theme or image, and
   developing it into "a sustained conceit often different in
   implication from the original." Surrey, apparently unin-
   terested in either Petrarch's transcendental attitude or
   Wyatt's realism, achieves neither the complexity of the
   former nor the intensity of the latter. His Petrarchan
   poems are predominantly literal, superficial, and static,
   reflecting an interest that is principally stylistic.

1960

GUIDI, AUGUSTO. "Introduzione," in his edition of Lirica
   Elisabettiana. Collana di Letterature Moderne, Vol. 12,
   directed by Elio Chinol. Naples: Edizioni Scientifische
   Italiane, pp. 3-39.
     The harshness and disjointedness that disturb the ear
   in Wyatt's translations/imitations might have been more
   appropriate in original compositions or less direct imitations. The man who comes through Wyatt's poetry is
   virile, passionate, introspective, bitter, and often
   allusive, almost cryptic in his expression; indeed Wyatt's
   poetry often seems an outlet, even a secret communication
   that suggests metaphysical poetry. It is not surprising,
   therefore, that he liked Serafino. Surrey is a more
   accessible and pliant poet, but he is now considered the
   more original of the two, and a more elegant and nimble
   translator, first of Petrarch, then of Virgil. And he is
   more refined than Wyatt in his original verse. [Includes
   biographical sketches, bibliographical note. In Italian.]

1 HARRIER, RICHARD C. "A Printed Source for 'The Devonshire
   Manuscript.'" RES, n.s. 11, 54.
      A group of poems in the MS. was probably borrowed from
   the 1532 edition of Chaucer by Thynne. The dates for
   these poems might be 1532-1537.

2 HUGHEY, RUTH. "Introduction," in her edition of The Arundel
   Harington Manuscript of Tudor Poetry. Vol. 1. Columbus,
   Ohio: The Ohio State University Press, 43-58, passim.
      The Manuscript contains 324 sixteenth-century composi-
   tions dating approximately from the last years of Henry
   VIII to the death of Elizabeth, and including 67 poems
   attributed to Wyatt (in the following order: sonnets,
   epigrams, miscellaneous poems, Satires, Psalms), 18 to
   Surrey ("lighter poems," Psalms, Ecclesiastes, in order).
   Evidence indicates that the Manuscript was "part of the
   same editorial movement" that produced Tottel's Miscellany, but that its texts are earlier and better, and that
   its Wyatt transcriptions derive directly from its companion, the Egerton MS. It was used by Nott for his
   edition [WS 1816.1] and also by the compilers of the Nugae
   Antiquae. [Includes two appendices corresponding to
   missing leaves from the Manuscript, one from Nott's
   transcription that contains a fragment of a Surrey poem,
   one from the Nugae Antiquae that includes poems by Wyatt.
   Vol. 2 contains notes to the poems, with extensive commentary on influences, characteristics, and doubtful poems of
   Wyatt and Surrey; and a glossary. See also WS 1935.1.]

3 PRINCE, F. T. "The Sonnet from Wyatt to Shakespeare," in his
   Elizabethan Poetry. Stratford-Upon-Avon Studies, No. 2,
   edited by John Russell Brown and Bernard Harris. New York:
   St. Martin's Press, pp. 12-17, passim.
      The rhythm of Wyatt's sonnets often results from the
   combination of the self-contained, "hobbling" movement of
   the medieval pausing line with the sustained flow of
   iambic pentameter and the "inevitability which is one of
   the chief aims of all sonnets." Surrey "devoted himself...
   with almost brutal determination" to the iambic pentameter
   line, and thus inspired its predominance in the poems of
   Tottel's Miscellany. He also led later sonnet writers
   away from Petrarch by establishing the freedom of the
   Shakespearean form and inspiring the use of the sonnet for
   subjects other than love.

1961

SEATON, ETHEL. "The 'Wyatt,' 'Surrey,' and Tottel Poems," in
her Sir Richard Roos[,] c. 1410-1482[:] Lancastrian Poet.
London: Rupert Hart-Davis, pp. 454-519, passim.
Based on the evidence of "single or double acrostic
anagrams," "parallels of thought and phrasing," and cor-
respondences with Wyatt's "known interests and preoccupations," it is probable that most of the poems now ascribed
to Wyatt, as well as "about half the short poems ascribed
to Surrey" and some two dozen other sixteenth-century
poems were written by Roos in the fifteenth century.

1 THOMPSON, JOHN. "Wyatt, Tottel, and Surrey," in his The
Founding of English Metre. New York: Columbia University
Press; London: Routledge and Kegan Paul, pp. 15-36.
The regularization of syllable numbers and stress patterns in Wyatt's Satires by the editors of Tottel's Miscellany indicate a "change of metrical principle": for
Wyatt, the ten-syllable iambic line functioned only to
throw into relief "the language of a man speaking," and
his alterations of those numbers and patterns were meant
to emphasize "the quality of living speech"; for the editors it was an absolute, and thus their changes not only
made his lines more regular, but often altered their tone
and meaning as well.
Surrey's metrical principles, on the other hand, were
very close to those of the Miscellany's editors, even in
the relatively free blank verse of his Aeneid translations.
However, Surrey's monotony derives not from strict adherence to metrical pattern, but from "a lack of energy
in the language, an aimless remoteness from speech," and
his legacy to later sixteenth-century poetry, as exemplified particularly by his poems in poulter's measure, was
an emphasis on metrical regularity at the expense of vigor
and strength.

1963

WILLIAMS, JOHN. "Preface: Three Phases of Renaissance
Poetry," in his edition of English Renaissance Poetry: A
Collection of Shorter Poems from Skelton to Jonson.
Garden City, New York: Anchor Books, pp. vii-xx.
Though responsible for introducing the "Petrarchan
mode" to English verse, Wyatt and Surrey belong mainly to
the "Native tradition." However, Wyatt, the better of the

two, sometimes goes beyond both traditions and looks forward to the final phase of Renaissance poetry, that which
"assimilates and completes the practices" of both.

1964

BROADBENT, J. B. "Wyatt" and "Interregnum," in his Poetic
Love. London: Chatto and Windus, pp. 57-65.
   Wyatt's Petrarchism is modified by "the more knowing,
realistic and public strain of Chaucer" and by the influence of the musical refrain, which keeps "Petrarchan mor-
bidity" out of his tone and dramatizes his lyrics. But he
does not possess the range or "intellectual framework" of
Chaucer or Donne. His strength is, rather, in his individual tone and in the "apprehension of local existence"
that is particularly strong in his Satires. Both Wyatt
and Surrey, finally, are limited by the static linguistic
and metrical situation in England after the Black Death
and the Wars of the Roses.

1967

BUXTON, JOHN. "Sir Thomas Wyatt" and "The Earl of Surrey,"
in his A Tradition of Poetry. London, Melbourne and
Toronto: Macmillan; New York: St. Martin's Press,
pp. 1-17, 18-35, passim.
   The poems of Wyatt the English gentleman are superior
to those of Wyatt the international courtier. The racy,
colloquial, proverbial "plain" style of the former came
from his own personality, and distinguished him from his
contemporaries in expressing succinctly and clearly the
"natural English prose order of words." Combined with his
gift for song and the influence of the native lyric tradition, this style is unaffected by Continental models.
Nevertheless, in "They flee from me," his best poem, the
Continental courtier and the plain-spoken gentleman
"miraculously fuse and combine," showing how his contact
with foreign influences "helped him to correct the irregularity and diffuseness...of his earlier poetry" and provided his "racy speech" with "a touch of urbanity."
   Surrey's intrinsic merits, his influence on later
poetry, and his rejection by twentieth-century criticism
all rest on his classicism rather than on contemporary/
Continental or medieval/native influence. His Aeneid
translations, as well as his shorter poems, invite attention to diction, syntax, and metrics rather than to his

1967

own personality, as is the case with Douglas' Eneados and
Wyatt's plain-style poems. Surrey's contrasting "literary
elegance," together with his "precocious sensitivity to
language" explain his artistic detachment, his interest
in strictly literary ends, his influence on later writers
of sonnets and blank verse, and his individual excellence.
His best poetry "can give pleasure not only for the suggestion of greater things to come, but for itself."

1   EVANS, MAURICE. "Wyatt and Surrey," in his English Poetry in
     the Sixteenth Century. New York: Norton, pp. 61-82.
        The poetry of Wyatt and Surrey, unlike that of Skelton,
     is largely private. Wyatt's experiences at court (espe-
     cially his relationship with Anne Boleyn) transformed him
     from ambitious courtier and writer of love poems into the
     disillusioned writer of the anti-court Satires. His
     lyrics, while tied to the literary and social conventions
     of courtly love, display a fundamental departure from
     their medieval predecessors in their Chaucerian realism
     and "dramatic immediacy." His sonnets are colloquial and
     similarly dramatic, displaying a roughness that is prob-
     ably intentional and an anti-Petrarchan attitude toward
     love. His Satires combine the Horatian style and Chaucer-
     ian echoes, thus merging the classical and native tradi-
     tions. He looks forward to Donne. Surrey is a less
     interesting poet but a more historically important one
     than Wyatt because he is more concerned with form and
     style than subject matter. His sonnet form led to Shake-
     speare's, his Aeneid translations "established the
     authentic High Style of English poetry," and his poems in
     poulter's measure represent historically important "aca-
     demic experiments." He looks forward to Jonson, Denham,
     and Waller.

2   PETERSON, DOUGLAS L[EE]. "Sir Thomas Wyatt" and "Tottel's
     Miscellany," in his The English Lyric from Wyatt to Donne:
     A History of the Plain and Eloquent Styles. Princeton,
     New Jersey: Princeton University Press, pp. 66-72, 87-
     119, and passim.
        The development of Wyatt's poetry represents a signifi-
     cant advance on the traditional medieval division between
     the eloquent and the plain lyric. While some of his songs
     and sonnets exemplify the meaningless ingenuity of the
     eloquent style, most belong to the plain tradition, ap-
     parently because of his ethical objections to court values.
     More significantly, he discovered in Petrarch the means of
     using metaphor as a means of investigating and qualifying
     the traditional sentiments of courtly love, and thus

produced in his better poems the first critical examination
in English of its content and style. In the process, his
poetry moves away from the preoccupation with style for
its own sake that is typical of the eloquent tradition
toward the serious consideration of ideas through complex
logical structures. He thus links the plain style for the
first time in English poetry with the anticourtly attitude
later associated with Googe, Turberville, Gascoigne, Ralegh, Donne and Herbert.

Surrey's sonnet to Geraldine and "Of Sardanopolis"
exemplify the structural methods of praise/dispraise recommended by the rhetorical handbooks, but his epitaph on
Wyatt and "SO cruel prison" are the "best examples" in
Tottel's Miscellany of "the confluence of the plain and
the eloquent traditions" in the elegy of lament. "Dyvers
thy death," on the other hand, fails because of its completely conventional adherence to eloquent techniques.

3   STACK, RICHARD CATESBY. 'The Development of the Sweet Line,'
in his "From Sweetness to Strength: A Study of the Development of Metrical Style in the English Renaissance,"
pp. 58-139.
The combination of "'loose,'" "'pausing,'" and iambic
rhythms in Wyatt's "Loue and fortune and my mynde, remem-
bre" exemplifies the important principle that meter functions "to indicate specific areas of poetic discourse"
and is not necessarily "the inevitable mode of expression
of a particular kind of discourse." That Wyatt "saw meter
as a function of genre as well as an expressive device" is
indicated by the differences between the "'loose'" or
"'pausing'" rhythms of his translations/adaptations and
the regular iambics of his lyrics, and by the differences
between the Egerton MS. versions of his Satires and the
smoother versions in Tottel's Miscellany. The differences between Wyatt's "The longe loue" and Surrey's "Loue
that doth raine" further exemplify the former's "refusal
to be bound by restrictive formal considerations," while
at the same time showing that Surrey belongs to the tradition of the "sweet line," with its emphasis on "language
as a mere component of form," its art as the manipulation
of "conventional linguistic and rhythmic counters," its
primary unit the line rather than the sentence, and its
separation of poetic language from the language of speech.

1968

LIEVSAY, JOHN L. The Sixteenth Century[:] Skelton through
Hooker. Goldentree Bibliographies in Language and Litera-
ture, edited by O. B. Hardison, Jr. New York: Appleton-
Century-Crofts, pp. 65, 102-104.
Selected bibliographies of Wyatt and Surrey.

1 SMITH, BARBARA HERRNSTEIN. Poetic Closure: A Study of How
Poems End. Chicago and London: University of Chicago
Press, pp. 57-68, 98-102.
Several Wyatt lyrics exemplify the various ways in
which poetic closure can be effected through minor alterations in "a succession of formally identical stanzas":
modification in the terminal refrain ("Fforget not yet");
manipulation of thematic elements ("In eternum"); and
repetition, with logical and thematic modifications, of
the first stanza at the end of the poem ("My lute awake").
Surrey's epigram to Martial demonstrates how the simplest
kind of "paratactic" structure, the list, can "acquire
closura force" through the device of a "frame" which is
signaled by the generalizing quality of opening and closing lines, and through the allusion to death, a "'natural'"
stopping place.

1969

BENDER, ROBERT M. "Sir Thomas Wyatt, 1503-1542" and "Henry
Howard, Earl of Surrey, 1517-1547," in his edition of Five
Courtier Poets of the English Renaissance. New York:
Washington Square Press, pp. 2-8, 180-184.
Discusses the various kinds of poems Wyatt wrote, but
sees the "independent greatness" of the native lyrics as
his principal achievement. Contrasts Wyatt's "irregular,
dramatic, and forceful" verse with Surrey's "smooth, restrained, and, at times, rather cold and formal" lines,
and finds Surrey deficient in originality. Finds Surrey's
main significance to lie in his Aeneid translations, which
probably contributed to the "classical restraint" of his
verse in general, and which represent his major contribution to later English poetry. [Includes brief biographies,
selective bibliographies.]

1 CERMAK, MARY MARGARET. "Terminal Structures in the Sonnets
of Wyatt and Surrey." Ph.D. dissertation, The Catholic
University of America, 212 pp.

1969

Analysis of the structure of the sonnets of Wyatt and Surrey through the examination of endings (couplet, sestet, or variations on those) reveals the following: (1) Wyatt's original sonnets are closer to the Shakespearean form, with a more independent couplet and a more apparent division between the first twelve lines and the couplet, but in general his sonnets are "anomalies," combining the structural features of both the 12-2 division of the English form and the 8-6 of the Italian; (2) Surrey's original sonnets are also closer to the Shakespearean form, and more regular in structure, but they also show a combination of both forms, and are therefore "Surreyan" rather than Italian or Shakespearean; (3) the couplet in the sonnets of both poets is not necessarily related to the Sheakespearean scheme or to quatrain divisions or to the "syntactical isolability" of the couplet.

2   FORSTER, LEONARD. The Icy Fire: Five Studies in European Petrarchism. Cambridge: Cambridge University Press, pp. 74-76, passim.
       Wyatt and Surrey imitated the more artifical sonnets of Petrarch rather than the better ones precisely because the devices in the former were imitable, and therefore helpful in the development of English poetic diction.

3   OSTRIKER, ALICIA. "Thomas Wyatt and Henry Surrey: Dissonance and Harmony in Lyric Form." NLH, 1: 387-405.
       Critical efforts to praise one poet at the expense of the other miss the point that Surrey and Wyatt represent two entirely different approaches to lyric form: Surrey's metrical regularity and cyclical organization, his subordination of persona to social, literary and historical givens and of meaning to pattern show him to be the "harmonious" type, who by formal methods "means to convey a sense of the world as essentially organized and beautiful"; Wyatt's metrical roughness and linear structure, his concentration on his persona's individual responses to given standards and contexts, his subordination of pattern to meaning mark him as the "dissonant" type, who either expresses contempt for the established order of things or sees "the unique personal experience of the poet as more significant than any generalizations about the cosmos."

1970

FOWLER, ALASTAIR. Triumphal Forms: Structural Patterns in
Elizabethan Poetry. Cambridge: Cambridge University
Press, pp. 70, 99–102, 188n.
Numerological analysis of Wyatt's "My lute awake" and
Surrey's Aeneid, "When Windsor walls," and his epitaphs on
Wyatt and Clere exemplify the departure from symmetrical
"renaissance style" to asymmetrical "mannerist structures."

1   MAZZARO, JEROME. Transformations in the Renaissance English
Lyric. Ithaca, New York, and London: Cornell University
Press, pp. 54–71, passim.
While Wyatt and Surrey (and Skelton) reproduce Petrarchan themes and situations, their lyrics, rather than medi-
tating on the deeper nature and spiritual implications of
love, treat it as a social and human phenomenon. As
various critics have pointed out, Wyatt's love lyrics are
influenced by the native and musical tradition rather than
the philosophical one exemplified in Petrarch. Surrey
then completes the "worldly descent" of Skelton and Wyatt
"by implicitly believing only in the literal level" of the
experience represented in the love lyric.

1971

FISHMAN, BURTON. "Recent Studies in Wyatt and Surrey." ELR,
1, no. 2 (Spring), 178–191.
Bibliography covering the years 1945 through 1969.
Provides information through prose commentary and "See
also" lists.

1   HUGHEY, RUTH. "The Life of John Harington of Stepney," in
her John Harington of Stepney: Tudor Gentleman[,] His
Life and Works. Columbus, Ohio: Ohio State University
Press, passim.
Notes the relationship of Harington to Wyatt and Surrey,
particularly his role in the collection and preservation
of their poetry in the Arundel Harington MS., BM Add. MS.
36529, and the 1549 printing of Wyatt's Penitential Psalms.
Also discusses the possibility that Wyatt left the Egerton
MS. with Harington and the relationship of Harington and
Nicholas Grimald to the Egerton and Tottel's Miscellany."
[Includes numerous references to Wyatt and Surrey in
"Notes" on the poems. See also WS 1935.1, 1960.2]

160

2 PARTRIDGE, A. C. The Language of Renaissance Poetry: Spenser, Shakespeare, Donne, Milton. London: Andre Deutsch,
pp. 42-48, 144-146, passim.
     The place of Wyatt and Surrey in the "reformation" of
English prosody was based on their use of iambic measures
and "the recognition of rhyme, not as an accessory ornament, but as the controlling medium in stanzaic verse."
Wyatt's metrical strength, less derivative than heretofore
recognized, was based on "his good ear, lyrical brevity
and avoidance of monotonous foot-patterns." He initiated
the establishment of an English poetic diction "distinct
from that of prose." The neoclassical Surrey, "more correct, but not a better poet than Wyatt," attained his
smooth versification by means of alliteration, antithesis
and the "comparative regularity" of his metrics. His
style is less conceited, his vocabulary less archaic, than
Wyatt's, and "he has a better sense than Wyatt of the
organic unity of mood and idea in lyric poetry." His
Aeneid translations would have been better with less
syllable-counting and less influence from Douglas' Eneados.

                              1972

RICHARDSON, DAVID ANTHONY. 'The Personalized Diction of
Wyatt' and 'Humanistic Intent in Surrey's Aeneid,' in his
"Decorum and Diction in the English Renaissance." Ph.D.
dissertation, University of North Carolina at Chapel Hill,
pp. 150-196, 197-240.
     Examination of the diction of "They fle from me,"
"Stond who so list," and portions of his Psalms shows how
Wyatt's plain language succeeds in communicating "personal
attitudes in convincing terms" without being "formulaic or
wholly conventional." Comparison of the texts of the
first two with the revised versions in Tottel's Miscellany reveals even more clearly Wyatt's "personal bent":
by altering their diction and syntax, the editor made the
mood and substance of the poems "less applicable to particular, personal situations" and "entirely alien to the
spirit of Wyatt's original[s]." Wyatt's own revisions of
the Psalms, on the other hand, render them even more
personal.
     Surrey's Aeneid represents "a truly artistic imitation"
in the humanistic sense: one which reproduced not only
Virgil's matter and form, but its "substance," "spirit,"
and "effect" as well. His fidelity to the original is
observable in his diction, metaphors, sentences, and
verse paragraphs, and in the differences between his

1972

version and the "more literal and prosaic" translation of
Gavin Douglas. Surrey's success was probably due to his
familiarity with classical rhetoric, "particularly with
the ideal of an elevated style for elevated poetic form
and matter." [See also S 1976.1.]

1973

POMEROY, ELIZABETH W. The Elizabethan Miscellanies: Their
Development and Conventions. Berkeley: University of
California Press, pp. 4, 5, 36-44, passim.
   At least five--perhaps all--of the short poems in The
Court of Venus are Wyatt's, and three of his poems were
later recast as moralizing pieces in The Court of Virtue.
Most of his poems included in Tottel's Miscellany are
those influenced by Petrarch and Serafino or by early
Tudor song lyric; the Italian pieces, however, are often
turned to "psychological drama" that suggests real experience, and his lyrics share a directness, a "simplicity of
phrase," and a rhythmical freedom that show the influence
of the song tradition. However, much of the effect of
that freedom is obscured by the metrical alterations of
the Miscellany's editor, and thus Wyatt's "technical diversity" was unknown to the later sixteenth century.
   Surrey's poems in the Miscellany show variety of meter
and stanza form, and because his "metrical principles were
apparently close to those of Tottel's editor," they were
less affected by the regularizing process, and thus more
influential to his immediate predecessors. Surrey's poems
also show careful structure, and his sonnets were of particular importance because of their balanced lines,
parallel constructions, and alliteration.

1974

HASHIGUCHI, MINORU. "Wyatt to Surrey--Eishi no Rhythm"
[Wyatt and Surrey: A Rhythm of English Poetry]. Eigo S.,
119, no. 11 (February), 62-64.
   Scansion of Wyatt's "The longe love" and Surrey's "Love
that doth raine" indicates that Wyatt gave up his efforts
to reconcile iambic pentameter with the native Anglo-Saxon
rhythm based on accent and stress, while Surrey attempted
to remain faithful to the iambic line even though aware
of the difficulties of reconciling the two kinds. [Bases
his scansion on Vladimir Nabokov's Notes on Prosody.
In Japanese.]

FOWLER, ALASTAIR. "Preface," "Obscurity of Sentiment in the
Poetry of Wyatt" and "Surrey's Formal Style," in his <u>Con-
ceitful Thought: The Interpretation of English Renaissance Poems</u>. Edinburgh: Edinburgh University Press,
pp. vii-viii, 1-37.
Despite "an appearance of straightforwardness if not
mere simplicity," Tudor poetry is perhaps more difficult
for modern readers to apprehend than has been heretofore
recognized. This difficulty is exemplified by the various
and contradictory modern interpretations of poems like
Wyatt's "Who so list to hunt," "For to love her," and
"They flee from me," which defy understanding precisely
because of the "cultural distance" between courtly sentiment and rhetoric and our own. Another variation on this
gap is apparent through close readings of Surrey's "The
soot season," "Wyatt resteth here," and "Norfolk sprang
thee," where the apparently simple and straightforward
formal structures cover far more intricate and subtle
patterns that were perhaps better understood and appreciated by Surrey's immediate successors than by modern
readers. Indeed, sixteenth-century readers may have found
in Surrey "models of indirection, of formal richness, of
subtle recourses to form, of distinctively poetic inex-
haustibility" that they did not find in Wyatt.

1976

BIELBY, NICHOLAS. "Introduction," in his edition of <u>Three
Early Tudor Poets: A Selection from Skelton, Wyatt and
Surrey</u>. Wheaton Studies in Literature. Oxford: Pergamon
Press; Elmsford, New York: A. Wheaton & Co., pp. 21-30,
35-46, passim.
The best approach to Wyatt's poetry is the thematic
one: for Wyatt, poetry was private, and there is in his
work a "continuity of theme" related to his search for "a
moral center," an inner source of permanence and harmony
amid a life of flux. The theme runs throughout his secular poetry, from the court lyrics and translations through
the Satires, and combines in the Psalms with the search
for "the deeper conclusion of peace with God." Thus
"secular and religious wisdom for Wyatt form an effective
continuum," one that represents an early stage of English
puritanism.
The principle basis for the study of Surrey is style.
Unlike Wyatt, he did not write socially significant lyrics,

nor did he, with Wyatt, attempt to "recreate in verse the
movement of thought, feeling and expression." His aesthetic detachment from his poetry, along with his stylistic
contributions to English humanism, mark his truly classical
poetic identity. [Provides cultural, historical, biographical, and literary background.]

1 STULL, WILLIAM. L. "Elizabethan Precursors of Donne's 'Divine Meditations.'" Comitatus, 6: 29-44.
  Wyatt's fourfold sonnet structure (two quatrains followed by an Italian volta, or "turn," at the ninth line
which introduces a sestet ending in a couplet) influenced
Donne's practice in the "Holy Sonnets." The form was
transmitted to Donne through the later editions of the
Songes and Sonettes and through the religious sonnets of
Henry Constable, Barnabe Barnes, and Henry Lok. Surrey,
who placed the full burden of resolution on the couplet,
exerted little influence on this development.

1978

PRESCOTT, ANNE LAKE. "Marot," in her French Poets and the
English Renaissance: Studies in Fame and Transformation.
New Haven and London: Yale University Press, pp. 3, 5,
8-9.
  Wyatt shares with Marot a "similarity of tone, an interest in fixed forms," an "openness to Petrarch and the
Italians, a courtier's urbanity," and, more significantly,
"moments of emotional depth or satirical force." Surrey
shares Marot's interest in more flexible structures.

Note to the Index

The Index includes authors and titles of all entries, works of Wyatt and Surrey mentioned in the annotations, and selected subjects. Its entries follow the organization of the main text: W = Wyatt section, S = Surrey section, WS = Wyatt and Surrey section; references refer first to the section, then to the year, then to the alphabetized entry within the year. Reviews are listed collectively under the books they discuss. Italicized entry numbers designate the fullest, or the most significant, treatments of their subjects. First lines of poems are, with a few exceptions, based on the first-line index in the Muir-Thomson edition of Wyatt [W 1969.3] and the table of contents in Emrys Jones' edition of Surrey [S 1964].

165

Index

The "Aeneid" of Henry Howard
Earl of Surrey (Ridley),
S 1963.2; Review S 1965
"A Face that should content me
wonders well," WS 1816.1
"After great storms the calm
returns," W 1968.5
Alamanni, Luigi, W 1913, 1925.2,
1929.2, 1952, 1961, 1963.2,
1970.6, WS 1909, 1910, 1955,
1956.1
"Alas, so all thinges nowe doe
holde their peace," WS 1935,
1952
Alden, Raymond Macdonald, WS 1899
Alscher, Rudolf, W 1886
"Amor che nel pensier mio vivo e
regna" (Petrarch, translated
by Wyatt and Surrey),
W 1946.1, S 1920, 1969
An Apologie for Poetrie (Sidney),
S 1595
"Anne Boleyn and Sir Thomas
Wyatt," W 1848
Anne of Cleves, W 1963.7
"Another Version of 'The Thinges
That Cause a Quiet Lyfe'"
(Camp), S 1937
"Anti-Petrarchism: A Study of
the Reaction against the
Courtly Tradition in English
Love-Poetry from Wyatt to
Donne" (West), W 1950.6
Aretino, Pietro, W 1920, 1953.4,
1970.6, WS 1955, 1956.1
Ariosto, Lodovico, W 1964.13,
1964.15

"A Robyn," W 1956.2, 1958.2,
1961.3, WS 1930
The Arte of English Poesie (Put-
tenham), S 1881, WS 1589,
1941
"The Art of Sir Thomas Wyatt"
(Smith), W 1946.1
Arundel Harington Manuscript,
W 1975.1, S 1975, WS 1935.1,
1960.2
The Arundel Harington Manuscript
of Tudor Poetry (Hughey),
WS 1960.2
Ascham, Roger, WS 1570
Ashton, Susan Eichenfeld, W 1973.1
"Th'Assyryans king, in peas with
fowle desyre," WS 1967.2
Athenae Oxonienses (A Wood), WS 1691
"Avising the bright beams of these
fair eyes," W 1890, 1891,
1966.1
À Wood, Anthony, WS 1691

"Balade de Bon Conseyl" (Chaucer),
W 1964.14
Baldi, Sergio, W 1953, 1961, 1966,
1966.1
Baldwin, T. W., W 1942
Baldwin, William, S 1923, 1973.1
Bale, John Christian, WS 1953
Balette (or Ballette or Balet),
W 1930.1, 1933, 1961
Ballade, W 1961
Ballatelle, W 1953
Bannatyne Manuscript, W 1945.1
Bannister, Edith, S 1936, 1936.5
Bapst, Edmond, S 1891
Barclay, Alexander, W 1923

167

Index

"The Bright Transparent Glass:
A Critical Study of the
Poetry of Sir Thomas Wyatt"
(Fiero), W 1968
Brilliant, A. N., W 1971.2
British Museum manuscripts, see
BM, Devonshire Manuscript,
Egerton Manuscript
Broadbent, J. B., WS 1964
Brodie, Philip T., W 1973.3
Brooks, Cleanth, Jr., S 1934
Brooks, Sarah W., WS 1889
Brownlow, E. B., W 1890, 1891,
1891.1
Bruce, John, W 1850, 1850.1
Bryan, Sir Francis, W 1950.1,
1964.13, 1974.8, 1978.1
Budé, Guillaume, W 1931, 1962.1
Bukofzer, Manfred F., W 1955
Bullett, Gerald, WS 1947
Bullock, Walter L., WS 1923
Buxton, John, WS 1967
Byrom, H. J., S 1936.1, 1939.1

"Caesar, when that the traitor of
Egypt," W 1966.1
California MS. AC 523, S 1964.1
"California MS. AC 523, Formerly
Phillipps MS. 3841" (Tucker),
S 1964.1
The Cambridge History of English
Literature (Child), WS 1909
Camden, William, S 1605
Camp, Truman W., S 1937
Campensis, Ioannes, W 1953.4,
1970.6, S 1971, WS 1953.1
Candelaria, Frederick H.,
W 1963.1
The Canon of Sir Thomas Wyatt's
Poetry (Harrier), W 1975.1;
Review, W 1976.2
Canzone, W 1963.4, 1964.8,
1964.13, S 1960.3
"The Canzone in Sixteenth Century
English Verse With Particular
Reference to Wyatt's Render-
ings from Petrarch's Canzon-
iere" (Mumford), W 1960.7
"A Carol of Anne Boleyn by Wyatt"
(Greene), W 1974.3

Casady, Edwin R., S 1936.2, 1938,
1939, 1939.1, 1939.2, 1939.3,
1939.4, 1939.6, 1940
Casson, Leslie F., S 1936.3
Castiglione, Baldassare, W 1975.3,
S 1929, 1956, WS 1941
Catherine of Aragon, W 1962.2,
1964.13
Catullus, W 1974.7
Cavalcanti, Guido, WS 1923
Cecchini, Antonio, WS 1935
Certain Bokes of Virgiles Aenaeis
turned into English metre,
S 1903, 1905, 1919, 1920.2,
1922.1, 1933, 1949, 1963,
1963.2
Certayne Chapters of the prouerbes
of Salomon drawen into metre
by Thomas sterneholde,
S 1965.1, 1971, 1975
Certayne Psalmes select out of the
Psalter of Dauid (Seager),
S 1975
Certayn Psalmes chosen out the
Psalter of David commonlye
called the vii Penytentiall
Psalmes, drawen into Englyshe
meter by Sir T. Wyat Knight,
W 1960.6, 1960.8, WS 1935.1
Chalker, John, S 1966
Chalmers, Alexander, WS 1810
Chambers, E. K., W 1933, 1935.1,
1935.2
Chapman, Hester W., S 1960.1,
1960.4
Chapman, Raymond, S 1952
Chapters on English Metre (Mayor),
S 1886
Charitean Petrarchanism,
W 1961.10, 1964.13
Chaucer, Geoffrey, W 1544, 1911,
1913, 1923, 1946.1, 1948,
1953.6, 1954, 1964.8,
1964.10, 1964.13, 1964.14,
1965.3, 1965.15, 1970.5,
1971, 1973.5, 1976.3, S 1920,
1920.1, 1960.3, WS 1917,
1941, 1951, 1953, 1956.2,
1959, 1960.1, 1964, 1967.1

Index

Cheneys and Wyatts: A Brief
History in Two Parts (Wyatt),
W 1959.5
Chiapelli, Carolyn, W 1977
Child, Harold H., WS 1909
Churchyard, Thomas, W 1978
Clere, Thomas, S 1605, 1969.1,
1976, 1977, WS 1970, 1975
Clerke, John, WS 1901.1, 1935
Clinard, Turner Norman, WS 1956
Colin Clouts Come Home Againe
(Spenser), W 1978.1
Collected Poems of Sir Thomas
Wyatt (Muir), W 1949.1,
1950.3; Reviews, W 1950.2,
1951, 1951.1
Collected Poems of Sir Thomas
Wyatt (Muir and Thomson),
W 1969.3; Reviews, W 1969.2,
1970.1, 1971.11, 1972.5
Collier, John Payne, WS 1820
Combellack, Frederick M., W 1959
"The Complaint to his Lady"
(Chaucer), W 1953.6
The Compleat Gentleman (Peacham),
WS 1622
Conceitful Thought: The Inter-
pretation of English Renais-
sance Poems (Fowler),
WS 1975
A Concordance to the Complete
Poetical Works of Sir Thomas
Wyatt (Hangen), W 1941; Re-
views, W 1941.1, 1942,
1942.1
Constable, Henry, WS 1976.1
"Contexts in Surrey's Poetry"
(Davis), S 1974.1
"Convention and Self: A Study
in the Poetry of Sir Thomas
Wyatt" (Birenbaum), W 1962
"Counterfeiting Chaucer: The
Case of 'Dido,' Wyatt, and
the 'Retraction'" (Miskimin),
W 1976.3
"The Course of the Particular:
Surrey's Epitaph on Thomas
Clere and the Fifteenth-
Century Lyric Tradition"
(Nathan), S 1977

Courthope, W. J., WS 1897
"Courtly Love in the English
Renaissance" (McDowell),
WS 1953.2
The Courtly Maker: An Essay on
the Poetry of Wyatt and His
Contemporaries (Southall),
W 1964.10; Reviews, W 1964,
1965.2, 1966.5, 1966.7,
1966.11
The Court of Venus, W 1956.1,
1966.6, 1975.1, WS 1973
The Court of Venus (Fraser),
W 1955.1
The Couurte of Vertue (Hall),
W 1565, WS 1973
"Covert Drama in Wyatt's 'They
flee from me'" (Plashberg),
W 1967.5
"A Critical History of the Pre-
Elizabethan English Sonnet"
(Clinard), WS 1956
"A Critical Survey of Scholarship
in the Field of English Lit-
erature of the Renaissance"
(Tuve), W 1943
Cromwell, Thomas, W 1964.13
Crosland, T. W., WS 1917
Curley, Stephen J., W 1974.1
Cutler, Edward J., W 1965.1
Cygnea cantio (Leland), W 1545

Daalder, Joost, W 1969, 1971.3,
1971.4, 1971.5, 1972.2,
1973.4, 1975, 1976.2, 1977.1
Daley, A. Stuart, W 1950.1
Dante, W 1964.15
Darrell, Elizabeth, W 1933,
1935.1
"Das Sonett in Der Englischen
Literature" (Schirmer),
WS 1926
Davies, M. Bryn, S 1960.2
Davis, Walter R., S 1974.1
Day, John, S 1554, 1905, 1919,
1920.2, 1922.1, 1933, 1963
De Consolatione (Boethius), W
1964.14
"Decorum and Diction in the
English Renaissance" (Rich-
ardson), WS 1972

170

"Deh le mie belle donne & amo-
rose" (Firenzuola), S 1965.4
De la Vega, Garcilaso, W 1974
De Marchi, Luigi, W 1895
Dembo, Pamela, W 1971.6
De Medici, Ippolito (or Francesco
de Molza), S 1924, 1933,
WS 1955
Denham, Sir John, WS 1967.1
De Pistoia, Cino, WS 1923
De remediis utriusque fortunae
(Petrarch), W 1962.2, 1971.2
De Sacrobosco, Joannes, W 1963.7
"The Design of Wyatt's 'They flee
from me'" (Moore), W 1952.1
De Sola Pinto, V., WS 1938
De Sphaera (de Sacrobosco),
W 1963.7
De Tranquillitate (Plutarch),
W 1971.2
Deux Gentilshommes-Poètes de la
Cour de Henry VIII (Bapst),
S 1891
"The Development of Blank Verse--
A Study of Surrey" (Emerson),
S 1889
"The Development of Sonnet-Pat-
terns in the Sixteenth
Century" (Potter), WS 1954.1
"The Development of the English
Lyric in the Sixteenth Cen-
tury: A Study of Styles and
Structure" (Peterson),
W 1957.3
Devonshire Manuscript (BM Add.
MS. 17492), W 1871, 1896,
1911, 1913, 1947.1, 1948.2,
1963.3, 1963.8, 1964.10,
1964.11, 1966.1, 1969.3,
1971.9, 1975.1, S 1906,
WS 1905, 1956.3, 1959, 1960.1
"The Devonshire Manuscript and
Its Medieval Fragments"
(Seaton), WS 1956.3
"The Devonshire Manuscript Col-
lection of Early Tudor
Poetry, 1532-41" (Southall),
W 1964.11
"Dialectical Traits in Sir Thomas
Wyatt's Poetry" (Kökeritz),
W 1965.8

"Die Handschriftliche Überliefer-
ung der Gedichte von Sir
Thomas Wyatt" (Flügel),
W 1896, 1897
Die Petrarcaübersetzungen Sir
Thomas Wyatts: Eine Sprach-
vergleichende Studie (Hietsch),
W 1960; Reviews, W 1961.8, 1966.8
1966.8
"The Direct Source of Wyatt's
Epigram: 'In Dowtfull
Brest...'" (Fucilla), W 1956
A Discourse of English Poetrie
(Webbe), S 1586
Dittes, Rudolf, S 1902
"Divers doth use as I have heard
and know," W 1971.9, WS 1956.2
Dobson, Austin, W 1891.4
Donne, John, W 1929.2, 1931.2,
1935, 1948, 1949.1, 1963.3,
1964.9, 1964.13, 1973.5,
WS 1909, 1952, 1964, 1967.1,
1967.2
"Donne's Relation to the Poetry
of His Time" (Praz), W 1931.2
"Douglas and Surrey: Translators
of Virgil" (Bawcutt), S 1974
"Drab age," WS 1954
Drayton, Michael, S 1619
Dryden, John, WS 1951
"Due Petrarchisti del Secolo XVI"
(Segrè), WS 1901.1
Duncan-Jones, E. E., W 1953.1
"Dyvers thy death," W 1557,
S 1969.1, 1974.1, 1976,
WS 1967.2

"Earle Surrey's Songs and Sonnets"
(Leach), S 1925
The Earlier Renaissance (Saints-
bury), WS 1928
"The Earl of Surrey in France"
(Chapman), S 1952
"The Early Fame of Gavin Douglas's
Eneados" (Bennett), S 1946
Early Sixteenth Century Lyrics
(Padelford), WS 1907
Early Tudor Criticism: Linguistic
and Literary (Sweeting),
WS 1940
Early Tudor Poetry (Berdan),
W 1920, S 1920

Merrill, L. R., S 1925.1
Merrill, Rodney Harpster, W 1970.3
Metaphysical poets, W 1943,
  WS 1960
"The Meter of Some Poems of
  Wyatt" (Schwartz), W 1963.6
The Metres of English Poetry
  (Hamer), WS 1930.1
"A Metrical Analysis of the Blank
  Verse of Henry Howard, Earl
  of Surrey" (Philbin),
  S 1963.1
Mickey, David H., W 1973.5
"The Migrations of a Sonnet"
  (Berdan), W 1908
Miles, Josephine, W 1945,
  WS 1948, 1951
Miller, Audrey Berryman, WS 1949
Milton, John, W 1954, S 1886,
  WS 1951
"The Mind in the Poem: Wyatt's
  'They Fle From Me'" (Fried-
  man), W 1967
"Mine own John Poins, since ye
  delight to know," W 1925,
  1957.1, 1963.2, 1971, 1978.1
"Mirando '1 Sol de begli occhi
  sereno" (Petrarch), W 1890,
  1891
The Mirror for Magistrates,
  W 1978
Miskimin, Alice S., W 1976.3
Moore, Arthur, W 1952.1
"The Moral Vision in the Poetry
  of Sir Thomas Wyatt"
  (Mickey), W 1973.5
"More About A Boke of Balettes,
  1547-1549" (Law), W 1956.1
"More about the 'Boke of Balettes'" (Law), W 1929.1
Morris, Harry, W 1960.1
Muir, Kenneth, W 1947.1, 1948.2,
  1949.1, 1950.3, 1951,
  1953.2, 1960.2, 1960.3,
  1960.4, 1960.5, 1961.4,
  1961.5, 1961.6, 1963.3,
  1963.8, 1965.9, 1965.14,
  1966.8, 1966.9, 1967.4,
  1969.2, 1969.3, 1970.1,
  S 1960.5, 1965.2

Mulliner Book, S 1956.1
Mumford, Ivy L., W 1956.2,
  1958.2, 1960.7, 1963.4,
  S 1956.1, 1965.3
"Musical Settings to the Poems
  of Henry Howard, Earl of
  Surrey" (Mumford), S 1956.1
"Musical Settings to the Poems
  of Sir Thomas Wyatt" (Mum-
  ford), W 1956.2
Music and Poetry in the Early
  Tudor Court (Stevens),
  W 1961.9
Music and Poetry of the English
  Renaissance (Pattison),
  W 1948.3
"My galley charged with forget-
  fulness," W 1971.10
"My heart I gave thee not to do
  it pain," WS 1935
"My lute awake," W 1565, 1961.1,
  1961.3, 1975.2, WS 1781,
  1968.1, 1970
"My mother's maids, when they
  did sew and spin," W 1966.2,
  1971.7, 1975.2, 1978.1
"My penne take Payne," W 1565,
  1928, 1961.1

Naeniae in mortem Thomae Viati
  equitis incomparabilis (Le-
  land), W 1542.1
Nagel, Heinrich, WS 1889.1
Nashe, Thomas, S 1594
Nathan, Leonard E., W 1965.12,
  S 1977
"The Necklace of Wyatt's 'Diere'
  (Candelaria), W 1963.1
Nelson, C. E., W 1963.5
"A New Biographical Criticism of
  Wyatt" (Harrier), W 1959.1
Newman, Joel, W 1957.2
The New Pollecye of Warre (Be-
  con), W 1542
The Nine English Worthies
  (Fletcher), WS 1606
Norfolk, Thomas Howard, Fourth
  Duke of, S 1554, 1964.2

"When Windesor walles sustained my wearied arme," WS 1970
"When youth had led me half the race," S 1956.1
Whipple, T. K., WS 1925
Whiting, George W., W 1960.10
"Whoso list to hunt I know where is an hind," W 1950, 1963.1, 1964.4, 1972, WS 1975
Whythorne, Thomas, WS 1576
Wiatt, William H., W 1952.2, 1958.3, 1960.11, 1961.12, 1966.12, 1968.7
Willcock, Gladys D., S 1919, 1920.2, 1922.1, 1935.1
Williams, John, WS 1963
Williams, Neville, S 1964.2
Winser, Leigh, W 1975.3
Winstanley, William, WS 1687
Wintermantel, Egon, WS 1903.1
Winters, Ivor, WS 1939
"With serving still," W 1953
The Works of Henry Howard Earl of Surrey and of Sir Thomas Wyatt the Elder (Nott), WS 1816.1; Review, WS 1816
The Works of the English Poets from Chaucer to Cowper (Chalmers), WS 1810
"Wrapt in my careless cloke, as I walke to and fro," S 1974.1
"Wyat resteth here," W 1542.2, S 1953, 1955, 1969.1, 1973.1, 1976, WS 1781, 1970, 1975
Wyatt, Sir Henry, W 1961.11
Wyatt, Sir Thomas,
  Bibliography, W 1970.4, WS 1938.1, 1968, 1971
  Biography, W 1831, 1848, 1850, 1850.1, 1854.2, 1868, 1889, 1920, 1925, 1929.2, 1930, 1933, 1934.1, 1935, 1935.1, 1949.1, 1952, 1952.2, 1953, 1955.1, 1958, 1959.1, 1959.5, 1961, 1961.11, 1961.12, 1963.3, 1964.5, 1964.9, 1964.13, 1968, 1968.7, 1972.4, 1974.2, 1975, 1976.1, WS 1679, 1687, 1691, 1723, 1781, 1810, 1816.1, 1897, 1901.1, 1903.1, 1935, 1960, 1969, 1976

Canon, W 1871, 1896, 1897, 1911, 1913, 1922, 1922.1, 1925.1, 1928, 1928.2, 1929.1, 1929.2, 1930.1, 1933, 1934.1, 1945.1, 1947.1, 1948.1, 1948.2, 1949.1, 1950.1, 1952, 1953, 1955.1, 1956.1, 1960.2, 1960.3, 1960.4, 1960.5, 1960.6, 1960.8, 1960.9, 1961.4, 1961.6, 1963.3, 1963.8, 1963.9, 1963.10, 1964.2, 1964.10, 1966.5, 1966.6, 1969.2, 1969.3, 1970.1, 1970.4, 1971.9, 1971.11, 1972.4, 1972.5, 1975, 1975.1, 1976.2, WS 1816.1, 1929, 1935.1, 1960.2, 1961,
Carols, W 1948.3, 1954.2, 1964.6, 1968.4, 1974.3
Defence, W 1935, 1963.3, WS 1816.1
Diction, W 1544, 1854.2, 1911, 1931, 1945, 1946.1, 1948, 1954.2, 1956.3, 1959.3, 1960, 1961.7, 1962.1, 1962.2, 1963.2, 1963.9, 1964.8, 1965.3, 1965.7, 1965.8, 1965.15, 1967.7, 1968, 1968.4, 1971.2, 1972.2, 1972.6, 1972.7, 1973.1, 1974.5, S 1920.1, WS 1589, 1902, 1907, 1909, 1941, 1941.1, 1948, 1951, 1953, 1959, 1961.1, 1964, 1967, 1967.3, 1969.2, 1971.1, 1972
Epigrams, W 1911, 1913, 1929.2, 1946.1, 1956, 1964.2, WS 1816.1, 1897, 1906.2, 1909, 1925, 1935.1, 1960.2
Imagery, W 1933, 1946.1, 1950, 1952.1, 1953.3, 1955.4, 1959, 1959.3, 1960.1, 1961, 1961.2, 1961.7, 1963, 1963.3, 1963.5, 1964.7, 1964.13, 1965.3, 1965.12, 1965.15, 1965.16, 1968, 1968.1, 1968.6, 1970.5, 1972, 1973.1, 1977, WS 1902, 1959.1
Letters, W 1850, 1934.1, 1949.1, 1963.3, 1973.1, 1975.2, 1978.3, WS 1816.1
Odes, W 1929.2, WS 1918

192